Pedagogies of Difference

Pedagogies of Difference

RETHINKING EDUCATION FOR SOCIAL CHANGE

EDITED BY
PETER PERICLES TRIFONAS

RoutledgeFalmer
New York • London

Published in 2003 by
RoutledgeFalmer
29 West 35th Street
New York, New York 10001
www.routledge-ny.com

Published in Great Britain by
RoutledgeFalmer
11 New Fetter Lane
London EC4P 4EE
www.routledgefalmer.com

RoutledgeFalmer is an imprint of the Taylor & Francis Group.

Copyright © 2003 by RoutledgeFalmer

Printed in the United States of America on acid-free paper.

10 9 8 7 6 5 4 3 2 1

Library of Congress Cataloging-in-Publication Data

Pedagogies of difference : rethinking education for social change / edited by Peter Pericles Trifonas.
    p. cm.
  Includes bibliographical references and index.
  ISBN 0-415-93148-7 — ISBN 0-415-93149-5 (pbk.)
    1. Critical pedagogy. 2. Multicultural education. 3. Postmodernism and education. I.
Trifonas, Peter Pericles, 1960–

LC196 .P45 2002
370.11'59—dc21

                                                                2002067932

To Effie, Peirce, Anthi, and Yanni

Contents

Acknowledgments

I would like to thank Bill Pinar, Henry Giroux, Michael Peters, Marla Morris, Megan Boler, Michalinos Zembylas, Kris Gutierrez, Carlos Tejeda, Manuel Espinoza, Jim Cummins, Roxana Ng, and Rinaldo Walcott who have participated in this anthology. We share the common hope that this book will enable educators—and all those interested in rethinking education for social justice—to reflect on the meaning of pedagogical practices and curricular policies in the context of recognizing the multiplicity of difference.

I would like to express my gratitude to Elefteria Balomenos for helping me to keep the task of writing going. Thank you.

This book would not have been possible without a grant from the Social Sciences and Humanities Research Council.

Introduction
Pedagogies of Difference:
Locating Otherness

The idea of difference has provided the conceptual groundwork for educational theorists of diverse ideological perspectives working toward the ethical purpose of actualizing equitable curricular contexts for teaching and learning that are responsive to individuals and groups within a society or culture regardless of race, class, gender, or sexuality (Apple 1990; Giroux 1992; Lather 1991; Pinar et al. 1995; Spivak 1993; hooks 1994; McLaren 1997). Yet this altruistic desire for securing equitable educational environments and opportunities is also the practical juncture at which feminist pedagogies, critical pedagogies, antiracist or postcolonial pedagogies, and gay and lesbian pedagogies begin to part company with respect to the concept of difference. Difference therefore becomes an intrinsic point of theoretical validation for asserting the legitimacy of such pedagogical discourses in practice by justifying the ethics of the methods each puts forward for the creation of equitable educational environments that seek to engage questions of social justice and alter the ideological preconditions of prejudice and discrimination.

For example, virtually all feminist pedagogies have validated the need to analyze the construction of sexual difference as a means for overcoming the bias of gender-role stereotyping (Luke and Gore 1992; Irigaray 1994). Some critical pedagogies have validated the importance of examining the sociopolitical ground for differences of subjectivity to illuminate the ideological subtext of human interactions (Freire 1970; Simon 1992; McLaren 1986, 1997), while others have concentrated on the economic distinction of class differences to address the bounds of social injustice and exploitation (Aronowitz and Giroux 1991; Apple 1993). Antiracist and postcolonial pedagogies have generally validated the necessity of acknowledging the uniqueness of racial differences as a heterogeneous marker of identity that gives a powerful voice to ethnic specificity in the face of discrimination against minorities and cultural hegemonies (Spivak 1993; hooks 1994; Bhabha 1994; McCarthy and Crichlow 1993). Gay and lesbian pedagogies have tended to validate the significance of recognizing differences of sexuality or sexual orientation to situate the essence of subjectivity at the psychic and somatic core of human desire (Pinar 1994; Sears 1992; Britzman 1991). Indeed, some aspect of difference has indeed informed the attempts of these pedagogical movements to break down and reconceptualize the normative basis of subjectivity that has been operationalized in strictly ethical terms by the Western conventions of schooling systems as a manifest curricular goal or outcome (Derrida 1990; Apple 1990; Spivak 1993).

Educational institutions have traditionally not tolerated the value of subjective differences among student populations. For the sake of securing the reproduction of the "cultural capital" of a society and its normative ideals and models, the institution of education in the West has promoted the vision of a relatively homogeneous community of learners working toward an idea of "academic excellence" narrowly defined according to standardized levels of progress and achievement (Bourdieu and Passeron 1992). Here I would contend that the history and spirit of curricular reconceptualization and progressive education that originally began with the social reconstructionist movement of the 1920s has continued to the present day in the form of feminist pedagogies, critical pedagogies, antiracist or postcolonial pedagogies, and gay pedagogies (Stanley 1992; Pinar et al. 1995). The focus of educational reform for achieving democracy and social justice has necessarily been retranslated over time, after John Dewey and his contemporaries, to include the recognition of the values of difference as a legitimate and integral feature of a modern civil society.) But a question arises, and its significance is paramount to the future of educational reform and to the future of critical democracy in the next millennia: To what extent can the idea of difference help us to redefine or rethink the principle of educational equity and the questions of social justice that it raises both within and outside of the classroom?

This question would assume that (1) as it stands, the principle of educational equity is not equitable and (2) to make the principle of educational equity more equitable we would need to address its precepts as they are put to practice in the classroom in terms of the idea of difference. Yet, if we only use difference as the main criterion through which to secure and evaluate equitable educational practice in the name of social justice, the problem of competing distinctions arises: How could we most properly adjudicate between the values of difference and their pedagogies to gauge both their argumentative and ethical validity as a way to educate students for social justice? It would not be possible to adhere to the democratic spirit of the principle of educational equity by arbitrarily choosing among differences of race, class, gender, or sexuality so as to privilege a pedagogy that appeals to some aspects of difference while marginalizing or rejecting others. The concept of a pedagogy of difference cannot be analyzed unproblematically and this is especially so when it is couched in the politically and ethically regressive terms of a desire for competing validation. If, as Henry Giroux (1992) suggests, "organizing schools and pedagogy around a sense of purpose and meaning that makes difference central to a critical notion of citizenship and democratic public life . . . [is] the basis for extending the struggle for equality and justice to the broader spheres of everyday life" (174), we then need to have some way of acknowledging the unifying threads of the divergent notions of difference and their pedagogical imperatives that I have previously detailed. This is the intellectual and pedagogical challenge of this edited collection: To rethink the terms of education for social justice via the recognition of difference as a basis for the education of subjectivity. It asks theorists and educational practitioners influenced by the schools of feminist pedagogy, critical pedagogy, antiracist or postcolonial pedagogy, and gay and lesbian pedagogy to reflect upon the possibilities of articulating pedagogies of difference. Such pedagogies of difference would highlight the need to acknowledge the specificity of difference as well as the need to try to bridge the negative values of difference that create competing theoretical and pedagogical discourses conducive neither to the principle or educational equity nor to education for social justice.

This edited collection takes as its premise that the cultural work of education—in theory and in practice—must move toward a reawakening of an ethical consciousness that opens the negative values of difference in an affirmative way, while still recognizing their uniqueness and particularity. To reduce the numbing sense of divisiveness permeating the public sphere of education requires the solidarity of a community of difference rather than a simple celebration of a community of differences perceived to exist, more or less, independently of each other as the multiple sites of isolated or marginalized subjectivities. This is crucial if we wish to enrich our knowledge of the border crossings of teaching and learning so as to adapt educational practices and institutional structures in a truly democratic way to the needs of all students regardless of race, class, gender, or sexuality—thereby ensuring the equitability of the principle of educational equity and education for social justice.

To date, there has been no sustained attempt, in educational theory or in its contextual grounding as praxis, to address the bridging of this gap of difference among the discourses of feminist pedagogy, critical pedagogy, antiracist and postcolonial pedagogies, and gay and lesbian pedagogy (Giroux 1992; Luke and Gore 1992; Spivak 1993). By researching the conceptual overlap and dissonance to synthesize and affirm the values of the theoretical perceptions of difference these pedagogies have put forward relative to the ethical bases of their practical educational aims, this edited collection works toward a rethinking of the concept of difference and pedagogy in light of the theorists' current work. *Pedagogies of Difference* works toward providing the groundwork for an inclusive articulation of difference through the conceptualization of pedagogical possibilities that create an openness toward the horizons of the other. Reconsidering the forms of difference and their pedagogical imperatives as cultural practice enables new directions for a rethinking of the traditional interpretation of the principle of educational equity in terms of a community of difference rather than in terms of a community of differences. In this way, *Pedagogies of Difference* makes a significant contribution toward a re-understanding of the importance of this relationship between pedagogy and difference and the principle of educational equity for securing the democratic future of schools through ethical educational reform for social justice.

Chapter one, "Toward a Decolonizing Pedagogy: Social Justice Reconsidered," outlines the parameters for what Paulo Freire might call a "pedagogy of freedom." Carlos Tejeda, Manuel Espinoza, and Kris Gutierrez detail the forms of violence that permeate the social sphere and negate the inherent potential of the subject to rise above injustice. They identify the "internal neocolonialism" present in the United States as a form of oppression constituted since the seventeenth century and normalized through the systemic exploitation of immigrant populations. A decolonizing pedagogy comes to be articulated in this chapter through Freire's struggle for a socially transformative praxis whereby the self-actualization of subjectivity and agency in the world can occur. Thus, it is argued that empowerment rests in rethinking approaches to education and the possibilities for self-determination and freedom through which social justice is defined.

Chapter two, "Challenging the Construction of Difference as Deficit: Where Are Identity, Intellect, Imagination, and Power in the New Regime of Truth?" considers the evolution of policy and practice that frequently focuses narrowly on instructional strategies designed to promote language learning and academic success to the neglect of issues related to the significance of societal power relations and the negotiation of identities between educators and students in classroom interactions. Jim Cummins argues that all classroom interactions can be viewed simultaneously through the twin lens of identity negotiation and knowledge generation. Furthermore, patterns of language learning and academic development cannot be understood when identity negotiation and its roots in societal power relations are omitted from consideration. A framework is presented that analyzes how patterns of power relations in the wider society affect both educator role definitions and educational structures that, in turn, determine the interpersonal spaces (zones of proximal development) that are constructed in the classroom interactions between teachers and students. Knowledge generation and identity negotiation are transacted in these interpersonal spaces. Cummins believes that the interactions between educators and students are never neutral. To varying degrees, they either always challenge or reinforce patterns of coercive power relations in the wider society. The practical implications for language policy and practice of this framework are discussed within the context of this theoretical purview.

In Chapter three, "Derrida, Pedagogy, and the Calculation of the Subject," Michael Peters considers the so-called deconstruction of the subject that is credited to the poststructural theorizing of Jacques Derrida. The chapter takes as its starting point the pedagogical implications of deconstruction as a theory of the formation of the subject. Peters surveys the philosophical underpinnings of the conception of subjectivity within Western epistemology and the implications it poses for pedagogy as a way to know the limitations of the difference between self and other. He follows the traces of the humanist subject through Hegel, Husserl, and Heidegger as a way into the Nietzchean period of antihumanism that culminated in France during the student revolts of May 1968. Peters looks to the proclamations of Michel Foucault and Jean-François Lyotard regarding "the death of man" in order to situate the ethico-political implications of Derrida's essay "The Ends of Man." Taking issue with the neoliberal backlash against deconstruction for the postmodern skepticism in a universal subjectivity, the chapter shows how the call for the "return of the subject" and the death of deconstruction has been misguided. Peters shows how the concept of difference in Derrida's writing is a determining factor for recognizing the ethics of deconstruction as a philosophical undertaking that never promoted or enacted the desire to kill off the subject, to make it simply disappear. Rather, the importance of poststructuralism, as is made evident in this chapter, is to recognize the multiple sites of subjectivity and the conditions of impossibility that requires us to keep open to difference and alterity, even in its most radical form: otherness.

Henry Giroux provides us with much to think about in relation to the politics of multiculturalism. Chapter four, "Pedagogies of Difference, Race, and Representation: Film as a Site of Translation and Politics," reconsiders the academic terrains of meaning over notions of multiculturalism that have redefined the term in theory and practice. The critical turn toward language, Giroux argues, has reinvigorated the debate over the public space of culture and how it is worked out via the institution as knowledge and social practices. The links between culture and power are not haphazard. We have known that for some time. Giroux shows us how power is articulated within relations predicated on colonizing the workings of consciousness via the imagination. He concentrates on media as a site where race and representation are united within the codic framework of film and the Hollywood industry where pedagogy becomes public, easily available for consumption by a mass audience. Giroux examines the filmic depictions of black youth and culture in the context of difference, race, and representation wherein ideology plays a determinate role in mythic depictions of the cultural self and the cultural other. The chapter calls for a pedagogy that links the linguistic or textual analysis of exploitation and injustice with its systemic, institutional, and economic manifestions.

Chapter five, "Discomforting Truths: The Emotional Terrain of Understanding Difference," outlines the preconditions for a pedagogy of discomfort—that is, a teaching that recognizes and problematizes the deeply embedded emotional dimensions that frame and shape daily habits, routines, and unconscious complicity with hegemony. Megan Boler and Michalinos Zembylas illucidate how to approach the ways in which we enact and embody dominant values and assumptions in our daily habits and routines via the emotions in order to identify unconscious privileges as well as invisible ways in which one complies with dominant ideology. Their perspective is quite unique. The chapter outlines how the liberal conceptualizes difference and its emphasis on individualism. Boler and Zymbylas frame the power of binary oppositions by looking at theories of difference ranging from Audre Lorde to Michel Foucault. They call for a pedagogy that embraces "ambiguity" in its critical conceptualization of identities so as to question the ground of contemporary certainties about subjectivity and normativity. A pedagogy of discomfort aims at encouraging a critical inquiry at a cognitive as well as an emotional level through the cultivation of acts of reflection promoting a self-awareness of differences and its inscriptions of otherness.

In Chapter six, "The Struggle for Happiness: Commodified Black Masculinities, Vernacular Culture, and Homoerotic Desires," Rinaldo Walcott addresses three different areas of knowledge claims: studies of gender—in particular masculinity studies, black studies, and queer theory. He puts forward the case for a reading practice of decipherment that can tolerate the postmodern complexities of the play of race and queer sexuality simultaneously. Arguing that the global proliferation of black male bodies as commodity and in service of commodities has come to dominate what black masculinities might look and act like, Walcott asserts a queer reading of masculinity studies as this sub-field of gender studies reproduces masculinities as only white or heterosexually black. His argument for refashioning masculinity studies resides in the ambivalent and draws from postcolonial and feminist studies.

William F. Pinar identifies the reluctance of the field of education to give up its versions of social reconstruction in chapter seven, "Inside Noah's Tent: The Sodomitical Genesis of Race in the Christian Imagination." This chapter outlines the tension between the pedagogical desire for high standards of excellence and the fact that this aim contradicts a curriculum for social justice. Pinar focuses on the psycho-cultural obsession with keeping issues related to sexuality out of the classroom while sublimating the question of alterity and otherness in the problem of "race," which is more palatable. Sexuality is located in the working out of racial politics. Pinar says as much, but takes it further to examine the genesis of race in a biblical episode that depicts, he argues, the homoerotic origins of human culture. The analysis is wide ranging and eclectic, bringing together sources drawn from American cultural history, black history, literature, psychoanalysis, and ecclesiastical hermeneutics.

Chapter eight, "Queer Pedagogies: Camping Up the Difference," is Marla Morris's contribution to this edited collection. In the chapter she defines contemporary theoretical trends to understand curriculum as a "symbolic representation." Morris takes up the issue of her sexuality to begin a conversation that places her as an exemplary figure within the opposition of seeing oneself as another. Being a lesbian woman teaching in the South, she wonders how her "queerness" is perceived by her students dealing as they are with a conservative consciousness of what it means. Morris takes us through the cultural history of sexuality via queer theory, settling on the cultural image of the vampire to convey the mythopoetic origins of camp in the curriculum that locates difference as vogue and parody. The vampire, Morris reminds us, is an outsider whose existence and identity depends both on heteronormativity and sexual ambivalence where camp and the threat of difference go hand in hand.

Roxana Ng examines and criticizes existing attempts in addressing inequality and difference, which usually focus on a single dimension of difference such as race, gender, or class. Chapter nine, "Toward an Integrative Approach to Equity in Education," recommends an approach to educational equity that is capable of addressing multiple and intersecting axes of inequality and difference. The key to this integrative approach is to understand power as a relational property that is produced in interactions. To illustrate this conceptualization, the author discusses how power operates in terms of race, gender, and class, and hints at how ability can be similarly conceptualized. In conclusion, the author puts forward—

tentatively—an approach called "against the grain," one which seeks to make power relations explicit in the educational process. By way of a conclusion, the implications of this approach are explored.

Chapter ten, "Toward a Deconstructive Pedagogy of *Différance*," elaborates how Jacques Derrida's grammatological overhauling of semiology enables us to rethink education, difference, and subjectivity. It is through the differential and deferred relations of the iterativity of the sign, its spatio-temporal "im-print" on the subject, that the excesses of difference manifest themselves in a recognition of alterity. The chapter shows how the teleological perspective of an "ego-logical" pedagogy cannot comprehend or care to admit such a radical opening-up of subjectivity to the horizons of otherness. I argue that the irreducibility of *différance* shows-up the infinite exteriority of the arche-trace of the Other through a *symploke*, or a weaving together of the diverse strands of deconstruction as a way to knowledge. Undecidability thus invades the transcendental preconditions of truth claims upon which episteme depends so as to be teachable by grounding what it means to know within self-certainty. A pedagogy of *différance* complicates the ancient thinking of the West that does not grant standing to the idea of the Other, *its infusing in the idea of perpetuity, stasis, and fixed order the semblance of an outside, exteriority, to a pedagogy of the Same.*

REFERENCES

Apple, Michael. 1990. *Ideology and Curriculum.* 2nd ed. New York and London: Routledge.

———. 1993. *Official Knowledge: Democratic Education in a Conservative Age.* New York and London: Routledge.

Aronowitz, Stanley, and Henry Giroux, eds. 1991. *Postmodern Education: Politics, Culture, and Social Criticism.* Minneapolis: University of Minnesota Press.

Bhabha, Homi K. 1994. *The Location of Culture.* New York and London: Routledge.

Bourdieu, Pierre, and Jean-Claude Passeron. 1992. *Reproduction in Education, Society, and Culture,* 2nd ed. London: Sage.

Britzman, Deborah. 1991. *Practice Makes Practice: A Critical Study of Learning to Teach.* Albany: State University of New York Press.

Derrida, Jacques. 1974. *Of Grammatology.* Trans. Gayatri Chakravorty Spivak. Baltimore: Johns Hopkins University Press.

———. 1988. "Afterword: Toward an Ethic of Discussion." In *Limited Inc.,* trans. Samuel Weber and Jeffrey Mehlman, ed. Gerald Graff. Evanston, Ill.: Northwestern University Press.

———. 1990. *Du Droit à la Philosophie.* Paris: Galilée.

Freire, Paulo. 1970. *Pedagogy of the Oppressed.* New York: The Seabury Press.

Giroux, Henry. 1992. *Border Crossings: Cultural Workers and the Politics of Education.* New York and London: Routledge.

Hooks, Bell. 1994. *Teaching to Transgress: Education as the Practice of Freedom.* New York and London: Routledge.

Irigaray, Luce. 1994. *Thinking the Difference: For a Peaceful Resolution.* Trans. Karin Montin. New York and London: Routledge.

Lather, Patti. 1991. *Getting Smart: Feminist Research and Pedagogy With/In the Postmodern.* New York and London: Routledge.

Luke, Carmen, and Jennifer Gore, eds. 1992. *Feminisms and Critical Pedagogy.* New York and London: Routledge.

McCarthy, Cameron, and Warren Crichlow, eds. 1993. *Race, Identity, and Representation in Education.* New York and London: Routledge.

McLaren, Peter. 1986. *Schooling as a Ritual Performance: Towards a Political Economy of Educational Signs and Gestures.* Boston: Routledge and Kegan Paul.

———. 1997. *Revolutionary Multiculturalism: Pedagogies of Dissent for the New Millenium.* New York: Westview.

Pinar, William F. 1994. *Autobiography, Politics, and Sexuality: Essays in Curriculum Theory, 1972–1992.* New York: Peter Lang.

Pinar, William F., William M. Reynolds, Patrick Slattery, and Peter M. Taubman. 1995. *Understanding Curriulum: An Introduction to the Study of Historical and Contemporary Curriculum Discourses.* New York: Peter Lang.

Sears, James, ed. 1992. *Sexuality and the Curriculum.* New York and London: Routledge.

Simon, Roger. 1992. *Teaching Against the Grain.* South Hadley, Mass.: Bergin & Garvey.

Spivak, Gayatri Chakravorty. 1993. *Outside in the Teaching Machine.* New York and London: Routledge.

Stanley, William B. 1992. *Curriculum for Utopia: Social Reconstruction and Critical Pedagogy in the Postmodern Era.* Albany: State University of New York Press.

Trifonas, Peter Pericles. 1993. "The Marks on the Page: Conceptions of Text and Textuality in Literary Theory from Structuralism to Poststructuralism." *Interchange,* 24 (4):381–95.

———. 1996. "The Ends of Pedagogy: From the Dialectic of Memory to the Deconstruction of the Institution." *Educational Theory,* 46 (3):303–33.

———. 2000a. *The Ethics of Writing: Derrida, Deconstruction, and Pedagogy.* Lanham, Md: Rowman & Littlefield.

———. (ed.). 2000b. *Revolutionary Pedagogies: Cultural Politics, the Institution of Education, and the Discourse of Theory.* New York and London: RoutledgeFalmer.

1

Toward a Decolonizing Pedagogy: Social Justice Reconsidered

CARLOS TEJEDA, MANUEL ESPINOZA, AND KRIS GUTIERREZ

Colonization, which sets out to change the order of the world, is, obviously, a program of complete disorder. But it cannot come about as a result of magical practices, nor of a natural shock, nor of a friendly understanding. Decolonization, as we know, is a historical process: That is to say it cannot be understood, it cannot become intelligible, nor clear to itself except in the exact measure that we can discern the movements which give it historical form and content. (Fanon 1963: 36)

I cannot be a teacher if I do not perceive with even greater clarity that my practice demands of me a definition of where I stand. A break with what is not right ethically. I must choose between one thing and another thing. I cannot be a teacher and be in favor of everyone and everything. I cannot be in favor merely of people, humanity, vague phrases far from the concrete nature of educative practice. Mass hunger and unemployment, side by side with opulence, are not the result of destiny. (Freire 1998: 93)

In the contemporary contexts of what many refer to as the United States, working-class indigenous and nonwhite peoples are often reduced to ontological foreigners in the very space and time they occupy. In these contexts, people are assaulted by multiple and mutually constitutive forms of violence in the various dimensions—the economic, the cultural, the political, the linguistic, the sexual, the spatial, the psychological, and epistemological—of their daily lives. Defining violence as "any relation, process, or condition by which an individual or group violates the physical, social, and/or psychological integrity of another person or group," Bulhan (1981: 53) explains that violence inhibits human growth, negates inherent potential, limits productive living, and causes death. We contend that one cannot ignore this violence when calling for social justice, and that it is necessary to define explicitly one's particular understanding of the term—in other words, the meaning of social justice that grounds one's politics and projects. Meanings are never neutral; they are always situated socially, culturally, and historically, and they operate within the logic of differing ideologies that imply differing sets of social practices. These practices, in turn, serve and sustain particular sets of interests, while they simultaneously work against others. Hence, we argue that any notion of social justice should be interrogated with the following questions: What ideologies underlie particular notions of social justice? Who benefits from the instantiation of those notions? At whose expense are those notions instantiated?

We argue for a notion of social justice that recognizes that the contemporary United States is essentially characterized by an internal neocolonialism (Almaguer 1974; Barrera 1979; Blauner 1972) that has its origins in the mutually reinforcing systems of colonial and capitalist domination and exploitation that enslaved Africans and dispossessed indigenous populations throughout the seventeenth, eighteenth, and nineteenth centuries. We insist on a notion of social justice that acknowledges that the forms of violence and "microaggressions" (Davis 1995) experienced by dominated and exploited groups in the context of everyday life are both normalized and officially sanctioned by dominant ideologies and institutional arrangements in American society. Most importantly, we argue for a notion of social justice that sees dismantling our internal neocolonial condition and abolishing its multiple forms of violence as preconditions to the existence of justice between all peoples inhabiting the contemporary United States.

Working-class indigenous and nonwhite peoples' interests cannot be represented by amnesia-ridden notions of social justice that ignore the current manifestations and effects of the corporal and cultural genocide that has been taking place in American society throughout the past four centuries. At worst, many of these notions are calls for social reform that ignore the racial and cultural dimensions of the social injustice we inherit from our colonial and capitalist past; at worst, they are calls for a more socially equitable (i.e., racially and ethnically diverse) participation in the existing structures of domination and exploitation. For us, the struggle for social justice is inextricably tied to the struggle for a politics and praxis of anticapitalist decolonization in the mutually constitutive terrains of social existence—in the economic, the cultural, the political, the juridical, and the educational. Focusing specifically on the educational terrain, we argue for engaging in the struggle for social justice through a decolonizing pedagogical praxis.

In this chapter, we outline an emergent theory of pedagogy—a decolonizing pedagogy—that stands in stark contrast to most social justice pedagogies currently in vogue. More specifically, we propose the concept of a decolonizing pedagogy to address the issue of social justice from and within the educational arena. We argue that an anticapitalist decolonizing pedagogical praxis is a concrete way to struggle for a social justice that serves the interests of working-class indigenous and nonwhite peoples in the internal neocolonial contexts of the contemporary United States. In what follows, we define our developing conception of a decolonizing pedagogy by providing a provisional definition of the term and outlining its constituent elements. This is followed by a discussion of some fundamental premises of our call for a decolonizing pedagogy and an outline of conceptual frameworks that currently inform its conceptualization. We conclude with a discussion of decolonizing pedagogical praxis that outlines its curricular contents and explicates its grounding in cultural-historical conceptions of learning and development.

WHY SOCIAL JUSTICE FROM A DECOLONIZING PERSPECTIVE?

In California's recent past, voter propositions designed to eliminate health and educational services to "undocumented, immigrant" populations (Proposition 187), to roll-back the limited civil rights gains of the 1960s (Proposition 209), and to prohibit the use of the home language in teaching and learning (Proposition 227) have been the order of the day. To some people, these propositions are mere vestiges of a racial discrimination and a social inequality that persist despite a long and concerted effort to uphold the founding ideals (e.g., liberty, democratic participation, and equality) of the American nation. To us, these policies are refurbished historical practices that produce racial and class domination and reiterate century-old questions: What are the value and place of nonwhite peoples in an Anglo-European nation and society? What should be the role of education for poor, indigenous, and nonwhite children?

These recent policies are manifestations of contemporary struggles and conflicting interests between differing groups in a neocolonial context that has been imposed, maintained, and dominated by Anglo-Europeans since the seventeenth century. They are manifestations of power, domination, conflict, and struggle that can be traced to European conquest, colonization, and imperialist expansion throughout the seventeenth, eighteenth, and nineteenth centuries.

While we acknowledge that the past is obviously not the present, we argue that the present can neither exist nor be understood outside of the past. It is impossible for social subjects to be ontologically disconnected; their being in the world cannot be detached from and unaffected by the time and space they have already occupied. In our recent past, social subjects, social relations, and forms of social organization have been so fundamentally marked by colonialism and capitalism that we believe it is naïve, erroneous, and even deceitful to contemplate our present existence without an analysis and understanding of the unfolding enconcretizations and effects of these. We are not, of course, arguing that we are living the actual colonialism or capitalist colonialism of the seventeenth, eighteenth, and/or nineteenth century. Clearly, many of the processes and practices of that colonial and capitalist domination and exploitation have evolved, have been altered, have been abandoned, or have been legally terminated. But it is also clear that essential features of that domination and exploitation continue to structure the social relations among differing groups in American society. We insist on discussing contemporary notions and issues of social justice from a decolonizing perspective because we understand that for working class indigenous and nonwhite peoples and their descendants the materialization of social justice, on the one hand, and the discrediting and dismantling of the lasting effects and contemporary manifestations of our capitalist colonialism, on the other hand, are inseparable.

FUNDAMENTAL PREMISES OF A DECOLONIZING PEDAGOGY

A basic premise of our call for a decolonizing pedagogy is that the dominant economic, cultural, political, judicial, and educational arrangements in contemporary American society are those of an internal neocolonialism produced by the mutually reinforcing systems of colonial and capitalist domination and exploitation that have organized social relations throughout the history of what today constitutes the United States. Given the underlying significance of this premise, we elaborate on the concept of internal neocolonialism.

The concept of internal neocolonialism we employ to characterize the dominant condition of social existence in the United States is indebted to the work of Barrera (1979) and Almaguer (1974). Barrera employs the concept in the development of a theory of racial inequality that is proposed as an alternative to the theories of deficiency, theories of bias, and theories of structural discrimination that attempted to explicate the issue of the Chicana/o inequality in the United States. In outlining this theory, he offers a discussion of colonialism and internal colonialism that is essential to the notion of internal neocolonialism we propose. Colonialism is defined by Barrera as follows:

> Colonialism is a structured relationship of domination and subordination, where the dominant and subordinate groups are defined along ethnic and/or racial !ines, and where the relationship is established and maintained to serve the interests of all or part of the dominant group (193).

Internal colonialism is distinguished from colonialism in the following terms:

> Internal colonialism is a form of colonialism in which the dominant and subordinate populations are intermingled, so that there is no geographically distinct, "metropolis" separate from the "colony." (194)

Almaguer (1974) links internal colonialism in the United States to advanced monopoly capitalism in a manner that is also essential to our developing concept of internal neocolonialism. In his examination of Chicana/o oppression in North America, Almaguer calls for a simultaneous analysis of capitalist and colonial structures, arguing that both the historical process of colonization (be it classical colonialism, neocolonialism, or internal colonialism) and the rise and spread of capitalism should be viewed as fundamental in the organization of social and economic power in the United States. He explains that the histories of oppressed peoples have been largely formed both by the rise of capitalism and the expansion of colonial domination, and he further theorizes that there is a dialectical relationship in the development of monopoly capitalism and the development of internal colonialism. He describes this relationship as follows:

> . . . the colonial expansionism by which the U.S. absorbed vast territories paved the way for the incorporation of its non-white colonial labor force. This contributed in turn to the accelerated process of capital accumulation. Necessary for the development of modern capitalism . . . not only did internal colonialism and monopoly capitalism develop concurrently, but . . . both processes are intimately interrelated and feed each other. At the same time that the utilization of non-whites as a controlled, colonized labor force contributed to the development of the U.S. as a major metropolis of the international capitalist system, the attendant class system in the U.S. provided a means of reinforcing a racially and culturally defined social hierarchy . . . (42)

As this passage indicates, capitalism did not simply develop side by side with internal colonial domination; it became inextricably interrelated with it. More significantly, Almaguer contends that capitalism is now the dominant mode of production and that it continues to systematically perpetuate a colonial domination in which the brunt of its oppression and class contradictions "have been largely carried over on racial terms and fall on the backs of colonized people of color" (1974: 42).

We define the dominant condition characterizing social existence in what today constitutes the United States as a colonial one because there continues to be a structured relationship of cultural, political, and economic domination and subordination between European whites on the one hand, and indigenous and nonwhite peoples on the other. What's more, this relationship (which was imposed and institutionalized throughout the seventeenth, eighteenth, and nineteenth centuries and has been maintained, in essence, up to the present) continues to serve primarily the interests of the dominant white, English-speaking, and Christian population. We qualify it as an internal colonial condition because the colonizing/dominant and colonized/subordinate populations coexist, are often socially integrated, and even share citizenship within the same national borders. What's more, we see this internal colonial condition, its forms of social organization, and its institutional apparatuses as inextricably tied to and perpetuated by capitalism and capitalist social relations—a capitalism that Almaguer discussed as advanced monopoly capitalism and we currently see as global capitalism (Stromquist and Monkman 2000; McLaren and Farahmandpur 2000). Our conception of internal colonialism, then, assumes the fundamentality of capitalism and capitalist social relations in the various dimensions of our neocolonial condition and social interaction.

We propose expanding the concept from internal colonialism to internal neocolonialism because we think it is necessary to distinguish between the forms of domination, oppression, and exploitation of the internal colonialism of the seventeenth, eighteenth, and nineteenth centuries, and the forms of domination, oppression, and exploitation that have characterized the internal colonialism of the twentieth and twenty-first centuries. Landmark legislation and its effects (e.g., the Emancipation Proclamation, the Fourteenth Amendment to the U.S. Constitution, the Indian Citizenship Act, Brown vs. Board of Education, the Civil Rights Act, the Voting Rights Act, the Indian Self-Determination and Education Assistance Act, and the Native American Languages Act) have altered the nature of the domination, oppression, and exploitation of subordinated groups. We think it is fundamentally important to acknowledge and account for significant changes in the condition that has characterized social existence in the United States. The past is obviously not the present, nor is the condition of the nineteenth century the same as the condition of the twenty-first century. We contend, however, that the condition characterizing the present maintains essential features of the condition that characterized social the past.

It is important to point out that our argument about the continuity of colonial relations is not grounded in simplistic representations of colonizing and the colonized populations. We are cognizant that the population of settling and invading Europeans was defined by difference and division along ethnic, linguistic, gender, and social class lines—not even the dominant population of Anglos was socially homogenous. Similarly, we are aware that there was tremendous diversity among both the indigenous population and African slaves. We are conscious that in referring to indigenous people, African slaves, and their descendants, we reference people from a plurality of groups with differing cultures, languages, and forms of social organization. Similarly, our conception of the processes and practices (both past and present) of colonialism acknowledges that not all European groups (nor differing social groups within the dominant Anglo population) have been equally complicit in the colonial relations of domination and exploitation that have taken place. Not all European groups have benefited equally from the establishment and perpetuation of the colonial/neocolonial condition. Our conception of internal colonialism in the United States (both past and present) also acknowledges that not all indigenous or nonwhite peoples and their descendants experienced or are experiencing colonialism in a uniform manner.

Another fundamental premise of our call for a decolonizing pedagogy is that the internal neocolonial condition of our social existence (i.e., our reality) can be transformed through *praxis*—guided action aimed at transforming individuals and their world that is reflected upon and leads to further action. This understanding of the malleability of social reality and the transformative potential of human praxis has its origins in the materialist philosophy of Marx and Engels and is clearly articulated in Freire's pedagogy for the oppressed.

Marx and Engels posit that human existence and society are produced by people and can be transformed by people. In a letter to one of his contemporaries, Marx asks, "what is society, whatever its form may be?" He then answers that society is "the product of men's[/women's] reciprocal activity!" (1973: 3). For Marx and Engels (1984) the activity of men and women in the world is the fundamental basis of human existence because it is at the center of the production of material life itself; it produces society and is the driving force of history. Their critique of the German idealism of their day clearly articulates the essential importance of human activity to the social existence and historical being of men and women in the world:

Since we are dealing with the Germans who are devoid of premises, we must begin by stating the first premise of all human existence, and therefore of all history, the premise, namely, that men[/women] must be in a position to live in order to "make history." But life involves before everything else eating and drinking, a habitation, clothing, and many other things. The first historical act is thus the production of the means to satisfy these needs, the production of material life itself. And indeed this is an historical act, a fundamental condition of all history, which today as a thousand years ago must daily and hourly be fulfilled merely in order to sustain human life. Even when the sensuous world is reduced to a minimum, to as stick as with Saint Bruno [Bauer] it presupposes the action of producing the stick. (48)

Marx and Engels argue that history *is made* by men and women who have secured the ability to live, but they do not argue that even having insured this ability these men and women can go about making history as they choose. In *El Dieciocho Brumario de Brumaire of Louis Bonaparte,* Marx points out that "men[/women] make their own history," but that they "are not free to make it as they please, under circumstances chosen by themselves." Those circumstances "are directly encountered, given, and transmitted from the past" (1978: 9; our translation from Spanish). Marx and Engels do not see men and women making history free from the social condition inherited from their past, but neither do they see that social condition absolutely determining the history they can make. While the past weighs heavily upon the present, it does not preclude men and women from radically altering the social existence imposed by their past. Marx and Engels explicitly posit this in their third thesis on Feuerbach:

The materialist doctrine concerning the changing of circumstances and upbringing forgets that circumstances are changed by men[/women] and that it is essential to educate the educator himself[/herself].

The coincidence of the changing of circumstances and of human activity or self-changing can be conceived and rationally understood only as *revolutionary practice.* (1984: 121)

Through this materialist philosophy and social theorization, we understand that the condition of our social existence in American society is a product of our most fundamental activity as living beings. We live an internal neocolonialism because we engage in colonial relations of domination and exploitation in the production and reproduction of our material existence and its cultural expression. We make the history of our internal colonial domination through the practice of our everyday lives. Our domination and exploitation do not reside exclusively in an ideological and discursive legacy; nor are these to be found only at the centers of power in American society. They reside and can be found in the labor and mundane displacements of our bodies. Our colonial domination and oppression materialize in the here and now of the processes and practices of our everyday lives—especially those related to securing the basic necessities of life. We also understand that we do not simply choose to engage in processes and practices that make and remake the internal colonialism we experience. We labor and relate to others in the production and reproduction of our social existence with the weight of a colonial and imperialist past squarely on our backs. It is within the circumstances inherited from that past that we reproduce the condition of our social existence and make our history. We are not, however, condemned to continue making and remaking the condition of our existence according to the circumstances imposed by our past. Those circumstances can be changed instead of merely reproduced and made anew. We understand that the very practice that makes possible our existence and characterizes its condition also holds the potential to radically transform these circumstances.

Mere practice, however, will not lead to a social transformation that effectively alters the internal neocolonialism we experience. It needs to be practice that is grounded in a critical consciousness of this condition and its possible transformation. This understanding finds clear expression in Freire's (1990) pedagogy for the oppressed and his call for a praxis of liberation. His pedagogical conception begins with the materialist theorization that social existence is the product of human action and can be transformed by human praxis:

> Just as objective social reality exists not by chance, but as the product of action, so it is not transformed by chance. If men[/women] produce social reality (which in the "inversion of praxis" turns back upon them and conditions them), then transforming that reality is an historical task, a task for men[/women].
>
> Reality which becomes oppressive results in the contradistinction of men[/women] as oppressors and oppressed. The latter, whose task it is to struggle for their liberation together with those who show true solidarity, must acquire a critical awareness of oppression through the praxis of this struggle. One of the gravest obstacles to the achievement of liberation is that oppressive reality absorbs those within it and thereby acts to submerge men's[/women's] consciousness. Functionally oppression is domesticating. To no longer be prey to its force one must emerge from it and turn upon it.

This can be done only by means of the praxis: reflection and action upon the world in order to transform it. (36)

In this passage we see the fundamental importance that Freire places on the development of a critical consciousness of social existence. An end to oppression, which is the fundamental objective of Freire's call for a socially transformative praxis, requires that men and women have the ability to perceive their existence in the world. He argues that their action in the world is largely determined by the way they see themselves within it, and that a correct perception necessitates of an ongoing reflection on their world. For Freire it is neither the mere action nor the mere reflection and critical consciousness of men and women that will transform the world and end oppression. This can only be achieved through "praxis: the action and reflection of men in the world in order to transform it" (66).

The ability to perceive correctly and arrive at a critical consciousness of the world, however, does not come automatically; it is itself the product of praxis. From this position Freire argues for an educational practice (a pedagogical praxis) that engages with the oppressed in reflection that leads to action on their concrete reality. He calls for a pedagogy that makes oppression and its causes objects of a reflection that will allow the oppressed to develop a consciousness of "their necessary engagement in the struggle for their liberation" (33). Freire clearly articulates the essential importance of critical consciousness to transformative action that is liberating:

> In order for the oppressed to be able to wage the struggle for their liberation, they must perceive the reality of oppression not a closed world from which there is no exit, but as a limiting situation which they can transform. This perception is a necessary but not a sufficient condition for liberation; it must become the motivating force for liberating action. (34)

He attributes to education an essential role in the development of developing critical consciousness that Freire ascribes to education:

> In problem posing education, men[/women] develop their power to perceive critically the way they exist in the world with which and in which they find themselves. They come to see the world not as static reality, but as reality in process, in transformation. Although the dialectical relations of men with the world exist independently of how these relations are perceived (or whether or not they are perceived at all) it is also true that the form of action men adopt is to a large extent a function of how they perceived themselves in the world. Hence the teacher-student and the students-teachers reflect

simultaneously on themselves and the world without dichotomizing this
reflection from action, and thus establish an authentic form of thought and
action. (71)

From Freire we understand that a social transformation that works in
the interests of working-class indigenous and nonwhite peoples necessitates a critical consciousness of social existence and the possibility of its
transformation. We argue that a critical decolonizing consciousness is fundamental to the transformation of the internal neocolonial condition of
social existence in the contemporary United States. One need only consider the level of post–September 11 patriotism and expressed belief in
official rhetoric (about America's moral righteousness and freedom loving
and defending tradition) among working-class indigenous and nonwhite
people to see the degree to which our internal neocolonial condition has
"submerged" the consciousness of men and women who live and experience the effects of that condition on a daily basis. The vast majority of
working-class indigenous and nonwhite people in the contemporary
United States cannot see the extent to which the essence of the colonialism that made them English-speaking, Christian individuals continues to
define their social existence. We agree with Freire that how men and
women act in the world is largely related to how they perceive themselves
in the world, and thus we understand that the existent potential to transform our internal neocolonial condition will remain unrealized if we fail
to appropriately perceive and develop a critical consciousness of this condition and its possible undoing. A social transformation that ends our neocolonial oppression and exploitation in American society will require a
cycle of emancipatory thought, action, and reflection—in other words, a
praxiological cycle. We build on Freire and contend that critical consciousness is developed through the struggle against internal neocolonialism both in the classroom and the larger social context.

TOWARD THE DEFINITION OF A DECOLONIZING PEDAGOGY

Critical pedagogy has put forth the notion that classroom practice integrates particular curriculum content and design, instructional strategies
and techniques, and forms of evaluation. It argues that these specify a particular version about what knowledge is of most worth, what it means to
know something, and how we might construct a representation of our
world and our place within it (McLaren 1998). From this perspective, the
pedagogical is inherently political. For us a decolonizing pedagogy encompasses both an anticolonial and decolonizing notion of pedagogy and an
anticolonial and decolonizing pedagogical praxis. It is an anticolonial and
decolonizing theory and praxis that insists that colonial domination and

its ideological frameworks operate and are reproduced in and through the curricular content and design, the instructional practices, the social organization of learning, and the forms of evaluation that inexorably sort and label students into enduring categories of success and failure of schooling. Thus, an anticolonial and decolonizing pedagogical praxis explicitly works to transform these dimensions of schooling so that schools become sites for the development of a critical decolonizing consciousness and activity that work to ameliorate and ultimately end the mutually constitutive forms of violence that characterize our internal neocolonial condition. For us, a decolonizing pedagogy addresses both the means and the ends of schooling.

THE CONCEPTUAL ORIENTATIONS OF A DECOLONIZING PEDAGOGY

The decolonizing pedagogy we propose must be guided by a conceptually dynamic worldview and a set of values that make it anticapitalist, antiracist, antisexist, and antihomophobic. It is informed by a theoretical heteroglossia that strategically utilizes theorizations and understandings from various fields and conceptual frameworks to unmask the logics, workings, and effects of internal colonial domination, oppression, and exploitation in our contemporary contexts. Among the most significant of these are postcolonial studies, spatial theory, critical pedagogy, critical race theory, and cultural-historical activity theory of learning and human development. In what follows, we briefly discuss the first four of these. The manner in which cultural historical theories of learning inform our conception of a decolonizing pedagogy is explained in our discussion of decolonizing pedagogical praxis.

POSTCOLONIAL STUDIES

While postcolonial studies is an increasingly divided and contested area of scholarship, elements of its critical focus on European colonialism's enduring effects contribute to our conception of a decolonizing pedagogy. In the past two decades, postcolonial theory has gained a significant ascendancy and legitimacy in the Western (i.e., British and American) academy. One can readily see its increasing significance in the expanding bibliography that theorizes, studies, critiques, or otherwise engages the reality and/or conceptual framework referred to as "postcolonial" (Afzal-Khan and Seshadri-Crooks 2000; Ashcroft, Griffiths, and Tifflin 1995; Gandhi 1998; Mongia 1996; Moore-Gilbert 1997; Singh and Schmidt 2000). This same bibliography, however, also reveals that there are differing conceptions of what constitutes a "postcolonial reality" or the "postcolonial theory" that explains it. Referring to the theoretical and methodological heterogeneity that characterizes the body of thought and work produced under its rubric, Gandhi (1998) explains why postcolonial is a "defuse and nebulous term":

> Over the last decade postcolonial studies has emerged both as a meeting point and battleground for a variety of disciplines and theories. While it has enabled a complex interdisciplinary dialogue with the humanities, its uneasy incorporation of mutually antagonistic theories—such as Marxism and post-structuralism—confounds any uniformity of approach. As a consequence, there is little consensus regarding the proper content, scope and relevance of postcolonial studies. Disagreements arising from usage and methodology are reflected in the semantic quibbling which haunts attempts to name post-colonial terminology. (viii)

Afzal-Kahn and Seshadri-Crooks explain why, despite its unquestionable growth, the field remains both undefinable and amorphous:

> It does not have a theory to speak of, concerned at it is with local cultural practices and political issues in the context of transnationalism. Unlike other area studies, postcolonial studies has no identifiable subject; it would be impossible to suggest that it pertains to one or the other area of the world or that it is confined to a genre, period, or theme; nor can it name a stable First or Third world subject as its legitimate speaker "(as can, e.g., women's studies, African American Studies, or gay and lesbian studies)." (2000: 19)

Moore-Gilbert writes that there even appears to be "a growing divide between postcolonial theory on the one hand and the rest of postcolonial criticism on the other" (1997: 1). Characteristic of this apparent divide are fervent disagreements over theory and method, as well as attacks on the politics and personal commitments of particular scholars (see Afzal-Khan and Seshadri-Crooks 2000; Gandhi 1998; Mongia 1996; Moore-Gilbert 1997). There are disagreements, for example, between those working from a poststructuralist perspective and those working from a Marxist perspective—the former privileging discourse; the latter political economy (Afzal-Khan and Seshadri-Crooks 2000; Gandhi 1998; Mongia 1996; Moore-Gilbert, 1997).

Without intending to minimize the significance of the conceptual and political issues related to the heterogeneity and antagonism in the field, we steer clear of these (at least for now) and highlight that which informs both our call for and our conception of a decolonizing pedagogy. It is, obviously, beyond the limitations of this chapter to engage in a thorough discussion of the varied ways in which postcolonial studies can inform us, but we want to signal at least two of these.

The first is the field's concern with recalling a colonial past and addressing its persisting effects. Gandhi argues that if postcoloniality can be said to be concerned with the "consequences of a self-willed historical amnesia," the theoretical value of postcolonial theory resides in its "ability to elaborate forgotten memories of this condition" (1998: 7–8). The capacity to recall and articulate forgotten memories of an internal colonial past is essential to the notion and praxis of a decolonizing pedagogy. Consider the following: how easily the average American can recall the heroic deeds of the Founding Fathers, while forgetting their ignoble practices and activities as slave-owning aristocrats (Franklin and Moss 1988); how most Americans know that the Founding Fathers and their contemporaries erected a democracy on the principles of liberty, justice, and the equality of all men, while ignoring that what they actually institutionalized and practiced was a democracy that excluded women, the nonpropertied, and all nonwhites (Zinn 1995); how American collective memory nostalgically remembers a Wild West that was tamed by pioneers in covered wagons and courageous cowboys on white horses, while it easily forgets about the presence of indigenous peoples on the continent, the Indian Wars, and the federal government's systematic removal and extermination of these Indians (Brown 1981; Churchill 1997).

Also consider how U.S. citizens see contemporary Mexicanos and Salvadoreños who cross U.S. borders as illegals, while they are blinded to American imperialists who conquered territories and imposed those borders in the first place (Acuña 1981; Powell 2000); how contemporary Americans remember the military attack on Pearl Harbor as "a day of infamy," while forgetting that the U.S. naval fleet was an occupying army in Hawaii (Zinn 1995); how in the recent past Americans condemned white rule and apartheid in South Africa, while maintaining a complicit naiveté and silence about white supremacist rule (Almaguer 1994; Horseman 1997) and Indian reservations in the United States (Deloria 1983); how present-day Americans are abhorred at terrorist attacks against America, while they find security in, or altogether ignore, the practices and activities of the Central Intelligence Agency (CIA) in foreign countries (Chomsky and Herman 1979).

That dominant American society fails to recall a colonial past and acknowledge its persisting effects explains why teachers in today's schools ingenuously lead choruses of school children to sing about a beautiful America from sea to shining sea; why students study U.S. history in high school yet graduate understanding none of the above; why Americans who studied U.S. history in high school place U.S. flags on car antennas to demonstrate that they stand united behind freedom and democracy, while they fail to consider all of the above. A decolonizing pedagogy challenges ahistorical memories of America's colonial past.

Secondly, we agree with the field's assertion that there is a direct and material relation between the political processes and social structures of colonialism on the one hand, and Western regimes of knowledge and representation on the other (Moore-Gilbert 1997). While postcolonial studies have addressed this relation primarily in terms of Western imperialist nations (e.g., England, France, and the United States) and their colonial territories outside the nation-state, this relation has also been essential to the domestic imperialism and internal colonialism of the United States. The brutal subordination, domination, and/or exploitation of indigenous and nonwhite peoples that were openly practiced and institutionally sanctioned in the seventeenth, eighteenth, nineteenth, and twentieth centuries were always accompanied and sustained (e.g., rationalized, legitimized, excused, and/or made commonsensical) by specific systems of knowledge and particular representations of peoples, their essence, their cultures, and their value as beings (Almaguer 1994: De Leon 1983; Dyer 1997; Fredrickson 1995; Seed 2001; Spring 2001b; Williams 1995).

Western epistemology and systems of knowledge have been integral to the internal colonial domination suffered by indigenous and nonwhite peoples. There were culturally specific systems of knowledge and underlying logics directly and materially related to the enslavement of Africans (Campbell and Oakes 1995; Trouillot 1995), the dispossession of Indigenous populations from the land (Seed 2001; Williams 1995) and the westward imperialist expansion of the United States (Almaguer 1994; Horseman 1997). Seed writes that Europeans who began seizing the resources of peoples in the New World after 1492 described the reasons for their seizure in terms of "fundamental international maxims" (2001: 4). The case was, however, that "what they characterized as 'international' or 'universal' were simply their own distinct European cultural traditions applied overseas" (4). Trouillot writes that by the early 1700s "the ideological rationalization of Afro-American slavery in the early 1700's relied increasingly on explicit formulations of the ontological order inherited from the Renaissance" (1995: 77). Colonization, he explains, provided a powerful "impetus for the transformation of European ethnocentrism into scientific racism" (77). Deloria asserts that the science founded on the Cartesian bifurcation of mind and matter "enabled atrocities of unimagined proportions to be administered" against darker-skinned people by slave owners and armies (1997: 6). He calls to mind a few examples of the type of hideous scientific practices (e.g., the experimentation with Indian cadavers, the testing of experimental drugs, and sterilization) exercised against indigenous peoples and he gives the following description of Western science's role in their continued domination and oppression:

> These practical examples of science gone mad are but minor points in the long run. More important for our purposes, while not forgetting the horrors of some scientific behavior, is the impact of scientific doctrine on the status of Indians in American society. Regardless of what Indians have said concerning their origins, their migrations, their experiences with birds, animals, lands, waters, mountains, and other peoples, the scientists have maintained a stranglehold on the definitions of what respectable and reliable human experiences are. The Indian explanation is always cast aside as a superstition, precluding Indians from having an acceptable status as human beings, and reducing them in the eyes of educated people to a prehuman level of ignorance. Indians must simply take whatever status they have been granted by scientists at that point which they have become acceptable to science. (7)

Representation of the other was an essential dimension of the relation between Western systems of knowledge and the political processes and social structures of colonialism in the United States. *Race* and *culture* were fundamental sites where British representations constructed an inferior Other that was integral to (although not necessarily the ultimate cause of) the colonial domination and the imperialist expansion that privileged white Europeans (primarily Englishmen) at the expense of indigenous and nonwhite peoples (Almaguer 1994; Campbell and Oakes 1995; De Leon 1983; Seed 2001; Spring 2001a; Williams 1995). As early as the sixteenth century, for example, the English had begun to represent Africans as "heathens" and "savages" devoid of civilization, as well as lewd, libidinous, and "almost bestial" (Campbell and Oakes 1997). By the early 1800s, these types of representations had been increasingly racialized and essentialized as constitutive of the racial character and inferiority of black slaves. The role of the notion of racial inferiority in rationalizing the institution of slavery is well documented and widely known. Less known is how fundamentally important the institution of slavery was to the economic development of the early United States and its westward imperialist expansion (Franklin and Moss 1988)—an economic development and an imperialist expansion that fundamentally benefited European whites at the expense of indigenous and nonwhite peoples.

The racial and cultural representation of indigenous peoples was no less ruthless. Almaguer (1994) explains that the European colonists who battled native peoples for control of the land in North America brought well-developed assumptions that allowed them to differentiate themselves from those they encountered. Those assumptions—Eurocentric binaries that differentiated between Christians and heathens, and civilized and savage—are said to have provided the cultural standard by which the colonists initially racialized the native population. They were later used to differentiate the cultural groups encountered by European Americans as they expanded into the Southwest. Almaguer points out that the representation of indigenous populations as "savage heathens was significant for the social organization of the colonial economy" (1994: 22). Nowhere was the material relation between the representation of indigenous people as "inferior others" and the political processes and the social relations of American colonialism more evident than in the dispossession of the land (Seed 2001; Spring 2001a; Williams 1997). The Europeans' assumed cultural superiority and what they believed it entitled them to vis-à-vis indigenous people is clearly explained by Seed (2001):

> Europeans uniformly explained that they were displacing Native Americans and seizing their labor, land and other valuable commodities because the conduct of the indigenous people failed to conform to the Europeans' expectations of society. Finding that natives failed to value or to exploit the resources the Europeans believed to be profitable, the Europeans declared natives to be ineffectual or unworthy users of their riches. . . . their qualifications stemmed from the inferiority of the "Indians." (5–6)

Of fundamental importance is that the scholars cited above (Almaguer 1994; De Leon 1983; Deloria 1997; Seed 2001; Spring 2001a; Trouillot 1995; and Williams 1997) argue that the systems of knowledge and modes of representation that accompanied and sustained the white-privileging internal colonialism and domestic imperialism of the United States are alive and well in the present. One need only to consider the following to see the veracity of their contention: the recent CIA support for genocidal wars against indigenous people in Guatemala, Nicaragua, and El Salvador; the passage of Proposition 187 in California; the daily deaths at the U.S.–Mexico border; the racial profiling and continuous murder of African Americans by police forces; the mascot of the professional football team from Washington, D.C.; the dominant regimes of knowledge in the academy; the discourse surrounding Indian casinos; and the "color" of the hands and the logics of the minds that administer the reins of economic, political, and cultural power in American society. That most contemporary descendants of both the colonizer and the colonized fail to see and understand how the past exists in the present speaks volumes to the brutal effectiveness of Anglo colonization and the genocidal efficiency of the processes and practices of deculturalization, Americanization, and ideological management that have found their clearest expression in American schooling (Spring, 1992, 2001a, 2001b). Today, for example, Mexicana(o)/Chicana(o) youth are much more likely to join the Armed forces of the United States than to identify as deculturalized descendants of indigenous peoples.

Theorizations and notions from postcolonial studies, then, contribute to our conceptualization of a decolonizing pedagogical praxis. As evidenced above, however, we ground these notions in the long tradition of scholarship and dissenting voices in African American Studies, Chicana/o Studies, and Native American Studies that predate the recent postcolonial vogue yet continue to be ghettoized within the mainstream academy.

SPATIAL THEORY

Our call for the conception and practice of a decolonizing pedagogy also incorporates and builds on the work of spatial theorists. A key premise of spatial theory is that *space matters fundamentally to social life;* it cannot be "reduced to a stage" on which social and historical actors play out their destiny (Carter 1995: 375–76). Space must be conceptualized as more than a "passive container of powerful economic and social processes" (Daniels and Lee 1996: 11). Haymes (1995), for example, argues that white supremacist discourses have racialized urban space and that those racialized urban spaces have affected both the positionality of blacks and black subjectivities. Theorizing the relationship between space and status, Spain contends that "gendered spaces" deny women access to knowledge employed by men to produce and maintain power and privilege (1992: 3). Rose (1993) interrogates geography's epistemological foundations and its conception of space, and then juxtaposes them with a review of feminist work on women and everyday spaces to argue that the space of geography's focus is riddled with a masculinism that has marginalized women from the field and the focus on women within the field. These scholars are articulating a theorization of space that can greatly inform our historical understanding of the domination and oppression of native peoples in the Americas (Tejeda 2000a) and is fundamental to our conception of social existence in the internal neocolonial context of the United States. This theorization posits that space matters with regards to social interaction, race, class, gender, identity formation, and power, and that it is integral to domination, oppression, and exploitation because it is inextricably bound to social existence. It cannot, "be dealt with as if it were merely an abstract arena on which things happen" (Keith and Pile 1993: 2).

The cornerstone of this insistence on the spatiality of social life is an ontological conception of space. This ontological conception, implied in the spatial assertions of various theorists (Foucault 1986; Spain 1992; Rose 1993; Keith and Pile 1993; Ligget and Perry 1995; Daniels and Lee 1996; Hamnett 1996), is best articulated by Soja (1989, 1996). He explains that taking space seriously requires "a deconstruction and reconstitution of critical thought and analysis at every level of abstraction, including ontology" (1989: 7). Soja (1989, 1996) calls for a critical sensibility toward space that is grounded in an ontological conception that situates spatiality right alongside historicality and sociality. According to this ontological conception, our being-in-the-world "is existentially definable as being that is simultaneously historical, social, and spatial" (1989: 73). From this conception of "being-in-the-world," it is no less important to think about the spatial acting on social and historical beings than it is to think about the social or the historical acting on spatial beings.

Space, we argue, is complicit in the domination, oppression, and exploitation of working-class indigenous and nonwhite peoples in the internal colonial contexts of the United States. As Daniels and Lee state, "geography has a history of complicity in socially destructive attempts to reshape the world" (1996: 5). Jacobs (1996) is even more explicit in signaling the importance of understanding colonialism from a spatial perspective. She writes that the expressions and negotiations of imperialism in contemporary first world cities do not simply occur in space, but are about "a politics of identity and power that articulates itself *through* space and is, fundamentally, *about* space" (1996: 1). She adds that people in contemporary cities are "connected by imperial histories" and that their interactions are "still regulated by imperialism's constructs of difference and privilege" (4). Camarillo made a similar argument about the existence of the past in the present. He wrote of the failure of scholars to recognize the influence of nineteenth century developments on twentieth century experiences" (1979: 4).

Space is more than simply *where* conquest and colonialism have occurred; it has been integral to the very operation of colonial domination and oppression. As Tejeda (2000b) argues,

> ... the conquering and subsequent domination of indigenous peoples throughout the Americas (which gave birth to the wandering, toiling, and undereducated Chicana(o)/Latina(o) of the 20th century—those in Mexico, Guatemala, and El Salvador, as well as those whose lives brushstroke the social landscapes of Los Angeles, San Antonio, and Chicago) occurred in and marked a space to no less a degree that it occurred in and marked a time. And

that space has in turn marked and acted on the indigenous peoples and their (mestizo/Mexicano/Chicano/Latino/Hispanic) descendants to no less a degree than time (history). (138)

Tejeda contends that the representation and production of native peoples as illegal aliens are a product of particularly defined and practiced space acting on social subjects to no less a degree than the "imagined community of the United States" is a product of social subjects acting on space. Theorizing the significance of the representation of space and the impact of spatial representation on bodies, Tejeda (2000a) posits the following:

> . . . to a large extent, the dominant discourses through which the spaces of Southern California are lived by their inhabitants are the white supremacist discourses that yesterday rationalized the Anglo conquest and colonization of the region (see Almaguer 1994) and today signify Anglos (white bodies) as a natural extension of those spaces, as entitled to the geography and its resources, while signifying Mexicano immigrants (brown bodies) as alien and un-natural to those spaces, as un-entitled. What's more, I would argue that the type of notions and practices theorized through the constructs of *whiteness* and *whiteness as property* (see McLaren 1997; Harris 1993) undergird and imbue both the anti-immigrant and anti-affirmative action discourses and social actions which currently undermine the educational opportunities and experiences of the ChCh/LL population—discourses which, inscribed on the very flesh of body/subjects (McLaren 1995), frame struggles that are essentially about social spaces (the academy, the workplace, the nation-state) and racialized body/subjects' access and entitlement to those spaces. (52–53)

Hence, we argue that the spatial dimension of our lives in the internal neocolonial context of the United States defines our social existence to no less a degree than the social and historical dimension of our lives. We further argue that there is a need to analyze, investigate, and understand the spatial dimension of our social existence in the internal neocolonial contexts of the United States with the same conceptual and methodological rigor that we analyze, investigate, and attempt to understand the social and historical dimension of this existence. Space matters fundamentally to social life, which is something indigenous people, at least those that have yet to be culturally and epistemologically colonized, have known all along.

In discussing a postcolonial psychology that acknowledges how the systematic genocide of the last five hundred years has devastated indigenous communities, Duran (1995) argues the following:

> One of the first ideas that must be kept in mind when thinking about the native American worldview from a Western perspective is that the native temporal approach to the world is different from that of Western people. Western thought conceptualizes history in a linear temporal sequence, whereas most Native American thinking conceptualizes history in a spatial fashion. Temporal thinking means that time is thought of as having a beginning and end; spatial thinking views events as a function of space or where the event actually took place. (14)

We are, unfortunately, not among those that have long known about the significance of space. We occupy indigenous bodies as we write; yet we come to know and understand things our indigenous ancestors have long known and understood, not from them but from those who voice from Euro-American academy. The brutality of colonization has meant for some of us that we must speak to and about ourselves through the colonizing other. In writing this chapter and arriving at this realization, we have come to see that our Indian bodies often move to the rhythms and the logics of a colonized mind. We have come to recognize that our indigenous corporality has enfleshed (McLaren 1995) a colonial mentality that is present in our very efforts toward the dissenting literacies of decolonizing pedagogy. We are forced to see that internal neocolonialism inhabits our minds and is enconcretized through our bodies. We can also see, however, that in developing this realization we have been engaging in decolonizing praxis.

CRITICAL RACE THEORY

We also draw on Critical Race Theory to understand better how an internal neocolonial condition (i.e., white privilege and control) is maintained through past and current formal and informal mechanisms of racial subjugation and inequality. In particular, this theoretical perspective allows us to understand how the legal system functions to sustain white privilege, or the status quo camouflaged as color-blind, across sociopolitical, economic, and educational contexts, practices, and institutions. This theory helps explain how, despite the changes brought about through the Civil Rights Movement and thereafter, white privilege and its attempts to nullify difference persevere.

Our lives and those of our students provide the context for our understanding the role the law has played in shaping and sustaining racial oppression in the U.S. Southwest. Experience alone, however, cannot account for everything. Conversely, theory in isolation from experience is deprived of the vigor of the situated perspective. It is in the coincidence of the two that helps ensure the robustness and validity of the analysis. Consequently, we draw upon the work of particular critical race scholars who prioritize the experiences poor, dark-skinned, and indigenous people have had with the U.S. legal system (Crenshaw 1995; Delgado 1995). Their work renders visible the mechanisms by which dominant color-blind interpretations of the Constitution serve to legitimate and maintain the social, economic, and political advantages that whites hold over other American citizens (Gotanda 1995). These critical race scholars documented how property rights and racial and economic subordination have collaborated since the birth of this country to create the racialized system of oppression that lives today (Harris 1993). Central to a decolonizing perspective is understanding how primitive and contemporary forms of capital accumulation and racism have enjoyed a symbiotic relationship. In other words, the motivation for expropriating indigenous people from their means of subsistence (i.e., the land that subsequently, through the magical language of the law, transformed into the settler's property) was never solely about capitalism or racism. Our decolonizing analysis, instead, focuses on the central role the relationship between capitalism and racism played in the birth and consolidation of the United States.

CRITICAL PEDAGOGY

McLaren describes critical pedagogy as a radical theory of education that is "irrevocably committed to the side of the oppressed" (1998: 164). He explains that it is a theoretical approach that is continuously annexing advances in social theory and developing new categories of inquiry and new methodologies to pose "a variety of important counterlogics to the positivistic, ahistorical, and depoliticized analysis employed by both liberal and conservative critics of schooling" (163). Various scholars have signaled that one of critical pedagogy's essential characteristics is that it cannot be reduced to a single conception or a homogenous set of theories and methodologies (McLaren 1998; Wink 1997; Leistyna, Woodrum, and Sherblom 1996). There are, nonetheless, a number of theoretical premises and positions orienting the work and politics of most critical pedagogues that can greatly inform our understanding of schooling in the internal neocolonial context of the contemporary United States.

The following are theorizations that inform our conception of schooling and its function in our internal neocolonial contexts: educational theories and practices should encourage and assist students and teachers to develop understandings of the relationships among culture, ideology, and power (Giroux 1981, 1988; Leistyna, Woodrum, and Sherblom 1996); schooling is characterized by complexities, contradictions, multiple realities, and change (Wink 1997); the processes and practices of schooling must be understood in their historical context and as a part of the existing social, political, and cultural fabric of society (McLaren 1998); schooling should be understood and analyzed as a process in which certain social groups are positioned within asymmetrical relations of power on the basis of race, class, and gender; schooling serves primarily the interest of the wealthy and powerful classes in society while working against the needs and interests of the poor, racial and ethnic minorities, and women (McLaren 1998; Wink 1997); the agency of social subjects should be a central focus in the analysis and understanding of schooling—in other words, teachers and students should be seen as participants in history, rather than merely objects that are acted upon, manipulated, and controlled (Giroux 1983a, 1983b; Leistyna, Woodrum, and Sherblom 1996); history is the product of social praxis and through social praxis a radically different world can be brought into existence; a fundamental objective of pedagogy should be to empower the oppressed and contribute to the transformation of the social relations and formations that produce social inequalities and injustices (McLaren 1998; Leistyna, Woodrum, and Sherblom 1996); schooling for self and social empowerment should be ethically prior to the mastery of technical skills (McLaren 1998; Leistyna, Woodrum, and Sherblom 1996); and, the modernist notions of objective inquiry, universal reason, and absolute truth should be challenged and the claims of a universal foundation for culture or truth should be rejected (McLaren 1995; Leistyna, Woodrum, and Sherblom 1996).

THE CURRICULAR CONTENTS OF A DECOLONIZING PEDAGOGICAL PRAXIS AND ITS CULTURAL-HISTORICAL CONCEPTION OF LEARNING AND COGNITION

Shortly after the military phase of the Spanish conquest, the Aristotelian philosopher Juan Gines de Sepulveda, the Dominican priest Bartolome de Las Casas, and their contemporaries debated whether "the Indian" should be educated and, if so, to what end (Hanke 1974). Conceptualizing indigenous people as children, Thomas L. McKenney, superintendent of Indian trade, argued that the creation of tribal school systems run by white missionaries could culturally transform Native Americans in one generation; his ideas were enacted by the U.S. Congress in the Civilization Act of 1819 (Spring 2001a). Those type of debates and arguments and their underlying ideologies of cultural and racial superiority have persisted into the present. They continue to largely define the educational opportunities and schooling experiences of indigenous and nonwhite peoples throughout the Americas. The United States, of course, is no exception.

One need only consider the recent propositions in the state of California to see how voices from the past speak loudly in our present. The electorate in the state actually voted to deny education to children who could not prove their legal status in the country. It then voted to rescind affirmative action programs that functioned to increase educational access and opportunity for nonwhite people. Most recently, the same electorate voted to deny the Spanish-speaking population in the state the opportunity to be educated in its own language. Indeed, the violence against indigenous and nonwhite peoples institutionalized during America's colonial past continues in its internal neocolonial present. We insist that there can be no social justice in the context of this violence, and that the struggle for social justice necessarily implies a struggle within and against the institutions that perpetuate, legitimize, or conceal the multiple forms of violence perpetuated against working-class indigenous and nonwhite peoples. This is not a struggle that will be waged with AK-47s; it is a struggle that must be waged with pedagogies, and we call for engaging in that struggle through a decolonizing pedagogical praxis in the classroom.

By calling for a decolonizing pedagogical praxis, it is not us who propose to politicize the curriculum and place the school at the service of political ends. The school in American society has been implicated in the politics of colonial domination from its inception. The deculturalization and Americanization that dominant groups saw as integral to cultural, political, and economic domination of indigenous and nonwhite peoples have always found a most hospitable site and effective mechanism in the school (Spring 2001a, 2001b).

THE CURRICULAR CONTENT OF A DECOLONIZING PEDAGOGY

What is the subject matter of a decolonizing pedagogy? What do teachers and students engaged in decolonizing pedagogical praxis teach and learn from one another? We contend that developing a critical consciousness of our internal neocolonial condition and its possible transformation is fundamental to what teachers and students do in decolonizing pedagogical spaces. This requires explicit attention to the history and contemporary manifestations of internal neocolonialism in a manner that clearly explicates their social origin and rejects their historical consequence. It also introduces students to robust theories and conceptual frameworks that provide them the analytical tools to excavate history and examine the present. It is a pedagogical content that must be guided by a conceptually dynamic worldview and a set of values that are anticapitalist, antiracist, antisexist, and antihomophobic.

We view the contents described above as necessarily contingent and context-specific. While internal neocolonialism indelibly marks all social existence and largely defines every dimension of life, it assumes diverse forms and is experienced differently in the various social spaces of American society. Hence, we contend that the specific history and specific manifestations of neocolonialism that students and teachers engage should be determined by the particular social spaces of their existence—the specific places and social contexts where they experience internal neocolonialism. Likewise, the specific theorizations and conceptual frameworks that students and teachers engage should be determined by the specificity of neocolonial domination and exploitation in the social spaces they inhabit. The content of a decolonizing pedagogical praxis on an Indian reservation, for example, would necessarily be different than the content of a decolonizing pedagogical praxis in the urban spaces of metropolitan Los Angeles. In other words, the content is situated and contingent and thus open to continuous modification and expansion.

While history and social science courses are seemingly ideal and most immediately relevant for addressing the history and current manifestations of internal neocolonialism, we call for decolonizing pedagogical praxis across the curriculum. All curricular subject matter (e.g., the social sciences, the humanities, and the natural sciences) can be used to examine neocolonial conditions or can be engaged in a manner that addresses the neocolonial production, utilization, and/or effects of its related bodies of knowledge. Whether we engage students in the learning of mathematics, history and social studies, language arts, chemistry, physics, or vocational skills, the content of our pedagogy highlights, examines, and discusses transforming the mutually reinforcing systems of neocolonial and capitalist domination and exploitation in the United States. Our proposed pedagogy also necessarily addresses how working-class indigenous and nonwhite teachers and students are assaulted by multiple and mutually constitutive forms of violence in the various dimensions of their daily lives. In this way, a decolonizing praxis seeks to provide students with a rich theoretical, analytical, and pragmatic toolkit for individual and social transformation.

While we argue for a specific curricular focus for a decolonizing pedagogical praxis, we are also committed to ensuring students the opportunity to master the traditional curriculum necessary for academic success within the present system of schooling. We do not, however, argue for ignoring or replacing the official curricular content for which students are held accountable. While we see the need to problematize and expose the official curriculum's complicity with neocolonial domination and exploitation, we know that failing to prepare students in the mastery of this curriculum only sets them up for academic failure and its related social consequences. The decolonizing pedagogical praxis we propose sets out, for example, to prepare high school students to dynamically critique and actively work against neocolonialism while preparing and making themselves eligible for admission to and success at the most prestigious universities in the United States. Such contradictions are inevitable in internal neocolonial contexts.

DECOLONIZING PEDAGOGICAL PRAXIS AND THE CULTURAL-HISTORICAL CONCEPTION OF LEARNING AND COGNITION

A decolonizing pedagogical praxis challenges not only the forms, content, and intent of other pedagogies and their historical antecedents, but also requires a complete reconceptualization of the social organization of learning in schooling institutions and fundamentally in classrooms. Such a reconceptualization calls for a transformation in the social and intellectual relationships among the participants both in schools and in particular communities in which the schools reside. To date, the most productive theory of human development from our perspective—one that aligns with a decolonizing perspective—is cultural-historical activity theory (Cole 1996; Gutierrez 2000; Moll 2000; Vygotsky 1978; Wertsch 1985, 1991). At its core, cultural-historical or sociocultural theory recognizes the fundamentally relational nature of teaching and learning, the microgenetic, sociohistorical, and cultural planes, and the centrality of culture in human development. Its dynamic and processual notion of culture requires a focus on everyday practice within larger systems of activity that are, of course, always socially and culturally organized. As Cole and Engestrom argue, "A natural unit of analysis for the study of human behavior is activity systems, historically conditioned systems of relations among individuals and their proximal, culturally organized environments" (1993: 8). From our perspective, these practices are inescapably organized within particular neocolonial spaces of domination and oppression.

From this perspective, teaching and learning cannot be disconnected from the larger contexts of their development, from the microgenetic or moment-to-moment and its larger sociohistorical context. This simultaneous focus on historicity and the quotidian requires us to understand the practices of schools as inseparable from our contemporary neocolonial contexts. For us, cultural-historical activity theory provides both a theoretical lens and methodological toolkit for examining and understanding how cultural artifacts that are both material and ideational mediate human beings' interaction with their social worlds. As such, tools or artifacts are never neutral and always a particular politic.

Conceptualizing teaching and learning as fundamentally situated and socially mediated forces us to always ground instructional practices in the present and past realities of teachers and students and to organize learning in ways that promote and assist their potential. Inherent in cultural historical theory is a pedagogy of potential in that its primary concern is on what students can accomplish with assistance in robust contexts of learning (Gutierrez, Baquedano-Lopez, and Tejeda 2000). But here we argue not for contexts that treat all contents, practices, and ways of organizing learning as neutral but rather we argue for contexts in which knowing and knowledge lead to a critical consciousness that guides action toward a transformation of our neocolonial condition.

Within a decolonizing perspective, cultural-historical activity theory can be used to examine and expose the ways the social constructs of race and ethnicity and its proxies, language and ability, achievement and underachievement, as well as the social practices of racism, discrimination, and privileging mediate the schooling outcomes of working-class indigenous and nonwhite students (Gutierrez et al. in press). In doing so, we create new social relations and systems of activity that move toward a fundamentally different instantiation of social justice—one that is defined by historically colonized peoples.

CONCLUSION

The discourses of equity, access, and democracy act as currency in the political economy of academia. The race, class, gender, and sexuality of those who traffic in these discourses weigh heavily on the development of these modes of thought. The question of social justice *by* whom begs us to ask the question: Social justice *for whom*? We move away from notions of social justice that seek to create social space for the poor, dark-skinned, and indigenous to be more like their oppressors.

The ideology that pervades liberal notions of social justice is that of a hopeful Americanism. For all its talk against the social ills of racism and economic inequalities, it fails to translate into a lived praxis that adequately contests the multiplicity of ways racism, capitalism, homophobia, privilege, and sexism are made manifest. We assert that these social ills cannot be combated simply by pressing the popgun of liberal, middle-class love against the bosom of oppressive social structures. Particular strains of social justice bestow upon capitalism immunity against criticism and anticapitalist action. We challenge progressive educators to walk with us, rather than defining the places, spaces, and modes for the inclusion of our voices and our experiences.

We seek to reposition to the center of this discourse those who have been silenced in the classroom—those who endure and have endured the internal neocolonial condition. We seek to reclaim our intellectual heritage and argue that any notion of social justice that informs education in the United States must be derivative of and informed by the experiences and interpretations of those living an internal neocolonial existence.

We argue the need for re-membering the brown body as central to social analysis and knowledge production. Thus, the integrity of the indigenous mind/body is the standard by which we measure the success of any decolonizing pedagogy.

REFERENCES

Acuña, R. 1981. *Occupied America: A History of Chicanos.* 2nd ed. New York: Harper and Row.

Afzal-Khan, F. and K. Seshadri-Crooks, eds. 2000. *The Preoccupation of Postcolonial Studies.* Durham, N.C.: Duke University Press.

Allen, J. and M. Pryke. 1996. "The Production of Service Space." In *Exploring Human Geography: A Reader.* ed. by S. D. R. Lee. New York: Halstead Press.

Almaguer, T. 1974. "Historical Notes on Chicano Oppression: The Dialectics of Racial and Class Domination in North America." *Aztlan* 5 (1 & 2):27–54.

———. 1994. *Racial Fault Lines: The Historical Origins of White Supremacy in California.* Berkeley: University of California Press.

Ashcroft, B., G. Griffiths, and H. Tifflin, eds. 1995. *The Post-Colonial Studies Reader.* New York: Routledge.

Barrera, M. 1979. *Race and Class in the Southwest: A Theory of Racial Inequality.* Notre Dame: University of Notre Dame Press.

Behdad, Ali. 2000. "Une Practique Sauvage: Postcolonial Belatedness and Cultural Politics." In *The Pre-Occupation of Postcolonial Studies,* ed. by F. A.-K. K. Seshadri-Crooks. Durham, N.C.: Duke University Press.

Blauner, R. 1972. *Racial Oppression in America.* New York: Harper and Row.

Brown, D. 1981. *Bury My Heart at Wounded Knee: An Indian History of the American West.* New York: Washington Square Press.

Bulhan, H. A. 1985. *Frantz Fanon and the Psychology of Oppression.* New York: Plenum Publishing.

Camarillo, A. 1979. *Chicanos in a Changing Society: From Mexican Pueblos to American Barrios in Santa Barbara and Southern California, 1848–1930.* Cambridge: Harvard University Press.

Campbell, J., and J. Oakes. 1997. "The Invention of Race: Rereading white over black." In *Critical White Studies: Looking Behind the Mirror,* ed. by R. D. J. Stefancic. Philadelphia: Temple University Press.

Carlson, D. 1987. "Teachers as Political Actors: From Reproductive Theory to the Crisis of Schooling." *Harvard Educational Review* 57 (3):283–307.

———. 1992. *Teachers and Crisis: Urban School Reform and Teachers' Work Culture.* London: Routledge.

Carter, P. 1995. "Spatial History." In *The Post-Colonial Studies Reader,* ed. by G. G. Bill Ashcroft and Helen Tifflin, 375–77. New York: Routledge.

Chomsky, N., and E. S. Herman. 1979. *The Washington Connection and Third World Fascism.* Boston: South End Press.

Churchill, W. 1997. *A Little Matter of Genocide: Holocaust Denial in the Americas 1492 to the Present.* San Francisco: City Lights Books.

Cole, M. 1996. *Cultural Psychology: A Once and Future Discipline.* Cambridge: The Belknap Press of Harvard University Press.

Cole, M. and Y. Engestrom. 1993. "A Cultural-Historical Approach to Distributed Cognition." In *Distributed Cognition: Psychological and Educational Considerations.* New York: Cambridge University Press.

Crenshaw, K. 1995. "Mapping the Margins: Intersectionality, Identity Politics, and Violence against Women of Color." In *Critical Race Theory: The Key Writings that Formed the Movement,* ed. N. G. Kimberlé Crenshaw, Gary Peller, and Kendall Thomas. New York: New Press.

Daniels, S., and R. Lee, eds. 1996. *Exploring Human Geography: A Reader.* New York: Halstead Press.

Davis, P. C. 1995. "Law as Microaggression." In *Critical Race Theory: The Cutting Edge,* ed. R. Delgado. Philadelphia: Temple University Press.

De Leon, A. 1983. *They Called Them Greasers: Anglo Attitudes toward Mexicans in Texas, 1821–1900.* Austin: University of Texas Press.

Delgado, R. 1995. "The Imperial Scholar: Reflections on a Review of Civil Rights Literature." In *Critical Race Theory: The Key Writings that Formed the Movement,* ed. N. G. Kimberlé Crenshaw, Gary Peller, and Kendall Thomas. New York: New Press.

Deloria, V. 1997. *Red Earth, White Lies: Native Americans and the Myth of Scientific Fact.* Golden, Colo.: Fulcrum Publishing.

Deloria, V., and C. M. Lytle. 1983. *American Indians, American Justice.* Austin: Texas University Press.

Dirlik, A. 1996. "The Postcolonial Aura: Third World Criticism in the Age of Global Capitalism." In *Contemporary Postcolonial Theory: A Reader,* ed. Padmini Mongia. New York: Arnold.

Driver, F. 1996. "Geography's Empire: Histories of Geographical Knowledge." In *Exploring Human Geography: A Reader,* ed. S. D. R. Lee. New York: Halstead Press.

Duran, E. and B. Duran, 1995. *Native American Postcolonial Psychology.* Albany: State University of New York Press.

Dyer, R. 1997. *White.* New York: Routledge.

England, V. L. 1997. "Getting Personal: Reflexivity, Positionality, and Feminist Research." In *Reading Human Geography: The Poetics and Politics of Inquiry,* ed. T. B. D. Gregory. New York: Arnold.

Fanon, F. 1963. *The Wretched of the Earth,* (trans. C. Farrington). New York: Grove Press.

Foucault, M. 1986. "Of Other Spaces." *Diacritics* 16:22–27.

Franklin, J. H., and A. A. Moss. 1988. *From Slavery to Freedom: A History of Negro Americans,* 6th ed. New York: Alfred A. Knopf.

Fredrickson, G. 1995. "White Images of Black Slaves (Is What We See in Others Sometimes a Reflection of What We Find in Ourselves?)." In *Critical Race Theory: The Cutting Edge,* ed R. Delgado. Philadelphia: Temple University Press.

Freire, Paulo. 1997 [1970]. *Pedagogy of the Oppressed.* Trans. by M. B. Ramos. New York: Continuum.

———. 1998. *Pedagogy of Freedom: Ethics, Democracy, and Civic Courage.* Trans. P. Clarke. Lanham, Md.: Rowman & Littlefield.

Gandhi, Leela. 1998. *Postcolonial Theory: A Critical Introduction.* New York: Columbia University Press.

Giroux, H. A. 1981. *Ideology, Culture, and the Process of Schooling.* Philadelphia: Temple University Press.

———. 1983a. "Theories of Resistance and Reproduction in the New Sociology of Education: A Critical Analysis." *Harvard Educational Review* 53 (3):261–93.

———. 1983b. *Theory and Resistance in Education: A Pedagogy for the Opposition.* New York: Bergin & Garvey Publishers.

———. 1988. *Schooling and the Struggle for Public Life: Critical Pedagogy in the Modern Age.* Minneapolis: University of Minnesota Press.

Gotanda, N. 1995. "A Critique of 'Our Constitution Is Color-Blind.' " In *Critical Race Theory: The Key Writings that Formed the Movement,* ed. N. G. Kimberlé Crenshaw, Gary Peller, and Kendall Thomas. New York: New Press.

Gutiérrez, K. 2000. "Teaching and Learning in the 21st Century." *English Education* 32 (4):290–98.

Gutiérrez, K., and J. Larson. 1994. "Language Borders: Recitation as Hegemonic Discourse." *International Journal of Educational Reform* 3 (1):22–36.

Gutiérrez, K., P. Baquedano-Lopez, and C. Tejeda. 2000. "Rethinking Diversity: Hybridity and Hybrid Language Practices in the Third Space." *Mind, Culture, & Activity: An International Journal* 6 (4):286–303.

Gutiérrez, K., Asato, J., Santos, M., and Gotanda, N. In press. "Backlash Pedagogy: Language and Culture and the Politics of Reform." *The Review of Education, Pedagogy, and Cultural Studies.*

Hamnett, C. 1996. *Social Geography: A Reader.* New York: Arnold.

Hanke, L. 1959. *Aristotle & the American Indians: A Study in Race Prejudices in the Modern World.* Chicago: Henry Regnery Company.

———. 1974. *All Mankind Is One: A Study of the Disputation between Bartolomé de Las Casa and Juan Ginés de Sepúlveda in 1550 on the Intellectual and Religious Capacity of the American Indians.* DeKalb, Ill.: Northern Illinois University Press.

Harris, Cheryl I. 1993. "Whiteness as Property." *Harvard Law Review* 106 (8):1709–91.

Haymes, S. 1995. *Race Culture and the City: A Pedagogy for Black Urban Struggle.* New York: State University of New York Press.

Horseman, R. 1997. "Race and Manifest Destiny: The Origins of American Racial Anglo-Saxonism." In *Critical White Studies: Looking Behind the Mirror,* ed. R. D. J. Stefancic. Philadelphia: Temple University Press.

Jacobs, J. 1996. *Edge of Empire: Postcolonialism and the City.* New York: Routledge.

Keith, M. and S. Pile, eds. 1993. *Place and the Politics of Identity.* New York: Routledge.

Leistyna, P., A. Woodrum, and S. A. Sherblom, eds. 1996. *Breaking Free: The Transformative Power of Critical Pedagogy.* Cambridge: Harvard Educational Review, Reprint Series No. 27.

Ligget, H. and D. C. Perry, eds. 1995. *Spatial Practices: Critical Explorations in Social/Spatial Theory.* Thousand Oaks, Calif.: Sage.

Marx, K. 1973. *Karl Marx on Society and Social Change.* Ed. N. J. Smelser. Chicago: The University of Chicago Press.

———. 1978. *El Dieciocho Brumario de Luis Bonaparte.* Pekin: Ediciones Lenguas Extranjeras.

Marx, K. and F. Engels. 1984. *The German Ideology.* Ed. C. J. Arthur. New York: International Publishers.

Massey, D. 1984. "Geography Matters." In *Geography Matters!: A Reader,* ed. D. M. a.J. Allen. Cambridge: Cambridge University Press.

McLaren, Peter. 1988. "On Ideology and Education: Critical Pedagogy and the Politics of Education." *Social Text* 19 & 20:153–85.

———. 1997. *Revolutionary Multiculturalism: Pedagogies of Dissent for the New Millennium.* Boulder: Westview Press.

———. 1998. *Life in Schools: An Introduction to Critical Pedagogy in the Foundations of Education,* 3rd ed. New York: Longman.

McLaren, Peter and R. Farahmandpur. 2000. "Critical Multiculturalism and Globalization: Transgressive Pedagogies in Gringolandia." In *Charting New Terrains of Chicana(o)/Latina(o) Education,* ed. C. Tejeda, C. Martinez and Z. Leonardo. New Jersey: Hampton Press.

McLaren, Peter, and Henry Giroux. 1995. *Critical Pedagogy and Predatory Culture.* London: Routledge.

Moll, L. 2000. "Inspired by Vygotsky: Ethnographic Experiments in Education." In *Vygotskian Perspectives on Literacy Research: Constructing Meaning through Collaborative Inquiry,* ed. C. L. P. Smagorinsky. New York: Cambridge University Press.

Mongia, P., ed. 1996. *Contemporary Postcolonial Theory: A Reader.* New York: Arnold.

Moore-Gilbert, B. 1997. *Postcolonial Theory: Contexts, Practices, Politics.* New York: Verso.

Powell, T. B. 2000. *Ruthless Democracy: A Multicultural Interpretation of the American Renaissance.* Princeton: Princeton University Press.

Rose, G. 1993. *Feminism and Geography: The Limits of Geographical Knowledge.* Minneapolis: University of Minnesota Press.

Seed, P. 2001. *American Pentimiento.* Minneapolis: University of Minnesota Press.

Simon, R. 1987. "Empowerment as a Pedagogy of Possibility." *Language Arts* 64 (4).

———. 1992. *Teaching against the Grain.* South Hadley, Mass.: Bergin and Garvey.

Singh, A. and P. Schmidt. 2000. *Postcolonial Theory and the United States: Race Ethnicity and Literature.* Jackson: University Press of Mississippi.

Soja, E. 1989. *Postmodern Geographies: The Reassertion of Space in Critical Social Theory.* New York: Verso.

———. 1996. *Thirdspace: Journeys to Los Angeles and Other Real and Imagined Places.* Cambridge: Blackwell Publishers.

Spain, D. 1992. *Gendered Spaces.* Chapel Hill: The University of North Carolina Press.

Spring, J. 1992. *Images of American Life: A History of Ideological Management in Schools, Movies, Radio, and Television.* Albany: State University of New York Press.

———. 2001a. *The American School: 1642–2000.* 5th ed. San Francisco: McGraw Hill.

———. 2001b. *Deculturalization and the Struggle for Equality: A Brief History of Dominated Cultures in the United States.* 3rd ed. San Francisco: McGraw Hill.

Stromquist, N. P., and K. Monkman, eds. 2000. *Globalization and Education: Integration and Contestation across Cultures.* Landham, Md.: Rowman & Littlefield.

Tejeda, C. 2000a. "Toward a Spatialized Understanding of the Chicana(o)/Latina(o) Educational Experience: Theorizations of Space and the Mapping of Educational Outcomes in Los Angeles." In *Charting New Terrains of Chicana(o)/Latina(o) Education,* ed. C. Tejeda, C. Martinez, and Z. Leonardo. N.J.: Hampton Press.

————. 2000b. "Mapping Social Space: A Study of Spatial Production in an Elementary Class-room." Doctoral Dissertation, University of California Los Angeles.

Trouillot, M. R. 1995. *Silencing the Past: Power and the Production of History.* Boston: Beacon Press.

Vygotsky, L. S. 1978. *Mind in Society: The Development of Higher Psychological Processes.* Ed. M. J. S. Cole, Vera. Cambridge: Harvard University Press.

Wertsch, J. 1985. *Vygotsky and the Social Formation of Mind.* Cambridge: Harvard University Press.

————. 1991. *Voices of the Mind: A Sociocultural Approach to Mediated Action.* Cambridge: Harvard University Press.

Whitty, G. 1985. *Sociology and School Knowledge, Curriculum Theory, Research and Politics.* London: Metheun.

Williams, R. A. 1995. "Documents of Barbarism: The Contemporary Legacy of European Racism and Colonialism in the Narrative Traditions of Federal Indian Law." In *Critical Race Theory: The Cutting Edge,* ed. R. Delgado. Philadelphia: Temple University Press.

Wink, J. 1997. *Critical Pedagogy: Notes from the Real World.* New York: Longman.

Wood, G. 1983. "Beyond Educational Cynicism." *Educational Theory* 32 (2):55–71.

Zinn, H. 1995. *A People's History of the United States: 1492–Present.* New York: Harper Perrennial.

2

Challenging the Construction of Difference as Deficit: Where Are Identity, Intellect, Imagination, and Power in the New Regime of Truth?

JIM CUMMINS

In virtually every country histories of education reveal a systematic and usually intentional process whereby dominant groups have organized the structure of educational provision in ways that construct the human differences that children bring to school—differences in race, class, culture, gender, language—as deficits that are invoked as explanation of these children's poor academic performance. Discourses mobilized in support of this coercive process range from crude overtly racist assertions of genetic inferiority to more sophisticated discussion of the impact of family socialization practices on children's intellectual potential and academic achievement. Common to all of these discourses is a process of blaming the victim (Ryan 1972). The school failure of subordinated or marginalized group students is attributed to alleged intrinsic characteristics of the group itself (genetic inferiority, parental apathy, bilingualism, etc.) or to social and educational programs that are intended to serve the interests of the group (e.g., affirmative action, bilingual education, etc.).

My primary focus in this chapter is on the discourse surrounding linguistic diversity in schools and its intersection with patterns of societal power relations. Drawing on more than thirty years of public debate in the United States regarding bilingual education, on the one hand, and the teaching of reading, on the other hand, I analyze how coercive power relations in the wider society penetrate into the role definitions of educators (e.g., their mindset, expectations, attitudes) and the organizational structures of schooling (e.g., curriculum, assessment, language of instruction, etc.). The interactions between educators and students that are envisaged within this discourse promote the production of certain kinds of student identities that, in turn, serve to reproduce existing patterns of social stratification. In other words, how are linguistic differences constructed in societal discourses related to education and national identity, and what impact is exerted by these discourses on the pedagogical relations that educators orchestrate with their students?

The "regime of truth" that has emerged in the popular media and in educational policies at federal, state, and local level attributes the underachievement of low-income bilingual children both to deficits that children bring to school and to the failure of schools to respond adequately to these deficits. The primary deficits are in children's command of English and in their phonological awareness (knowledge of the constituent sounds of the language). These deficits have been compounded, according to this discourse, by the failure of schools to teach basic English and phonics skills adequately. In response to this construction of the problem of underachievement and spurred on by high-stakes standardized tests, many inner-city school districts in states such as California and Texas, have opted for all-English instruction and scripted phonics instruction that strongly discourages teachers from deviating from the assigned script (as in the *Open Court* reading program).

I suggest that the major problem with this approach is that when we frame the universe of discourse about underachievement primarily in terms of children's deficits in some area of psychological or linguistic functioning, we expel culture, language, identity, intellect, and imagination from our image of the child. Similarly, these constructs are nowhere to be found in our image of the effective teacher of these children, nor in policies that might guide instruction.

Furthermore, a focus on student and community deficits, together with the scapegoating of educators, deflects critical scrutiny from the social conditions that are associated with educational underachievement. The impact of these socioeconomic disparities and associated patterns of racial discrimination can be seen in the strong correlation between academic failure and the collective poverty level of children in a school (Snow, Burns, and Griffin's 1998 review: 126). Yet, there has been little political will to push for equality of access to funding as a means of raising achievement in underfunded inner-city schools. It is much safer to focus on the presumed deficits that low-income children bring to school (e.g., lack of phonological awareness) and teachers' alleged lack of competence to remediate these deficits than to highlight inequities in the distribution of economic and educational resources as causal factors in students' underachievement.

The chapter also addresses the extent and ways in which educators can challenge the historical pattern whereby differences are transformed into deficits. I argue that despite working in conditions that are frequently oppressive both for them and their students, educators have choices in the ways they define their roles in relation to marginalized students and communities and in the kinds of interactions they orchestrate in their classrooms. These interactions construct an interpersonal space within which knowledge is generated and identities are negotiated. This process is never neutral with respect to societal power relations; teacher-student interactions can always be located on a continuum between reinforcement of coercive relations of power in the wider society or promotion of collaborative relations of power.

In order to locate the theoretical discussion of the intersections of linguistic diversity and societal power relations within a concrete context, I briefly outline the evolution of the debate on bilingual education in the United States since the late 1960s to the present.

EVOLUTION OF THE BILINGUAL EDUCATION DEBATE

The debate about the merits or otherwise of bilingual education has preoccupied educators, politicians, the media (and occasionally the general public) in the United States for more than thirty years. Many commentators have warned that bilingual education is not only educationally ill-advised, it also threatens the social and political stability of the nation. Newspaper editorials across the country have detailed a catastrophic scenario of Latino/Latina activists demanding ever-more intensive bilingual education as a ploy both to prevent bilingual children from learning English and to fuel separatist tendencies, resulting ultimately in the disintegration of the United States.

To outsiders, this paranoia about bilingual education might seem absurd, especially in view of the prevalence and high status of bilingual programs in many countries around the world (see Baker and Prys Jones 1998; Cummins and Corson 1997). However, within the United States these arguments are taken very seriously. The roots of this bilingual paranoia can be seen in the evolution of the policy debate through four phases during the past thirty years.

PHASE I. 1967–1974

Initially, as Troike (1978) observed, bilingual education was instituted in the late 1960s on the basis of what appeared to be a self-evident rationale, namely that "the best medium for teaching a child is his or her mother tongue," but with relatively little hard evidence to back up this rationale. The reaction of many press commentators in the initial years of this experiment was one of wait-and-see; they didn't particularly like the idea but were willing to give it a chance to prove its potential for reducing educational inequities. Some were concerned, however, that bilingual education might have the opposite effect, namely of preventing Spanish-speaking students from entering the mainstream of English-speaking America, and also that it might give rise to the divisiveness that appeared to be associated with bilingualism in Canada. However, in general, this first phase of the modern bilingual education debate was marked by a tolerance for the educational potential of bilingual education and, although doubts were certainly raised, its rationale was not disputed in any sustained or systematic way.

PHASE II. 1974–1986

The bilingual education debate became considerably more volatile after the *Lau v. Nichols* case in 1974. The judgment of the Supreme Court in this case acknowledged that the civil rights of non-English-speaking students were violated when the school took no steps to help them acquire the language of instruction.

> . . . there is no equality of treatment merely by providing students with the same facilities, textbooks, teachers, and curriculum; for students who do not understand English are effectively foreclosed from any meaningful education. Basic English skills are at the very core of what these public schools teach. Imposition of a requirement that, before a child can effectively participate in the educational program, he must already have acquired those basic skills is to make a mockery of public education. We know that those who do not understand English are certain to find their classroom experiences wholly incomprehensible and in no way meaningful (Crawford 1992: 253).

The Supreme Court did not mandate bilingual education but it did mandate that schools take effective measures to overcome the educational disadvantages resulting from a home–school language mismatch. The Office of Civil Rights, however, interpreted the Court's decision as effectively mandating transitional bilingual education unless a school district could prove that another approach would be equally or more effective. This interpretation of the Court decision by the Office of Civil Rights sparked outrage among media commentators and educators in school districts that, for the most part, were totally unprepared to offer any form of bilingual instruction.

The ensuing debate was (and continues to be) volatile. The concern with political divisiveness resulting from bilingual education was articulated clearly in a *New York Times* editorial entitled "Bilingual Danger" on November 22, 1976:

The disconcerting strength gathered by separatism in Canada contains a relevant lesson for the United States and its approach to bilingual education. . . . It is no exaggeration to warn that the present encouragement given to making [Spanish-speaking] enclaves permanent, in the mistaken view that they are an expression of positive pluralism, points the road to cultural, economic and political divisiveness (quoted in *The Linguistic Reporter,* January 1977: 1).

As the debate evolved, the sociopolitical concerns of many commentators were backed up by psychoeducational arguments against bilingual education and in favor of all-English immersion programs. The argument in favor of bilingual education that was reflected in the Supreme Court's decision, namely, that "children can't learn in a language they don't understand," was no longer regarded as self-evident. As Noel Epstein (1977) pointed out, apparent counterevidence had appeared in the findings from French immersion programs in Canada that showed that English-background children who were taught initially through French in order to develop fluent bilingual skills did not suffer academically as a result of this home–school language switch (see Swain and Lapkin 1982; Cummins and Swain 1986). To many commentators in the United States, these results suggested that English immersion programs were a plausible educational alternative to bilingual programs.

The bilingual approach appeared to imply a counterintuitive "less equals more" rationale in which less English instruction is assumed to lead to more English achievement. To many opponents of bilingual education it appeared more logical to argue that if children are deficient in English then they need maximum instruction in English, not their native language. School failure was assumed to be caused by insufficient exposure to English (largely at home) and thus it made little sense to further dilute the amount of English to which bilingual students were exposed by instructing them through their first language (L1) at school. Unless such students are immersed in English at school, they will not learn English; consequently they will be prevented from participating in the mainstream of American society.

In summary, during this second phase the battle lines were drawn between two opposing but apparently equally plausible arguments: on the one hand, the *linguistic mismatch* hypothesis, which argued that children can't learn in a language they don't understand; on the other, the *maximum exposure* hypothesis, which argued that if children are deficient in English, then surely they require maximum exposure to English in school. These psychoeducational hypotheses remain prominent in the third phase of the debate—but in this phase the relatively narrow concern with bilingual education has joined forces with a broader set of concerns in relation to the more general infiltration of cultural diversity into American institutions.

PHASE III. 1987–1998

During the 1980s and 1990s, the U.S. English organization coordinated much of the opposition to bilingual education, initiating and passing referenda in nineteen states to make English the official language (see Crawford 2000 for detailed analysis of the U.S. English movement).

The urgency of the U.S. English mandate was enhanced during the late 1980s by publications of a variety of neoconservative academics (e.g., D'Souza 1991; Hirsch 1987; Schlesinger 1991) who warned about the dangers cultural diversity posed to the American way of life. These authors articulated a form of intellectualized xenophobia intended to alert the general public to the infiltration of the Other into the heart and soul of American institutions. Cultural diversity had become the enemy within—far more potent and insidious in its threat than any external enemy. Most influential was E. D. Hirsch's (1987) *Cultural Literacy: What Every American Needs to Know,* which argued that the fabric of nationhood depended on a set of common knowledge, understandings, and values shared by the populace. Multilingualism represented a threat to cultural literacy and, by extension, nationhood:

> In America, the reality is that we have not yet properly achieved *mono*literacy, much less multiliteracy. . . . Linguistic pluralism would make sense for us only on the questionable assumption that our civil peace and national effectiveness could survive multilingualism. But, in fact, multilingualism enormously increases cultural fragmentation, civil antagonism, illiteracy, and economic-technological ineffectualness (92).

Hirsch's cultural literacy represented a call to strengthen the national immune system so that it could successfully resist the debilitating influence of cultural diversity. Only when the national identity has been fortified and secured through cultural literacy should contact with the Other be contemplated—even then educators should keep diversity at a distance, always vigilant against its potent destructive power.

It is in this context that we can understand statements such as the following from Arthur Schlesinger Jr. (1991) in his book *The Disuniting of America:*

> In recent years the combination of the ethnicity cult with a flood of immigration from Spanish-speaking countries has given bilingualism new impe-

tus. . . . Alas, bilingualism has not worked out as planned: rather the contrary. Testimony is mixed, but indications are that bilingual education retards rather than expedites the movement of Hispanic children into the English-speaking world and that it promotes segregation rather than it does integration. Bilingualism shuts doors. It nourishes self-ghettoization, and ghettoization nourishes racial antagonism. . . . Using some language other than English dooms people to second-class citizenship in American society. . . . Monolingual education opens doors to the larger world. . . . Institutionalized bilingualism remains another source of the fragmentation of America, another threat to the dream of "one people" (108–109).

The claims that "bilingualism shuts doors" and "monolingual education opens doors to the wider world," are laughable if viewed in isolation, particularly in the context of current global interdependence and the frequently expressed needs of American business and security agencies (e.g., the CIA) for multilingual "human resources." Schlesinger's comments become interpretable only in the context of a societal discourse that is profoundly disquieted by the fact that the sounds of the "other" have now become audible and the hues of the American social landscape have darkened noticeably.

Despite its disdain for empirical evidence, this discourse is broadcast through the media into every classroom in the nation. There is anger that schools have apparently reneged on their traditional duty to render the Other invisible and inaudible. Under the guise of equity programs initiated in the 1960s, diversity infiltrated into the American classroom and became legitimated. In view of demographic projections that diversity will increase dramatically during the next thirty years, there is extreme urgency to curtail the infiltration of diversity and particularly one of its most visible manifestations—bilingual education.

PHASE IV. 1998–2002

The bilingual education debate across the United States changed dramatically in June 1998 with the passage in California of Proposition 227. In November 2000, Arizona voters followed suit with the passage of Proposition 203. These initiatives aimed to eliminate the use of bilingual children's first language for instructional purposes except in very exceptional circumstances. In its place, a transitional program of structured English immersion, normally to last only one year, has been implemented. Proposition 227 also mandated that any teacher who willfully and repeatedly refused to implement the law could be personally sued in court.

The debate leading up to the Proposition 227 referendum crystallized all of the arguments that had been advanced for and against bilingual education in the previous quarter century. Both sides claimed equity as their central guiding principle. Opponents of bilingual programs argued that limited English-proficient students were being denied access to both English and academic advancement as a result of being instructed for part of the day through their L1. Exposure to English was being diluted and, as a result, it was not surprising that bilingual students continued to experience difficulty in academic aspects of English. Only maximum exposure to English (frequently termed time-on-task) could remediate children's linguistic difficulties in that language on entry to school.

Proponents of bilingual education argued that L1 instruction in the early grades was necessary to ensure that students understood content instruction and experienced a successful start to their schooling. Reading and writing skills acquired initially through the L1 provided a foundation upon which strong English-language development could be built. Transfer of academic skills and knowledge across languages was evidenced consistently by the research literature on bilingual development (e.g., Cummins 2001). Thus, L1 proficiency could be promoted at no cost to children's academic development in English. Furthermore, the fact that teachers spoke the language of parents increased the likelihood of parental involvement and support for their children's learning. This, together with the reinforcement of children's sense of self as a result of the incorporation of their language and culture in the school program, contributed to long-term academic growth.

In the context of Proposition 227, bilingual advocates argued that bilingual education itself could not logically be regarded as a cause of continued high levels of academic failure among bilingual students since less than 30 percent of limited English proficient students in California were in any form of bilingual education. Less than 18 percent were in classes taught by a certified bilingual teacher, with the other 12 percent in classes most likely taught by a monolingual English teacher and a bilingual aide. Thus, they argued that educational failure among bilingual (particularly Latino/Latina) students was more logically attributed to the absence of genuine bilingual programs than to bilingual education in some absolute sense.

Proposition 227 has not succeeded in eliminating bilingual education from California, although it has reduced the number of programs significantly. Prior to Proposition 227, 29 percent of English learners were in a bilingual program but this figure dropped to 12 percent one year later. A number of school districts have continued to offer bilingual education by using a provision of the law that permits parents to sign a waiver requesting that their child be educated bilingually. However, only 67 percent of districts formally notified parents of this option. Some districts have set up charter schools that offer dual language or two-way bilingual programs involving both English L1 and minority language L1 (e.g., Spanish, Korean) students. Despite the negative social climate around bilingualism and bilingual education, dual language programs increased in California from 95 in 1997–1998 to 119 in 1999–2000. According to the California Department of Education (2000), these programs have increased almost 300 percent since 1990.

In summary, virtually since its inception in the 1960s as a programmatic response to discriminatory educational policies and practices, bilingual education has evoked strong negative reactions from dominant sectors of U.S. society. How can the discourse surrounding bilingual education be conceptualized in the context of broader theoretical principles? In order to legitimately analyze the opposition to bilingual education as a form of coercive relations of power, the empirical evidence relating to the claims of both sides must be examined. For example, if it were the case that bilingualism caused cognitive confusion or that instruction through two languages resulted in lower academic achievement, then the opposition to bilingual education could claim credibility based on what is in the best interests of bilingual students. However, if these arguments are spurious, then the discourse can be analyzed in terms of its sociopolitical goals rather than its psycholinguistic rationalizations.

In the next section, the research on bilingual education is briefly summarized.

THE APPLIED LINGUISTICS RESEARCH CONSENSUS

The following points express a consensus among applied linguists who have examined the research on bilingual education, although they might be expressed differently according to the theoretical orientation of individual researchers.

1. *Bilingual programs for minority and majority language students have been successfully implemented in countries around the world.* As documented in many sources (e.g., Baker and Prys Jones 1998; Cenoz and Genesee 1999; Cummins and Corson 1997; Dutcher 1995; Skutnabb-Kangas 2000; Williams 1996), students educated for part of the day through a minority or lower status language do not suffer adverse consequences in the development of academic skills in the majority or higher status language.

2. *Bilingual education, by itself, is not a panacea for students' underachievement.* Underachievement derives from many sources and simply providing some L1 instruction will not, by itself, transform students' educational experience. Bilingual instruction *can* make a

significant contribution but the predominant model of bilingual education in the United States (quick-exit transitional programs) is inferior to programs that aim to develop bilingualism and biliteracy, such as developmental (late-exit) and dual language programs. Dual language programs also serve English-background students in the same classes as minority language students, with each group acting as linguistic models for the other (Christian et al. 1997; Lindholm-Leary 2001).

3. *The development of literacy in two languages entails linguistic and perhaps cognitive advantages for bilingual students.* There are close to 150 research studies carried out since the early 1960s that report significant advantages for bilingual students on a variety of metalinguistic and cognitive tasks (see Cummins 2001).

4. *Significant positive relationships exist between the development of academic skills in L1 and L2.* This is true even for languages that are dissimilar (e.g. Spanish and Basque; English and Chinese; Dutch and Turkish). These cross-lingual relationships reflect the transfer of academic and conceptual knowledge across languages as well as the fact that the same cognitive and linguistic processing system operates on the acquisition and use of both languages (Huguet, Vila, and Llurda 2000; Verhoeven 1992).

5. *Conversational and academic aspects of language proficiency are distinct and follow different developmental patterns.* Several large-scale studies (Cummins, 1981; Hakuta, Butler, and Witt 2000; Thomas and Collier 1997; Worswick 2001) have shown that it usually takes at least five years for second language learners to catch up academically to their native English-speaking peers but conversational fluency in English is often attained within two years of intensive exposure to the language. Thus, the claims of proponents of Proposition 227 that one-year of intensive immersion in English is sufficient for second language learners to catch up academically are without foundation (see Krashen 2001).

This sketch of the literature on bilingual education is not meant to imply that all bilingual programs, as implemented, have been successful. In fact, the results of many so-called bilingual programs in the United States are mixed. The majority of bilingual programs instituted in the United States are quick-exit programs that make minimal or no attempt to promote literacy in students' L1. This weak variety of bilingual education is a consequence of the political pressure to remove students from bilingual programs as quickly as possible. Other so-called bilingual programs may involve little more than a classroom assistant who works with the bilingual students (in either L1 or L2) while the classroom teacher instructs those who are fluent in English. Under these conditions, it is hardly surprising that students fall behind since they seldom interact with the teacher or get access to mainstream curriculum content. However, in general, both large-scale and small-scale studies in the United States and elsewhere consistently show that strong promotion of bilingual students' L1 throughout elementary school contributes significantly to students' academic success. They also show overwhelmingly that there is no evidence for the maximum exposure hypothesis that claims a direct relationship between the amount of instructional exposure to the majority language and academic achievement in that language.

In view of the overwhelming evidence against the maximum exposure hypothesis and in favor of the legitimacy of bilingual education, it is appropriate to ask what sociopolitical functions are served by the vehement opposition to such programs. This issue is analyzed in the next section.

NEGOTIATION OF IDENTITY IN THE CONTEXT OF SOCIETAL POWER RELATIONS

The framework presented in figure 1 (Cummins 2001) views the interactions between educators and students (termed micro-interactions) as the most immediate determinant of student success or failure in school. These interactions can be viewed through two lens: (1) the lens of the teaching–learning relationship in a narrow sense, represented by the strategies and techniques that teachers use to promote reading development, content knowledge, and cognitive growth; (2) the lens of identity negotiation, which is represented by the messages communicated to students regarding their identities—who they are in the teacher's eyes and who they are capable of becoming. A central proposition is that the ways in which identities are negotiated between educators and students is at least as fundamental in determining student achievement as any of the myriad techniques for teaching reading or any other academic content. Only teacher-student interactions that generate maximum identity investment on the part of students, together with maximum cognitive engagement, are likely to be effective in promoting achievement.

The framework proposes that relations of power in the wider society (macro-interactions), ranging from coercive to collaborative in varying degrees, influence both the ways in which educators define their roles and the types of structures that are established in the educational system. Coercive relations of power refer to the exercise of power by a dominant group (or individual or country) to the detriment of a subordinated group or country. The assumption is that there is a fixed quantity of power that

**COERCIVE AND COLLABORATIVE RELATIONS
OF POWER MANIFESTED IN MACRO-INTERACTIONS BETWEEN
SUBORDINATED COMMUNITIES AND DOMINANT GROUP INSTITUTIONS**

↙   ↘

EDUCATOR ROLE DEFINITIONS ↔ EDUCATIONAL STRUCTURES

↘   ↙

**MICRO-INTERACTIONS BETWEEN
EDUCATORS AND STUDENTS**

forming an

INTERPERSONAL SPACE

**within which
knowledge is generated
and
identities are negotiated**

EITHER

REINFORCING COERCIVE RELATIONS OF POWER

OR

PROMOTING COLLABORATIVE RELATIONS OF POWER

Figure 1. Coercive and Collaborative Relations of Power Manifested in Macro- and Micro-Interactions

operates according to a zero-sum logic—the more power one group has the less is left for other groups.

By contrast, collaborative relations of power operate on the assumption that power is not a fixed pre-determined quantity but rather can be generated in interpersonal and intergroup relations. In other words, as illustrated in loving relationships (e.g., parents and children), participants in the relationship are empowered through their collaboration such that each is more affirmed in her or his identity and has a greater sense of efficacy to create change in his or her life or social situation. Power is created in the relationship and shared among participants. The power relationship is additive rather than subtractive. Power is created with others rather than being imposed on or exercised over others. Empowerment can thus be defined as the collaborative creation of power. In the classroom, this happens (or doesn't happen) in the interactions between teachers and students.

Role definitions refer to the mindset of expectations, assumptions, and goals that educators bring to the task of educating culturally diverse students. Educational structures refer to the organization of schooling in a broad sense that includes policies, programs, curriculum, and assessment. This organization is established to achieve the goals of education as defined primarily by the dominant group in the society. For example, the historical patterns of educational segregation in Canada, South Africa, the United States and many other countries were designed to limit the opportunities that subordinated groups might have for educational and social advancement. By contrast, bilingual education in the United States was instituted to promote equality of educational opportunity at a time (in the late 1960s, early 1970s) when there was some degree of consensus in the society that this was a valid and important goal.

Educational structures, however, are not static; as with most other aspects of the way societies are organized and resources distributed, educational structures are contested by individuals and groups. The debates surrounding bilingual education illustrate just how volatile these issues can become.

Educational structures, together with educator role definitions, determine the micro-interactions between educators, students, and communities. These micro-interactions form an interpersonal or an interactional space within which the acquisition of knowledge and formation of identity is negotiated. Power is created and shared within this interpersonal space (or zone of proximal development) where minds and identities meet. As such, the micro-interactions constitute the most immediate determinant of student academic success or failure.

These micro-interactions between educators, students, and communities are never neutral; in varying degrees, they either reinforce coercive relations of power or promote collaborative relations of power. When they reinforce coercive relations of power they contribute to the disempowerment of culturally diverse students and communities. When they promote collaborative relations of power, the micro-interactions enable educators, students, and communities to challenge the operation of coercive power structures.

The relationships among variables articulated in this framework are not just empty theoretical speculation of the kind frequently dismissed or, more benignly, ignored by the positivistically correct. There is a vast amount of research data and hard-nosed theoretical synthesis to support these relationships that can be found within the disciplines of anthropology, sociology, and psychology (Cummins 2001; Delpit 1995; Ladson-Billings 1994; Nieto 1996, 2001; Portes and Rumbaut 2001).

ALTERNATIVE DIRECTIONS FOR EDUCATIONAL CHANGE

In the context of the theoretical framework elaborated above, the societal discourse that demonizes bilingualism and bilingual education as major causes of children's educational underachievement can be interpreted as both reflecting and constituting coercive relations of power. Broadcast into the classroom, this discourse directly affects the ways in which identities are negotiated between educators and bilingual students; specifically, it acts to constrict the interpersonal space such that total assimilation to the dominant culture and language is the only identity option offered to any student who aspires to academic success. Educators who view bilingualism and biculturalism as opening doors rather than closing doors are required to challenge this coercive discourse in order to co-construct alternative identity options with their students.

What directions for change are implied by the present framework as compared to more typical analyses of educational underachievement that focus on remediation of student or community deficits? Currently the deficit of choice in mainstream educational discourse has become low-income students' alleged lack of phonological awareness as a result of growing up in a print-deprived environment. Students' deficits have been compounded, according to this view, by the failure of schools to adequately develop these skills through rigorous phonics instruction (see Cummins 2001; Gee 1999).

Thus, the current mainstream discourse of the popular media invokes twin causes of underachievement among bilingual and low-income students:

- Ineffective teaching of reading as a result of the educational system's failure to implement rigorous phonics instruction; the alleged neglect of phonics for many years is attributed to the previous prevalence of whole-language instructional methods in the schools.
- Failure to teach English effectively as a result of the fact that limited English proficient students have been trapped in bilingual education programs that expose them only minimally to English.

Once the phenomenon and its causes have been framed in this way, the solutions are clear:

- Require all schools to teach phonics in a systematic direct way (preferably through prescribed "teacher-proof" reading programs such as *Open Court*).
- Require schools to immerse all English learners in English-only instructional programs that will enable them to overcome the disadvantage of speaking a language other than English at home.

This framing of the problem of underachievement as deriving from student and community deficits and the associated pedagogical solution involving more rigorous top-down scripting of teacher-student interactions, policed by standardized tests, entails very different directions for change than the analysis of identity negotiation and societal power relations outlined in the current framework.

We can highlight some of these directions by examining images of the student, the teacher, and the society reflected in the different approaches.

CONSTRUCTIONS AND CONSTRICTIONS OF IDENTITY IN POLICY AND CLASSROOM INTERACTIONS

Implied by the notion of negotiating identities, is the fact that as educators, our interactions with students are constantly sketching a triangular set of images:

- an image of our own identities as educators.
- an image of the identity options we highlight for our students.
- an image of the society we hope our students will help form.

The intersection of these three images and the ways in which instruction opens up or shuts off identity options can be illustrated in the findings of large-scale studies of classroom interaction in the United States. These studies suggest that teacher-centered transmission of information and skills remains the predominant mode of instruction (e.g., Goodlad 1984; Ramírez 1992). The current era of teaching to the high stakes test has surely reinforced this pattern, at least in low-income urban schools if not in their suburban counterparts. Sirotnik, in discussing the implications of Goodlad's study, points to the fact that the typical American classroom contains:

> [A] lot of teacher talk and a lot of student listening . . . almost invariably closed and factual questions . . . and predominantly total class instructional configurations around traditional activities—all in a virtually affectless environment. It is but a short inferential leap to suggest that we are implicitly teaching dependence upon authority, linear thinking, social apathy, passive involvement, and hands-off learning (1983: 29).

In other words, an image of the society that students will graduate into and the kind of contributions they can make to that society is embedded implicitly in the interactions between educators and students. When the problem is conceptualized only in terms of lack of phonological awareness in English and the solution assigns a central role to scripted phonics and

English-only instruction enforced directly by monitors in the school and more remotely by high-stakes testing focused on those skills, what are the consequences for students and teachers? What is left out of students' educational experience that as a society we might consider valuable? What is the image of the teacher as educator and student as learner implied by this approach?

Clearly, for teachers, the top-down imposition of scripts represents an attempt to teacher-proof the curriculum. It reflects a profound distrust of teachers and an extremely narrow interpretation of the teaching-learning process. Nowhere in this anemic instructional vision is there room for really connecting at a human level with culturally diverse students; consigned to irrelevance also is any notion of affirming students' identities, and challenging coercive power structures, by activating what they already know about the world and mobilizing the intellectual and linguistic tools they use to make sense of their worlds. This kind of programming reduces instruction to a technical exercise. No role is envisaged for teachers or students to invest their identities (affect, intellect, and imagination) in the teaching/learning process.

Notions such as identity don't appear in the positivistic scientific research for the simple reason that the best scientific minds haven't figured out how to operationalize and measure them. Does scientific logic therefore dictate that the negotiation of identity in schools is irrelevant to academic achievement? Or should we hold our noses and acknowledge the vast amount of nonpositivistic scientific research that highlights identity and investment of self as central variables in determining academic engagement and achievement (see Cummins 2001 for a review)?

The same reasoning applies to imagination. Imagination can be defined as "the act or power of creating mental images of what has never been actually experienced" (Egan 1986: 7). Egan (1986, 1999) makes an extremely persuasive case that school curricula have excluded the "most powerful and energetic intellectual tools children bring to school" (1986: 18). He suggests that we need to reconstruct our curricula and teaching methods in light of a richer image of the child as an imaginative as well as a logico-mathematical thinker. Children's imaginations are revealed in their capacity for highly abstract and sophisticated thinking in relation to engaging stories (e.g., *Star Wars, Harry Potter*), yet we systematically restrict throughout schooling their opportunities to exercise these imaginative intellectual powers. We view children, and particularly children of poverty, as relative intellectual incompetents ignoring our everyday experience of their creative intellectual energy and imaginative powers (1986: 22). One might add that the new regime of truth also constructs teachers as relative intellectual incompetents who must be policed to ensure that they do not deviate from the official script.

We have become much more vigilant in constricting imagination, intellect, and identity in low-income inner-city schools than in suburban schools. Gee (in press) points out that standards-driven, teacher-proof, direct instruction pedagogy is largely directed at poor and minority students and evaded by children in private schools, magnet schools, charter schools, schools in affluent suburbs, and by those students identified as gifted—a category seldom penetrated by minority and poor students.

When we frame the universe of discourse only in terms of children's deficits in English and in phonological awareness (or deficits in any other area), we expel culture, language, identity, intellect, and imagination from our image of the child. Similarly, these constructs are nowhere to be found in our image of the effective teacher of these children, nor in policies that might guide instruction. The positivistically correct seem to believe that identity and imagination can't be relevant because they can't be measured. In fact, in the current era, imagination might be regarded as a negative quality in a teacher because imaginative teachers simply won't parrot top-down imposed scripts; they will quit, resist or subvert this way of constricting their identities, the identities of the children they teach, and the entire teaching-learning process.

In contrast to an approach founded on presumed deficits in low-income children's phonological awareness, an instructional focus on empowerment, understood as the collaborative creation of power, starts by acknowledging the cultural, linguistic, imaginative, and intellectual resources that children bring to school. These resources reflect the funds of knowledge abundantly present in children's communities (Moll et al. 1992). Educators explore, with individual children and parents, how these resources might be developed and expanded in classroom interactions. If educators' image of the child includes her capacity to become fluently bilingual and biliterate, they will orchestrate classroom interactions to communicate this potential to the child (e.g., by encouraging the writing and classroom publication of child-authored bilingual stories). When structures reflecting coercive relations of power have been imposed (e.g., English-only instruction as a result of Propositions 227 and 203), educators will redouble their efforts to affirm students' bilingual and bicultural identity. When curriculum is implemented that constructs the child as a cultural, linguistic, intellectual, and imaginative *tabula rasa,* educators will search for cracks in the structure to communicate a very different message to children. The research suggests that this is exactly what effective schools do (e.g., Freeman 1998; Lucas, Henze, and Donato 1990; Lucas and Katz 1994).

This approach implies an image of society as needing all the intelligence, imagination, and multilingual talent it can get. Effective citizenship requires active intelligence, critical literacy, and a willingness to challenge power structures that constrict human possibility. This perspective suggests an answer to the question posed in the title of this chapter. Identity, intellect, imagination, and power are absent from the new regime of truth because they potentially challenge the smooth operation of coercive power structures. Few people have expressed our contradictory orientations to literacy, and some of the fundamental choices we face as educators and as a society, more incisively than James Moffett (1989):

> Literacy is dangerous and has always been so regarded. It naturally breaks down barriers of time, space, and culture. It threatens one's original identity by broadening it through vicarious experiencing and the incorporation of somebody *else's* hearth and ethos. So we feel profoundly ambiguous about literacy. Looking at it as a means of transmitting our culture to our children, we give it priority in education, but recognizing the threat of its backfiring we make it so tiresome and personally unrewarding that youngsters won't want to do it on their own, which is of course when it becomes dangerous . . . The net effect of this ambivalence is to give literacy with one hand and take it back with the other, in keeping with our contradictory wish for youngsters to learn to think but only about what we already have in mind for them. (85)

The bottom line is that effective schools create instructional spaces where identity, intellect, and imagination are negotiated between teachers and students in ways that actively challenge coercive relations of power in the wider society. In the words of Adriana and Rosalba Jasso (1995: 255) commenting on their experiences in one such classroom: "Our classroom was full of human knowledge. We had a teacher who believed in us; he didn't hide our power, he advertised it."

REFERENCES

Baker, C., and S. Prys Jones. 1998. *Encyclopedia of Bilingualism and Bilingual Education.* Clevedon, England: Multilingual Matters.

California Department of Education. 2000. "California Two-Way Bilingual Immersion Programs Directory." Sacramento: California Department of Education.

Cenoz, J., and F. Genesee, eds. 1999. *Beyond Bilingualism: Multilingualism and Multilingual Education.* Clevedon, England: Multilingual Matters.

Christian, D., C. L. Montone, K. J. Lindholm, and I. Carranza. 1997. "Profiles in Two-Way Immersion Education." Washington, D.C.: Center for Applied Linguistics and Delta Systems.

———. 1992. *Language Loyalties: A Source Book on the Official English Controversy.* Chicago: University of Chicago Press.

Crawford, J. 2000. *At War with Diversity: U.S. Language Policy in an Age of Anxiety.* Clevedon, England: Multilingual Matters.

Cummins, J. 1981. "Age on Arrival and Immigrant Second Language Learning in Canada: A Reassessment." *Applied Linguistics* 1:132–49.

———. 2001. *Negotiating Identities: Education for Empowerment in a Diverse Society,* 2nd Ed. Los Angeles: California Association for Bilingual Education.

Cummins, Jim, and Dave Corson, eds. 1997. *Bilingual Education.* 8 vols. Vol. 5, *Encyclopedia of Language and Education,* Ed. D. Corson. Dordrecht, The Netherlands: Kluwer Academic Publishers.

Cummins, Jim, and Merril Swain. 1986. *Bilingualism in Education: Aspects of Theory, Research and Practice.* London: Longman.

Delpit, Lisa. 1995. *Other Peoples' Children: Cultural Conflict in the Classroom.* New York: The New Press.

D'Souza, Dinesh. 1991. *Illiberal Education: The Politics of Race and Sex on Campus.* New York: Vintage Books.

Dutcher, N. 1995. *The Use of First and Second Languages in Education: A Review of International Experience.* Washington, D.C.: The World Bank.

Egan, Kieran. 1999. *Children's Minds, Talking Rabbits & Clockwork Oranges: Essays on Education.* New York: Teachers College Press.

———. 1986. *Teaching as Story Telling: An Alternative Approach to Teaching and Curriculum in the Elementary School.* Chicago: The University of Chicago Press.

Epstein, N. 1977. *Language, Ethnicity and the Schools.* Washington, D.C.: Institute for Educational Leadership.

Freeman, R. D. 1998. *Bilingual Education and Social Change.* Clevedon, England: Multilingual Matters.

Gee, James Paul. 1999. "Critical Issues: Reading and the New Literacy Studies: Reframing the National Academy of Sciences Report on Reading." *Journal of Literacy Research* 31 (3): 355–74.

———. In press. "Literacies, Schools, and Kinds of People in the New Capitalism." In *Language, Literacy, and Power in Schooling,* ed. T. McCarty. Albany: SUNY Press.

Goodlad, John I. 1984. *A Place Called School: Prospects for the Future.* New York: McGraw Hill.

Hakuta, K., Y. G. Butler, and D. Witt. 2000. *How Long Does It Take English Learners to Attain Proficiency?* Santa Barbara: University of California Linguistic Minority Research Institute.

Hirsch, E. D. Jr. 1987. *Cultural Literacy: What Every American Needs to Know.* Boston: Houghton Mifflin Co.

Huguet, A., I. Vila, and E. Llurda. 2000. "Minority Language Education in Unbalanced Bilingual Situations: A Case for the Linguistic Interdependence Hypothesis." *Journal of Psycholinguistic Research* 29 (3): 313–33.

Jasso, A., and R. Jasso. 1995. "Critical Pedagogy: Not a Method, But a Way of Life." In *Reclaiming Our Voices: Bilingual Education, Critical Pedagogy & Praxis,* ed. J. Frederickson, 253–59. Los Angeles: California Association for Bilingual Education.

Krashen, Steve. 2001. "Are Children Ready for the Mainstream after One Year of Structured English Immersion?" *TESOL Matters,* (Sept.–Oct.–Nov.) 1, 4.

Ladson-Billings, G. 1994. *The Dreamkeepers: Successful Teachers of African American Children.* San Francisco: Jossey-Bass Publishers.

Lindholm-Leary, K. J. 2001. *Dual Language Education.* Clevedon, England: Multilingual Matters.

Lucas, T., and A. Katz. 1994. "Reframing the Debate: The Roles of Native Languages in English-Only Programs for Language Minority Students." *TESOL Quarterly* 28 (3): 537–62.

Lucas, T., R. Henze, and R. Donato. 1990. "Promoting the Success of Latino Language-Minority Students: An Exploratory Study of Six High Schools." *Harvard Educational Review* 60: 315–40.

Moffett, J. 1989. "Censorship and Spiritual Education." *English Education* 21: 70–87.

Moll, L. C., C. Amanti, D. Neff, and N. González. 1992. "Funds of Knowledge for Teaching: Using a Qualitative Approach to Connect Homes and Classrooms." *Theory into Practice* 31 (2): 132–41.

Nieto, S. 1996. *Affirming Diversity: The Sociopolitical Context of Multicultural Education,* 2nd Ed. White Plains, N.Y.: Longman.

———. 2001. *Language, Culture, and Teaching: Critical Perspectives for a New Century.* Mahwah, N.J.: Lawrence Erlbaum Associates.

Portes, A., and R. G. Rumbaut. 2001. *Legacies: The Story of the Immigrant Second Generation.* Berkeley: University of California Press.

Ramírez, J. D. 1992. "Executive Summary." *Bilingual Research Journal* 16: 1–62.

Ryan, W. 1992. *Blaming the Victim.* New York: Vintage.

Schlesinger, A. Jr. 1991. *The Disuniting of America.* New York: W. W. Norton.

Sirotnik, K. A. 1983. "What You See Is What You Get—Consistency, Persistency, and Mediocrity in Classrooms." *Harvard Educational Review* 53: 16–31.

Skutnabb-Kangas, T. 2000. *Linguistic Genocide in Education—or Worldwide Diversity and Human Rights.* Mawah, N.J.: Lawrence Erlbaum Associates.

Snow, C. E., M. S. Burns, and P. Griffin, eds. 1998. *Preventing Reading Difficulties in Young Children.* Washington, D.C.: National Academy Press.

Swain, Merril, and Sharon Lapkin. 1982. *Evaluating Bilingual Education.* Clevedon, England: Multilingual Matters.

Thomas, W. P., and V. Collier. 1997. *School Effectiveness for Language Minority Students.* Washington, D.C.: National Clearinghouse for Bilingual Education.

Troike, R. 1978. "Research Evidence for the Effectiveness of Bilingual Education." *NABE Journal* 3: 13–24.

Verhoeven, L. 1992. "Assessment of Bilingual Proficiency." In *The Construct of Language Proficiency,* ed. L. Verhoeven and J. H. A. L. De Jong, 124–36. Amsterdam: John Benjamins Publishing Company.

Williams, E. 1996. "Reading in Two Languages at Year 5 in African Primary Schools." *Applied Linguistics* 17 (2): 183–209.

Worswick, C. 2001. *School Performance of the Children of Immigrants in Canada, 1994–98.* Ottawa: Statistics Canada.

3

Derrida, Pedagogy, and the Calculation of the Subject

The assumption of one single subject is perhaps unnecessary; perhaps it is just as permissible to assume a multiplicity of subject, whose interaction and struggle is the basis of our thought and our consciousness in general? A kind of aristocracy of "cells" in which domination resides? To be sure, an aristocracy of equals, used to ruling jointly and understanding how to command?

My hypothesis: *The subject as multiplicity.*

—Nietzsche (1968: 270)

I believe that at a certain level both of experience and of philosophical and scientific discourse, one cannot get along without the notion of the subject. It is a question of knowing where it comes from and how it functions.

—Derrida (1970: 271)

INTRODUCTION

Luc Ferry and Alain Renaut argue that "the philosophy of 68" eliminates and leaves no room for a positive rehabilitation of human agency necessary for a workable notion of democracy. In their preface to the English translation of *La pensée 68,* Ferry and Renaut (1990: xvi), refer to the philosophy of the 1960s as a Nietzschean-Heideggerian antihumanism that is structurally incapable of taking up the promises of the democratic project inherent in modernity. Their criticisms are specifically aimed at Jacques Derrida and are intended as a path back to a form of humanism, liberalism, and individualism (the doctrine of human rights) that they think can sustain a notion of political agency required for democracy.

Derrida provides us with resources for understanding and responding to these criticisms. He denies a simple-minded nihilism as it applies to the subject, to notions of political agency and to the idea of democracy. He also argues that the anti-Nietzschean polemical attack on the critique of the subject is misplaced; that poststructuralism never "liquidated" the subject but rather rehabilitated it, decentered it, and re-positioned it, in all its historico-cultural complexity. As he argues: "There has never been The Subject for anyone . . . The subject is a fable . . . but to concentrate on the elements of speech and *conventional* fiction that such a fable presupposes is not to stop taking it seriously (it is the serious itself) . . ." (Derrida 1995b: 264). This chapter explores these issues in relation to the project for a critical pedagogy.

DERRIDA, HUMANISM, AND DECONSTRUCTION[1]

The American reception of deconstruction[2] and the influential formulation of poststructuralism in the English-speaking world, quickly became institutionalized from the point at which Derrida delivered his essay "Structure, Sign and Play in the Discourse of the Human Sciences" to the International Colloquium on Critical Languages and the Sciences of Man at John Hopkins University in October 1966. Richard Macksey and Eugenio Donato (1970: x) described the conference as "the first time in the United States that structuralist thought had been considered as a cross-disciplinary phenomenon." Even before the conclusion of the conference, there were clear signs that the ruling transdisciplinary paradigm of structuralism had been superseded, yet only a paragraph in Macksey's "Concluding Remarks" signaled the importance of Derrida's "radical reappraisals of our [structuralist] assumptions" (320).

In the now classic essay "Structure, Sign and Play," Derrida (1978) questioned the structurality of structure or notion of center, which, he argued, has served to limit the play of structure:

> . . . the entire history of the concept of structure . . . must be thought of as a series of substitutions of center for center, as a linked chain of determinations of the center. Successively, and in a regulated fashion, the center receives different forms or names. The history of metaphysics, like the history of the West, is the history of these metaphors and metonymies. Its matrix . . . is the determination of being as *presence* in all senses of this word. It could be shown that all the names related to fundamentals, to principles, or to the center have always designated an invariable presence—*eidos, arche, telos, energeia, ousia* (essence, existence, substance, subject) *aletheia,* transcendentality, consciousness, God, man, and so forth (279–80).

In this one paragraph Derrida both called into question the previous decade of French structuralism and intimated the directions of his own intellectual ambitions. The decade of French structuralism, beginning with Claude Lévi-Strauss and his structural anthropology, had its complex cultural prehistory in Nietzsche's critique of modernity, in the development of European structural linguistics, and in early twentieth-century modernism, especially formalism and futurism as it took form in both pre-revolutionary Russia and Italy.[3]

The decentering of structure, of the transcendental signified, and of the sovereign subject, Derrida suggests—naming his sources of inspiration—can be found in the Nietzschean critique of metaphysics and, especially, of the concepts of Being and truth, in the Freudian critique of self-presence, as he says, "the critique of consciousness, of the subject, of self-identity and of self-proximity or self-possession" (1978: 280), and, more radically, in the Heideggerean destruction of metaphysics, "of the determination of Being as presence" (1978: 280). In the body of the essay, Derrida considers the theme of decentering in relation to Lévi-Strauss's ethnology and concludes by distinguishing two interpretations of structure. One, Hegelian in origin and exemplified in Lévi-Strauss's work, he argues, "dreams of deciphering a truth or an origin which escapes play and the order of the sign" and seeks the "inspiration of a new humanism." The Other, "which is no longer turned toward the origin, affirms play and tries to pass beyond man and humanism . . ." (Derrida, 1978: 292).

In another well-known essay "The Ends of Man," given as a lecture at an international colloquium in New York two years later (1968), Derrida (1982: 114) addresses himself to the question "Where is France, as concerns man?" and he provides an account that interprets the dominant motif of post-war French philosophy as a philosophical humanism authorized by anthropologistic readings of Hegel, Marx, and Heidegger. Sartre's "monstrous translation" (115) of Heidegger's *Dasein* legitimated an existentialist humanism, and even the critique of humanism, itself a major current of French thought in the post-war era, presented itself more as an amalgamation of Hegel, Husserl, and Heidegger with the old metaphysical humanism. Derrida argues "the history of the concept man is never examined. Everything occurs as if the sign 'man' had no origin, no historical, cultural, or linguistic limit" (116). This statement gives a strong indication as to Derrida's own motivations and directions: a movement toward an ever clearer specification of the subject in historical, cultural, and linguistic terms and an excavation of the history of the subject.[4]

Derrida reconsiders the *relève* of man in the thought of Hegel, Husserl, and Heidegger to demonstrate that in each case there is a clear critique of anthropologism. In particular, Heidegger's thought is guided by the double motif of being as presence and of the proximity of being to the essence of man (128). He suggests that if we are not simply to restore the ordering of the system by recourse to humanist concepts or to destroy meaning, we face two strategic choices: (1) "To attempt an exit and a deconstruction without changing terrain, by repeating what is implicit in the founding concepts and the original problematic . . . ," and (2) "To decide to change terrain, in a discontinuous and irruptive fashion, brutally placing oneself outside, and by affirming an absolute break and difference" (135). And he says, in an oft-quoted remark: "A new writing must weave and interlace these two motifs of deconstruction. Which amounts to saying that one must speak several languages and produce several texts at once" (135). What we need to "change the terrain," he claims, finally quoting Nietzsche, "is a change of 'style'; and if there is style, Nietzsche reminded us it must be *plural*" (135).[5]

The relation of both Derrida and deconstruction to pedagogy is as clear as it is fundamental: Derridean philosophy offers an active interpretation, resistance, and reevaluation of humanist pedagogy, of forms of pedagogy based on the sovereign subject—which is to say, the predominant forms of pedagogy existing today that structure our pedagogical institutions, theories, and practices. I shall argue that the question of pedagogy is never far from Derrida's concerns; that when he poses the question of style,[6] of new styles of writing and thinking, he is engaged in rethinking traditional humanist pedagogical practices and the founding principles of our educational institutions. This is most straightforwardly the case with applied forms of deconstruction in its relation to pedagogy and Derrida's investigations into the nature of writing as *différance*,[7] such as the deconstruction of the authorial–authoritarian subject.[8] It is the case in Derrida's questioning of the politics and unity of the proper name (see Derrida 1985). It is also the case in personal or autobiographical terms, where he has deliberated over the *form* of "philosophical discourse"—its "modes of composition, its rhetoric, its metaphors, its language, its fictions"—to investigate the ways in which the institutional authority of academic philosophy, and the autonomy it claims, rests upon a "disavowal with relation to its own language" (Derrida 1995: 218).[9]

Derrida has never disowned the subject or its relevance either to philosophical or scientific discourse. He has, however, radically questioned the sovereign subject and the philosophical tradition of consciousness that left its indelible imprint on a variety of post-war humanisms. Inspired by Nietzsche and Heidegger, and befriended by Levinas, Derrida has interrogated the humanist construction of the sovereign subject—its genealogy and its authorial functions—in his attempt to develop a science of writing that both deconstructs and moves beyond "man" as the full presence of consciousness in being. His work has been misinterpreted by those christening themselves anti-Nietzscheans who claim that Derrida (and poststructuralism in general) has liquidated or eliminated the subject and, therefore, endangered agency and posed a consequent threat to a workable notion of democracy.

FRENCH ANTI-NIETZSCHEANISM

Luc Ferry and Alain Renaut published *La Pensée 68* in 1985, poorly translated into the English title as *French Philosophy of the Sixties: An Essay on Antihumanism* (1990). In the preface to the English translation, Ferry and Renaut maintain that French intellectual history since World War II has been dominated by "a critique of the modern world and the values of formal democracy" (xi) inspired by Marx and Heidegger, which resulted in a common rejection of humanism. They claim that Nietzschean-Heideggerianism dates the advent of modern humanism from Descartes rather than from the rise of capitalism, and works to deconstruct the subject defined as conscience and will, as "the author of his acts and ideas" (xii). In their description of the trajectory of French post-war thought, they assert that the critique of modern rationality was intimately bound up with the critique of the subject: Marxism had interrogated the universalism of the Enlightenment, based upon claims of the emancipation of man, in the light of Eurocentrism and European colonialism. When Marxism collapsed the Heideggerian critique took over. They argue, "the retreat of Marxism has made the presence of Heideggerianism in France more and more visible" (xv) and that what happened to Marxism in the 1970s is happening to Heidegger today. In relation to both Marxism and Heideggerianism they summarize their position thus:

> *Whether conducted in the name of a radiant future or a traditionalist reaction, the total critique of the modern world, because it is necessarily an antihumanism that leads inevitably to seeing in the democratic project, for example, in human rights, the prototype of ideology or the metaphysical illusion, is structurally incapable of taking up, except insincerely and seemingly in spite of itself, the promises that are also those of modernity* (xvi; emphasis in the original).

They claim that in their philosophical paradigm—what we can describe as a French neoliberalism—it is necessary "to grant a minimum of legitimacy to a reference to the subject which is inherent in democratic thought" (xvi) and to bypass the confusion between metaphysics and humanism. It is, they claim, after Marx, Nietzsche, Freud, and Heidegger, today more than anything "a question of rethinking . . . the question of the subject" (xvi).

The antihumanism of French philosophy of the 1968 period is tracked out by reference to Derrida's "The Ends of Man," Foucault's declaration in *The Order of Things* of "the death of man," and Lyotard's scepticism of anthropologism. Antihumanism holds that "the autonomy of the subject is an illusion" (xxiii) and the problem that now confronts us, Ferry and Renaut suggest, "consists of searching for conditions for what a *non-metaphysical humanism* might be" that involves "conferring a coherent philosophical status on the promise of freedom contained in the requirements of humanism" (xxviii). Ferry and Renaut wish to invent a form of modern humanism that is not metaphysical and permits the ascription of universal moral and political judgments and rights without further appeals to essentialist notions of human nature.

In this first attempt, Ferry and Renaut dissipate much of their energies by criticising the Nietzschean-Heideggerianism. While they legitimately question the Heideggerian critique of subjectivity—the meaning of the metaphysics of subjectivity—and inquire as to what can replace the metaphysical subject after its deconstruction (212), there are more rhetorical (and less savory) elements in their attack that seek to damn Derrida and deconstruction by association with Heidegger's Nazism or Nietzsche's irrationalism and illiberalism.[10] These rhetorical moves aside, there is little sustained engagement with Derrida's texts and their work seems excessively negative or mired in critique, without positively identifying, beyond the most schematic form, in what modern humanism might consist. For instance, toward the end of their book, they argue that "It does not follow that, having established that man is not really . . . autonomous . . . , one has to go to the extreme of withdrawing all meaning and function . . . from the Ideal of autonomy" (211). Or, again, in the conclusion, they indicate that the critique of humanism and of the subject has revealed a surprising simplicity, suggesting that a history of the subject still has yet to be written.

As Mark Lilla (1994) comments in respect to Ferry and Renaut,

what they mean by the "subject" is often obscured in their writings, which up to now have mainly been critical and directed against their adversaries. They have yet to develop their own theory of subjectivity or respond to the objections that all such theories inevitably confront. Still it is clear what they wish such a theory of subjectivity to undergrid: a new defense of universal, rational norms in morals and politics, and especially a defense of human rights. (19–20)

Lilla clarifies that "such a defense would not be based upon the notion of an isolated individual as possessor of rights and therefore would not be compatible with classical liberalism" (20). Instead, they appeal to a French republicanism that is to be articulated through a new humanism. To date, this project has remained entirely programmatic, schematic, and its content has been unfulfilled.[11]

The sorts of criticisms articulated by Ferry and Renaut represent a wider set a criticisms against Derrida and, more broadly, poststructuralism for its theoretical antihumanism and its alleged lack of a subject that can provide either for a notion of political agency and resistance or for the ascription of human rights and the workability of democracy. Indeed, strangely, it is on the basis of this generalized criticism that liberals of all persuasions—old fashioned, feminists, social democrats, and neoliberals—and humanist or disaffected structuralist Marxists and communitarians join hands. This new alliance can be given the generic term anti-Nietzscheans. It is, perhaps, most obvious in the work of Ferry and Renaut (1991), who in the early 1990s published a collection of essays with the title *Pourquoi Nous ne Sommes pas Nietzschéens,* including essays by Vincent Descombes, Alain Boyer, and Phillippe Raynaud, among others. Yet it is also clear in the more general attack mounted against Derrida by Barry Smith, the editor of *The Monist* and the inaugurator of the infamous letter that sparked what Derrida called "the Cambridge Affair."[12] In the foreword to a selection of essays edited by Smith (1994) for instance, he claims that the present ills facing American academic life are due directly to Foucault, Derrida, Lyotard, and others:

Many current developments in American academic life—multiculturalism, "political correctness," the growth of critical theory, rhetoric and hermeneutics, the crisis of scholarship in many humanities departments—have been closely associated with, and indeed, inspired by, the work of European philosophers such as Foucault, Derrida, Lyotard and others. In Europe itself, in contrast, the influence of these philosophers is restricted to a small coterie, and their ideas have certainly contributed to none of the wide-ranging social and institutional changes we are currently witnessing in some corners of American academia.

This set of extraordinary claims are advanced without evidence of any kind; they are, after all, empirical statements rather than analytic ones, and therefore, in terms Smith would accept, the establishment of their truth would necessarily require some historical evidence and analysis.

In the Smith (1994) collection mentioned above, Dallas Willard (1994: 15), attempting to address the question of causation implied in Smith's assertions, concludes that to suppose that deconstructionism is *the* cause of the university crisis is a misdiagnosis. Yet he reiterates the charge in Smith's letter that deconstruction is not a method of thought. These are general attacks that do not proceed from a direct criticism of the Nietzscheanism assumed, often unproblematically, to exist as a source and inspiration for Derrida and to account for an antiliberalism in Derrida's thought (and that of other poststructuralists). The essay by Pascal Engel (1994) "The Decline and Fall of French Nietzscheo-Structuralism" in Smith (1994) is a clearer example, that echoes many of the criticisms raised by Ferry and Renaut. Engel (1994: 36–37, fn 3) distinguishes between what he calls Heideggero-Nietzscheanism (Derrida) and Metaphysical-Nietzscheanism (Deleuze) and formulates his criticisms in terms of a series of theses said to be the basis of Nietzscheo-Structuralism: there is no such thing as meaning, truth, epistemology (theses 1, 3, 4); nothing exists but forces (thesis 2); consciousness and subjectivity are just effects (of affects) (thesis 5); philosophy creates concepts (thesis 6). Engel (1994: 34) comments upon the "catastrophic consequences in political philosophy" of entertaining these theses (as if Deleuze or Derrida actually holds such crudely stated theses).

The new liberal alliance is also strongly evidenced in a recent essay by Charles Taylor (1994) on multiculturalism contributed to a collection edited by Amy Gutmann (1994), including Jürgen Habermas, K. Anthony Appiah, Susan Wolf, Micheal Walzer, and others. Taylor, for instance, makes casual and off-hand remarks concerning neo-Nietzscheans, at one point referring to "subjectivist, half-baked neo-Nietzschean theories" (1994: 70). He mentions Derrida and Foucault only once and then without reference to specific texts and in derogatory terms.[13] Taylor argues that citizenship cannot be regarded as a basis for universal identity as people are both unique, self-creating individuals as well as bearers of culture. Both qualifications could easily be given a Nietzschean perspective. Indeed, the question of cultural difference has been most thoroughly theorized, one might argue, by Derrida and a host of other poststructuralists (for example, Foucault on micropractices, Lyotard on the *differend*, Deleuze on repetition and difference).

Derrida, for instance, constitutes an important place in the history of the subject when he invents the concept of *différance* and plots the linguistic limit of the subject. *Différance*, as Derrida (1981: 8–9) remarks, as both the common root of all the positional concepts marking our language and the condition for all signification, refers not only to the "movement that consists in deferring by means of delay, delegation, reprieve, referral, detour, postponement, reserving" but also and finally to "the unfolding of difference," of the ontico-ontological difference, which Heidegger named as the difference between Being and beings.

Amy Gutmann (1994: 13) characterizes the concern for cultural difference and for the public recognition of particular cultures within liberal democracies as one that is forever counterbalanced by the concern for the protection of universal rights, and she translates the issue into the educational sphere as a dispute over the core curriculum and the content of courses when she sets up the debate in terms of the essentialists and the deconstructionists. Gutmann (1994) suggests that the deconstructionists argue:

> That to preserve the core by excluding contributions by women, African-Americans, Hispanics, Asians, and Native Americans as if the classical canon were sacred, unchanging, and unchangeable would be to denigrate the identities of members of these previously excluded groups and to close off Western civilization from the influences of unorthodox and challenging ideas of the sake of perpetuating sexism, racism, Eurocentrism, close-mindedness, the tyranny of truth (with a capital T), and a host of related intellectual and political evils. (13–14)

To construct the debate in this way as one between the opposite poles of essentialism and deconstructionism allows Gutmann to safely impugn both and to come out on the side of liberal democracy. The debate over the core or multicultural curriculum is largely a reflection over the philosophy of the subject: essentialist or deconstructionist? There are a number of buried premises in the argument concerning the liberal theory of education and schooling, the education of reason, the shaping of selves, and so on. Gutmann does not make these theoretical connections. Whether she is kind to essentialists I will leave for others to judge. Her take on deconstructionists follows an analogous form to the problem of agency argument: "deconstructionists erect a different obstacle to liberal democracy when they deny the desirability of shared intellectual standards, which scholars and students might use to evaluate our common education"; "they [deconstructionists] view common standards as masks for the will to political power of dominant, hegemonic groups" (18). Gutmann asserts that such an argument is self-undermining, both logically and practically, for deconstructionism itself reflects the will to power of deconstructionists. Her quarrel with deconstructionism is that, first, "it denies *a priori* any reasonable answers to fundamental questions," and, second, "it reduces everything to an exercise of political power" (20).

The difficulty is that Gutmann deconstructionists are faceless; she never mentions Derrida or any theorist in association with deconstructionism. In other words, she sets up a strawman deconstructionism, which alleviates her of the scholarly responsibility to read or refer to specific texts, only to fiercely knock it down in the name of liberal democracy. We are entitled, for instance, to ask Gutmann: can Foucault really be considered a deconstructionist? Is the will to power a motivating concept in Derridean deconstruction or Foucauldian genealogy? Where does Derrida explicitly address the theme of ethnocentrism and what does he say concerning it? Gutmann has homogenized the differences between those she calls deconstructionists and while appropriating the term deconstructionism she has ignored any reference at all to Derrida's work. If Gutmann had investigated Derrida's work, she may have discovered that ethnocentrism and phallocentrism are seen to accompany the logocentrism that defines historically the attempt in the West to determine being as presence and that Nietzsche's influence, in Derrida's eyes, has been to free the signifier from the logos.[14]

The anti-Nietzscheanism, perhaps, reached its peak in the early 1990s with Ferry and Renaut's (1991) *Pourquoi Nous ne Sommes pas Nietzschéens*. In the preface to the 1992 French edition, Ferry and Renaut (1997: vii–viii) suggest that an appropriate retitling of the collection of essays might be "to think Nietzsche against Nietzsche" for they identify Nietzsche as the inventor of the genealogy, the thinker, above all, who inspired the so-called master thinkers of the 1960s, who standing in the shadows of Nietzsche believed that they too could philosophize with a hammer, smashing the last idols of metaphysics and thereby move beyond humanism. Yet, while they assert that "today nobody believes in Absolute Knowledge, in the meaning of history, or in the transparency of the Subject" (presumably the thinking of Nietzsche), it is also the case that "philosophy is not condemned to infinite deconstruction" (the thinking of Nietzsche against Nietzsche). They continue: "philosophy renews the ancestral desire for rationality, which the relativism of the modes of thought of difference invited us, too facilely, to renounce."

Only Vincent Descombes (1997) deals with Nietzsche's "French moment" and his analysis focuses upon Foucault and Deleuze to the exclusion of Derrida. Descombes generalizing to poststructuralism—an "unnatural alliance" of Nietzscheanism with orthodox structuralism—suggests that Nietzscheanism introduces no new principles apart from those of the modern project and its "critique of consciousness doesn't go beyond

Cartesian mind philosophy" (90). As he says, "The superior individual is inconceivable outside the idealist philosophy of autonomy" (90).

Ferry and Renaut (1997) bypass the so-called master thinkers, or any one of them, to concentrate on Nietzsche in relation to the question of democracy. They distinguish two attitudes to democracy: the development or enlargement of the model of argumentative deliberation in either its theoretical or practical dimensions (Habermas, Apel, Rawls); and the investigation of the possibility of the emergence of a contemporary analogue to a traditional universe through the development of the critique of democratic modernity (Strauss, MacIntyre, and the communitarians—Taylor, Sandel, etc.). Nietzsche's case is interesting, they argue, especially in terms of critically investigating the neotraditionalist path because he articulates the critique of democratic modernity (and the argumentative foundation of democratic norms) while rejecting the neotraditionalist possibility of a contemporary analogue of tradition, in an age characterized by the death of God. This is an interesting and productive essay but one that hardly touches Derrida—or Derrida's Nietzsche.[15]

DERRIDA'S RESPONSE: THE CALCULATION OF THE SUBJECT[16]

I shall argue that the anti-Nietzschean polemical attack on the critique of the subject is misplaced, for poststructuralism never liquidated the subject but rather rehabilitated it, decentered it, and repositioned it, in all its historico-cultural complexity. While Ferry and Renaut talk of returning to the question of the subject, their critique of poststructuralism and their nonmetaphysical humanism singularly lacks any resources for doing so. There is in Ferry and Renaut's work nothing that might suggest a reworking of the question of the subject in any guise except an innocent, historically naive, and unproblematic return to a (neoliberal) human agency.

Jean-Luc Nancy (1991) comments in his Introduction to *Who Comes After the Subject?*:

> I did not send my question ("Who comes after the subject?") to those who would find no validity in it, to those for whom it is on the contrary more important to denounce its presuppositions and to return, as though nothing had happened, to a style of thinking that we might simply call humanist, even where it tries to complicate the traditional way of thinking about the human subject. (3)

For Nancy, the contributors (including Deleuze, Derrida, Blanchot, Lyotard, Levinas, Irigaray, Descombes, and many others) do not stand in a tradition or belong to a school, but rather "each entertains a complex rap-

port" to "the Husserlian, the Marxian, the Heideggerian, and the Nietzschean traditions" (3). When Nancy writes of "those who return, as
though nothing had happened, to the humanist subject," clearly he has
Ferry and Renaut in mind.

In an interview with Nancy, Derrida (1995: 256) disputes Nancy's
interpretation of the "liquidation of the subject," and, discussing the discourse concerning "the question of the subject" in France over the past
twenty-five years, suggests instead the slogan, "a return to the subject, the
return of the subject."[17] He begins the interview by briefly tracing the place
of the subject in Lacan (the decentering of the subject), in Althusser (its
interpellation), and in Foucault ("a history of subjectivity" and "a return
to a certain ethical subject").[18]

> For these three discourses (Lacan, Althusser, Foucault) and for some of the
> thinkers they privilege (Freud, Marx, Nietzsche), the subject can be reinter-
> preted, re-stored, re-inscribed, it certainly isn't "liquidated." The question
> "who," notably in Nietzsche, strongly reinforces this point. This is also true
> of Heidegger, the principle reference or target of the *doxa* we are talking
> about. The ontological questioning that deals with the *subjectum,* in its
> Cartesian and post-Cartesian forms, is anything but a liquidation. (Derrida,
> 1995: 257)

The attribution of the liquidation of the subject to a Nietzschean poststructuralism—an attribution underlying the polemical attacks of Ferry
and Renaut and also of a French kind of neoliberalism—operates polemical to identify its target only by ignoring the time, place, and logical space
of the subject, its multiple genealogy within the history of modern philosophy and its active reinterpretation and re-inscription. What this tells
us is that the *problematique* of the subject, as it has developed in France
over the last twenty-five years, cannot be reduced to homogeneity.

Derrida's response to Nancy in the interview is both complex and
detailed, covering extensive territory and raising fresh sources for inquiry.
While it may be true to say that Derrida's discussion focuses upon an explication of themes in Heidegger (and Levinas to a lesser degree) in relation
to a certain responsibility and the question of the subject, he makes reference to the entire history of the metaphysics of subjectivity, mentioning
along the way many of the most prominent thinkers in the last twenty-five
years of French philosophy. I think it is useful to linger a while to consider
Derrida's (1995) description of the way in which the central hegemony of
the subject was put into question again in the 1960s at a point when the
question of time and of the other became linked to the interest in Husserl's
discourse:

It was in the 1950s and 1960s, at the moment when an interest in these difficulties [i.e., the dislocation of the absolute subject from the other and from time] developed in a very different way (Levinas, Tran-Duc-Thao, myself) and following moreover other trajectories (Marx, Nietzsche, Freud, Heidegger), that the centrality of the subject began to be displaced. . . . But if certain premises are found "in" Husserl, I'm sure that one could make a similar demonstration in Descartes, Kant, and Hegel. . . . This would have at least the virtue of de-simplifying, of "de-homogenizing" the reference to something like The Subject. (264)

Derrida is turned to Heidegger by Nancy, and he refers to the act by which Heidegger substitutes a concept of *Dasein* for a concept of the subject simultaneously recalling "the essential ontological fragility of the ethical, juridical, and political foundations of democracy" (266) that "remain essentially sealed within a philosophy of the subject" (266). The question and task, Derrida suggests, is to develop an ethics, a politics, and an "other" democracy—he refers elsewhere to a "democracy to come" based upon Nietzsche's understanding (see below)—that is, "another type of responsibility" that would safeguard us against the worst antidemocratic intrusions (i.e., meaning National Socialism in all its forms). As Derrida (1995) puts it:

> In order to recast, if not rigorously re-found a discourse on the "subject," on that which will hold the place (or replace the place) of the subject (of law, of morality, of politics—so many categories caught up in the same turbulence), one has to go through the experience of deconstruction. (272)[19]

Significantly, Derrida suggests that *Dasein,* in *Being and Time,* in spite of the questions it has raised and the spaces it has opened up for thinking, still occupies a place similar or analogous to that of the transcendental subject because it has been determined on the basis of a series of oppositions not sufficiently scrutinized. These oppositions include all the essential predicates of which subjects are the subject and which are ordered around being-present [*étant-present*] such as "presence to self . . . ; identity to self, positionality, property, personality, ego, consciousness, will intentionality, freedom, humanity, etc." (274). We shall not follow Derrida in any detailed way into his excursus on the "yes, yes" or the affirmation, as he says, not addressed first to a subject but rather bids to a certain responsibility not reducible to and beyond the traditional category of the subject. Suffice it to say here that Derrida locates this responsibility in "that to which one cannot and should not submit the other in general; in the who of friendship that provokes conscience and therefore opens up responsibility" (275). This who of friendship, he claims, belongs to the existential structure of *Dasein* and "precedes every subjectal determination" (275), referring to both Nancy's *Inoperative Community* and Blanchot's *The Unavowable Community.* He says clearly:

> The origin of the call that comes from nowhere, an origin in any case that is not yet a divine or human "subject," institutes a responsibility that is to be found at the root of all ulterior responsibilities (moral, juridical, political), and of every categorical imperative. (Derrida 1995: 276)

This figure of responsibility can be approached also through Levinas's understanding of subjectivity of the *hostage* where "the subject is responsible for the other before being responsible for himself as 'me' " (279).

While the discourses of Heidegger and Levinas disrupt a certain traditional humanism they remain "profound humanisms *to the extent that they do not sacrifice sacrifice*" (279). In other words, both thinkers tend to be humanists to the extent that only sacrifice of human life is forbidden, not life in general. Let me quote Derrida (1995) yet again—a tortuous passage but one that rescues (finally) the significance of the title "Eating Well" and casts light upon the remarks above.

> If the limit between the living and the nonliving now seems to be as unsure . . . as that between "man" and "animal," and if . . . the ethical frontier no longer rigorously passes between the "Thou shalt not kill" (man, thy neighbour) and the "Thou shalt not put to death the living in general," . . . then, as concerns the "Good" [*Bien*] of every morality, the question will come back to determining the best, most respectful, most graceful, and also the most giving way of relating to the other and of relating the other to the self. For everything that happens at the edge of the orifices (of orality, but also of the ear, the eye—and all the 'senses' in general) the metonymy of "eating well" [*bien manger*] would always be the rule. (281)[20]

The explication of "who" in relation to sacrifice at once allows Derrida to emphasize the originality of Heidegger's and Levinas's discourses while recognizing their humanisms, and the way they break from traditional humanism. (He suggests that Heidegger was a Judeo-Christian thinker). At the same time it allows Derrida to foreshadow the notion of responsibility for an ethics, and politics to come, which springs from the relation to the other.[21] Certainly it is the case, against Ferry and Renaut and other anti-Nietzscheans that Derrida does not do away with the subject. He does not eliminate or liquidate although he does deconstruct the sovereign subject and the history of the subject. For Derrida, as his comment almost thirty years ago should remind us—a comment I used to open this chapter—the notion of the subject is something one cannot get along without. It is never a question of doing without it so much as "knowing where it comes from and how it functions."

In relation to the question of democracy, Derrida (1994a: 41–42) resists the temptation to conclude that Nietzsche is an enemy of democracy in general and has nothing to offer in the name of "a democracy to come." "I don't consider Nietzsche to be an *enemy of democracy in general.*" Derrida suggests that this move is to open up the difference between a notion of democracy, "which while having something in common with what we understand by democracy today . . . is reducible neither to the contemporary reality of 'democracy' nor to the ideal of democracy informing this reality or fact." It is this difference that Derrida indicates he has explored at length in *Spectres de Marx* (1993). While, as Derrida maintains, one cannot subscribe to all of what Nietzsche has written concerning the democracy of his day, he identified "particular risks in what he foregrounded under the name of 'democracy' " and "There are at the same time critical and genealogical motifs in Nietzsche that *appeal to a democracy to come*" (Derrida 1994a: 41–42).[22]

Richard Beardsworth observes that Derrida's work in distinction to both Nietzsche and Heidegger, affirms both technology and democracy and he asks the following question:

> Although the promise of democracy is not the same as either the *fact* of democracy or the regulative *idea* (in the Kantian sense) of democracy, deconstruction does "hear" *différance* more in a democratic organisation of government than in any other political model; and there are no new models to be invented. If I understand you correctly, your affirmation of democracy is, in this respect, a demand for the sophistication of democracy, such a refinement taking advantage, in turn, of the increasingly sophisticated effects of technology. (Derrida 1994a: 18)

Beardsworth poses the question in relation to a number of pertinent observations: first, that "democratic institutions are becoming more and more unrepresentative in our increasingly technicised world;" second, that "the media are swallowing up the constitutional machinery of democratic institutions, furthering thereby the depoliticisation of society and the possibility of populist demagogy;" third, that "resistance to this process of technicisation is at the same time leading to virulent forms of nationalism and demagogy in the former Soviet empire;" finally, that "the rights of man would seem an increasingly ineffective set of criteria to resist this process of technicisation (together with its possible fascistic effects) given this process's gradual effacement of the normative and metaphysical limit between the human and the inorganic" (18).

Derrida responds by contemplating the nature of contemporary acceleration of technicization and the relation between technical acceleration—a product of the so-called technosciences—and politico-economic processes, which relates rather to the structure of decision making. In relation to these two kinds of acceleration Derrida asks, "what is the situation today of democracy?" His response is worth noting:

> "Progress" in arms-technologies and media-technologies is incontestably causing the disappearance of the site on which the democratic used to be situated. The site of representation and the stability of the location which make up parliament or assembly, the territorialisation of power, the rooting of power to a particular place, if not to the ground as such—all this is over. The notion of politics dependent on this relation between power and space is over as well, although its end must be negotiated with. I am not just thinking here of the present forms of nationalism and fundamentalism. Technoscientific acceleration poses an absolute threat to Western-style democracy as well, following its radical undermining of locality. Since there can be no question of interrupting science of the technosciences, it's a matter of knowing how a democratic response can be made to what is happening. This response must not, for obvious reasons, try to maintain at all costs the life of a democratic model of government which is rapidly being made redundant. If technics now exceeds democratic forms of government, it's not only because assembly or parliament is being swallowed up by the media. This was already the case after the First World War. It was already being argued then that the media (then the radio) were forming public opinion so much that public deliberation and parliamentary discussion no longer determined the life of a democracy. And so, we need a historical perspective. What the acceleration of technicisation concerns today is the frontiers of the nation-state, the traffic of arms and drugs, everything that has to do with inter-nationality. It is these issues which need to be completely reconsidered, not in order to sound the death-knell of democracy, but in order to rethink democracy *from within these conditions*. (Derrida 1994a: 57–58)

Derrida maintains that since technics have obliterated locality, the future of democracy must be thought in global terms. It is no longer possible to be a democrat at home and wait to see what happens abroad. In emphasizing the call to a world democracy Derrida suggests the stakes of a democracy to come can no longer be contained within frontiers or depend upon the decisions of a group of citizens or a nation, or group of nations. The call is for something new that is both more modest and yet also more ambitious than any overriding concept of the universal, the cosmopolitan, or the human. Derrida distinguishes the difference between a rhetorical sense of democracy as politics that transcends borders (as one might speak of the United Nations) and what he calls a "democracy to come." The difference exhibits itself in decisions made in the name of the rights of man, which, he suggests, "are at the same time alibis for the continued inequality between singularities." He indicates that we need to invent new concepts—concepts other than that of state, superstate, citizen, and so forth for what he has called the "new international" (Derrida 1993). He says:

> The democracy to come obliges one to challenge instituted law in the name of an indefinitely unsatisfied justice, thereby revealing the injustice of calculating justice whether this be in the name of a particular form of democracy or of the concept of humanity. (Derrida 1994a: 60–61)

Elsewhere Derrida (1994b) explains what he means by deconstructing the foundations of international law. While international law is a good thing, it is nevertheless rooted in the Western concept of philosophy—as he says, "in its mission, its axiom, in its languages"—and the Western concept of state and sovereignty, which acts as a limit. In order to rethink the international order and think of a "democracy to come" we must deconstruct the foundations of international law and the international organizations built upon it. The second limit is that the international organizations are governed by a number of powerful, rich states, including the United States.

Derrida here is attempting "to deconstruct the political tradition not in order to depoliticize but in order to interpret differently the concept of the political."

> So justice and gift should go beyond calculation, which doesn't mean that we shouldn't calculate, we should calculate it as rigorously as possible but there is a point or a limit beyond which calculation must fail. . . . And so what I tried to think or to suggest is a concept of the political and of democracy which would be compatible, which could be articulated with these impossible notions of the gift and justice. (Derrida 1994b: 34)

It might be argued that the prospect of a critical pedagogy of difference, of a genuinely multicultural and internationalist pedagogy suitable for the future, is located at the interstices and in the interplay between a "democracy to come" and a "subject to come," a global subject whose critical function it is to both initiate and interrogate the new international.

NOTES

1. This section is drawn from my essay "Humanism, Derrida, and the New Humanities" (Peters 2001).
2. For a clear account of deconstruction and its American reception and mediation (especially at the hands of Paul de Man) as a school of literary criticism see Rorty (1995). Rorty provides an exemplary account of both deconstructionist theory and the two main lines of (analytic) criticism against Derridean philosophy.
3. See my "Poststructuralism and the Philosophy of the Subject," chapter 1, in Peters (1996).
4. Judith Butler's (1987: 175) comment is entirely apposite here: "The twentieth-century history of Hegelianism in France can be understood in terms of two constitutive moments: (1) the specification of the subject in terms of finitude, corporeal boundaries, and temporality and (2) the 'splitting' (Lacan), 'displacement' (Derrida), and eventual death (Foucault, Deleuze) of the hegelian subject."
5. For an account on the importance of Nietzsche to poststructuralist thought and to Derrida see Behler (1991), Large (1993), and Schrift (1995, 1996); also see "Naming the Multiple: Poststructuralism and Education," (Peters 1998) and Trifonas (1998) for an account of Derrida educational writings, especially "The Age of Hegel."
6. "The Question of Style" is the title of Derrida's presentation to the Nietzsche conference at Cerisy-la Salle in 1972, which was later extended into *Spurs: Nietzsche's Styles* (1978).
7. There have been a number of attempts to apply Derrida's ideas to pedagogy. Gregory Ulmer (1985) has outlined a project after-Derrida, especially in the areas of media and cultural studies, that he calls applied grammatology where students are encouraged to experience theory directly in performance. See his home page at www.ucet.ufl.edu/~gulmer. See also Vincent Leitch (1996), especially chapters "Teaching Deconstructively" and "Postmodernism, Pedagogy and Cultural Criticism."
8. This is Schrift's (1995: 24) construction. He writes, "Derrida develops his deconstructive critique of the subject as a privileged center of discourse in the context of his project of delegitimizing authority, whether that authority emerges in the form of the author's domination of the text, or the tradition's reading of the history of philosophy" (25). Derrida's deconstructive critique of authority—both the authority of the text and of the history of philosophy—has an obvious relevance to pedagogy as a critique of authority of educational institutions and those that assume positions of authority in its name.
9. His questioning of pegagogical forms of writing is, perhaps, clearest in "The Time of the Thesis: Punctuations" (Derrida 1983), the text of a presentation given at the opening of a thesis defense based on published works at the Sorbonne in 1980. There Derrida divides his work into four phases: 1957–1962; 1963–1967, 1968–1974, and the years after 1974. He says he registered his thesis with the title of "The Ideality of the Literary Object" in 1957, which was concerned with using techniques of transcendental phenomenology to elaborate a new theory of literature. During the second period he says that he was trying to work out a "not wholly formalizable ensemble of rules for reading, interpretation and writing" (40). During each period he relates his own activities to the form of the thesis and the structure of the *universitas,* which, he says, "has an essential tie with the ontological onto-encyclopedic system" (43). Later he states that deconstruction "was not primarily a matter of philosophical contents, themes or theses, philosophemes, poems, theologemes or ideologemes, but especially and inseparably meaningful frames, institutional structures, pedagogical or rhetorical norms, the possibilities of law, of authority, of evaluation, and of representation in terms of its very market" (44–54).
10. See, for example, their reference in the preface to the English translation, to Victor Farias (xv). They also later became emboiled in the so-called Heidegger affair when Farias's book sparked a

debate in the 1980s concerning alleged new revelations of Heidegger's Nazi involvement. See Ferry and Renaut's (1990) *Heidegger and Modernity.*

11. Lilla (1994) makes the following useful remark:

> Ferry and Renaut have made two, not always compatible appeals to previous philosophies of the subject. One is to Kant, and specifically to the *Critique of Judgment,* wishing to avoid the transcendental presuppositions of the First Critique and the rigors of the Second, they have followed the increasingly common strategy of seeking in the Third an "aesthetic" model for reflection on morals and politics. . . . A second appeal is to Fichte, specifically to his earliest work: here they discover a "non-metaphysical" philosophy of the subject that makes room for intersubjective experience and permits a critical analysis of history (32, fn 38).

   The first appeal might be considered curious in the light of the fact that Lyotard first moved in this direction in the early 1980s to sustain his notion of heterogenous language games. See his essay "Answering the Question; What is Postmodernism?" an appendix to *The Postmodern Condition* (1984).

12. For the full text of the letter and Derrida's response, originally published in the *Cambridge Review* in 1992 see Derrida's (1992) *"Honoris Causa:* 'This is *also* extremely funny.' " For a recent and balanced account of the affair see Joseph Margolis (1994).

13. For a full discussion of this matter see "Monoculturalism, Multiculturalism and Democracy: The Politics of Difference or Recognition?," chapter 10 in Peters (1996).

14. See, for example, Derrida's (1976: 19) comment: "Radicalizing the concepts of *interpretation, perspective, evaluation, difference,* and all the 'empiricist' or nonphilosophical motifs that have constantly tormented philosophy throughout the history of the West, and besides, have had nothing but the inevitable weakness of being produced in the field of philosophy, Nietzsche, far from remaining simply (with Hegel and as Heidegger wished) within metaphysics, contributed a great deal to the liberation of the signifier from its dependence or derivation with respect to the logos and the related concept of truth or the primary signified, in whatever sense that is understood." Derrida begins the "Exergue" to his *Of Grammatology* by focusing our attention on the ethnocentrism that has controlled our notion of writing and addresses the notion further in *Part II Nature, Culture Writing.* This would be an appropriate starting point for Gutmann if she was interested in deconstructionism in relation to the question of ethnocentrism. Still the best short commentary, in my view, on Derrida in relation to Nietzsche, Heidegger, and Freud is Gayatri Chakravorty Spivak's (1976) "Translator's Preface" to *Of Grammatology.*

15. Of all the essays, perhaps the most interesting and most relevant for my purposes here is Phillippe Raynaud's (1997) "Nietzsche as Educator." Raynaud wants to approach Nietzsche's oeuvre directly rather than through his French admirers to ask about the kind of philosophy possible today, Nietzsche's relation to the Enlightenment, and his critique of modern ideals. His interpretation is, I think, insightful: "The task for democratic political thinking is analogous to that which I have tried to define for philosophy: as an antidote to the modern spirit, Nietzsche's thought should be taken by modernity as a privileged means for self-criticism. It is in that respect, more than as a master of truth, that Nietzsche is an *educator.*"

16. This section is based upon an expansion and reconsideration of a couple of points I first advanced in "Introduction: Naming the Multiple" (Peters 1998).

17. The interview with Jean-Luc Nancy entitled " 'Eating Well,' or The Calculation of the Subject" was originally published in *Cahiers Confrontation* 20 (Winter 1989), an issue called "Après le subjet qui vent" (After the subject who comes). All references in this chapter are to the full interview now published in *Points . . . Interviews, 1974–1994* (Derrida 1995). A note (Derrida 1995: 473) recording the circumstances and bibliographic history surrounding the interview, used to first present the interview in *Cahiers,* is repeated in *Points.* I think it is worth repeating here: "Jacques Derrida was unable to write a text in time for *Topoi* (the journal in which this interview was initially published in English translation in October 1988 [vol. 7, no. 2]; the issue has since been re-edited as a book: *Who Comes After the Subject?* Ed. Eduardo Cadava, Peter Connor, and Jean-Luc Nancy (New York: Routledge, 1991). He proposed that we do an interview instead. The latter, however, took place too late to be integrally transcribed and translated in *Topoi,* which was able to publish only about half of it. It appears here almost in its entirety (although not without the omission of certain developments whose themes were

announced in *Topoi:* the whole would have been both too long and occasionally too far afield from the main theme)."

18. Derrida (1995: 256) notes "As for Foucault's discourse, there would be different things to say according to the stages of its development." This remark is important for it reveals the complexity of the question of the subject in the thought of *one* thinker, which demonstrates the inadequacy of the generalized description the liquidation of the subject as it applies to the whole of post-war French philosophy. On the stages of the history of subjectivity in the discourses of Heidegger and Foucault (and the parallels between them) see Dreyfus (1998: 1), who in particular, demonstrates I think the inadequacy of the notion that the subject has been liquidated in either Heidegger or Foucault. He writes, "Whatever their similarities and differences, one thing that Heidegger and Foucault clearly have in common is that they are both critical of the Cartesian idea of a self-transparent subject and the related Kantian ideal of autonomous agency. Yet neither denies the importance of human freedom. In Heidegger's early work the subject is interpreted as Dasein—a non-autonomous-thrown way of being, yet who can change the field of possibilities in which it acts. In middle Heidegger, thinkers alone have the power to disclose a new world, while in later Heidegger anyone is free to step back from the current world, enter one of a plurality of worlds and facilitate a change in the practices of one's society. For early Foucault the subject is reduced to a function of discourse; for middle Foucault writing can open up new worlds, and in later Foucault freedom is understood as the power to question what is currently taken for granted, plus the capacity to change oneself. In short, while both Heidegger and Foucault reject the Enlightenment idea of an autonomous subject, they have a robust notion of freedom and action." Dreyfus's observation expressed in his last sentence is important for pedagogy and educational theory for Heidegger and Foucault, it suggests that it is possible to posit a notion of the subject which is not autonomous in the traditional Cartesian–Kantian sense, yet nevertheless free and capable of action. What would a pedagogy based on such a subject look like?

19. Invoking a certain notion of responsibility that is excessive in that it "regulates itself neither on the principles of reason not on any sort of accountancy," Derrida (1995: 272) suggests that the subject is also "a principle of calculability"—hence part of the title of the interview "The Calculation of the Subject." As he suggests "the subject is also a principle of calculability—for the political (and even, indeed, for the current concept of democracy, which is less clear, less homogenous, and less of a given than we believe or claim to believe, and which no doubt needs to be rethought, radicalized, and considered as a thing of the future), in the question of legal rights (including human rights, about which I would repeat what I have just said about democracy) and in morality" (Derrida 1995: 272). Yet, for us to arrive at a notion of responsibility that might carry with it the new possibilities and new meanings for the political and the moral, the calculation of the subject must pass through deconstruction.

20. The translators note (475, note 15) says "The phrase in play here, '*Il faut bien manger*' (which is also the original title of the interview), can be read in at least two ways: 'one must eat well' or 'everyone has to eat.' In addition, when the adverb *bien* is nomialized as '*le Bien*,' there results the sense of 'eating the Good.' It is this multivalent sense that Derrida explores in the succeeding sentences." I shall not attempt to precis Derrida's stunning and surprising "turns" but will simply leave it as an enticement.

21. I think it is useful to refer to the way in which Derrida recognizes how the question of the subject and of the living "who," as he says, is at the heart of the most pressing concerns of modern societies. I shall summarize: decisions over birth and death involving, the treatment of sperm or ovum, surrogacy, genetic engineering, bioethics, biopolitics, euthanasia, organ removal, and transplant.

22. Compared with Hollingdale's (1968: 89) remark: "*Democracy:* Nietzsche is known to be anti-democratic and is thought in this to be perversely opposing as the whole general movement of the modern world. No need to agree or disagree here either: when Nietzsche was criticized for his moral theories he replied by asking 'whether we have in fact become more moral,' " and we might likewise ask ourselves whether we have in fact become more democratic and whether in fact we want to. Do you consider every man and woman your equal, in every respect, in any respect? What does political democracy *mean?* Is it separable from industrial democracy? Who really *rules* (do you rule?). Are we any closer now to *cultural* democracy, to an actual equivalence of capacity between man and man, than we were in 1888 when *Twilight of the Idols* and *The Anti-Christ* were written?

REFERENCES

Behler, Ernest. 1991. *Confrontations: Derrida, Heidegger, Nietzsche.* Trans. S. Taubeneck. Stanford: Stanford University Press.

Cadava, Eduardo, Peter Connor, and Jean-Luc Nancy, eds. 1991. *Who Comes After the Subject?* New York: Routledge.

Derrida, Jacques. 1970. From the discussion following "Structure, Sign and Play in the Discourses of the Human Sciences." In *The Structuralist Controversy,* trans. Richard Macksey, ed. Richard Macksey and Eugenio Donato, 271. Baltimore: John Hopkins University Press.

———. 1976. *Of Grammatology.* Trans. G. C. Spivak. Baltimore and London: The John Hopkins University Press.

———. 1978. "Structure, Sign and Play in the Discourses of the Human Sciences." In *Writing and Difference,* trans. A. Bass, 278–93. Chicago: University of Chicago Press.

———. 1978. *Spurs: Nietzsche's Styles.* Trans. B. Harlow. Chicago: Chicago University Press.

———. 1981. *Positions.* Trans. A. Bass. Chicago: University of Chicago Press.

———. 1982. "The Ends of Man." In *Margins of Philosophy,* trans. A. Bass 109–136. Chicago: University of Chicago Press.

———. 1983. "The Time of the Thesis: Punctuations." In *Philosophy in France Today,* ed. Alan Montefiore, 34–50. Cambridge: Cambridge University Press.

———. 1985. "Octobiographies: The Teaching of Nietzsche and the Politics of the Proper Name." In *The Ear of the Other: Otobiography, Transference, Translation,* trans., Avital Ronell, Christie V. McDonald, and Peggy Kamuf, 1–38. New York: Schocken Books.

———. 1994a. "Nietzsche and the Machine: An Interview with Jacques Derrida by Richard Beardsworth." *Journal of Nietzsche Studies* 7: 7–66.

———. 1994b. "Roundtable Discussion with Jacques Derrida." Transcr. J. Christian Guerrero, Villanova University, October 3, 1994. Located at: http://www.lake.de/home/lake/hydra/vill1.html.

———. 1995a. "*Honoris Causa:* 'This Is Also Extremely Funny.' " In *Points . . . Interviews, 1974–1994,* ed. E. Weber, trans. P. Kamuf and others, 399–421. Stanford: Stanford University Press.

———. 1995b. " 'Eating Well,' or the Calculation of the Subject." In *Points . . . Interviews, 1974–1994,* ed. E. Weber, trans. P. Kamuf and others, 255–87. Stanford: Stanford University Press.

———. 1995c. "Is There A Philosophical Language?" In *Points . . . Interviews, 1974–1994,* ed. E. Weber, trans. P. Kamuf and others. Stanford: Stanford University Press.

———. 1997. "Nietzsche's French Moment." In *Why We Are Not Nietzscheans,* ed. Luc Ferry and Alain Renaut, trans. R. de Loaiza, 70–91. Chicago and London: The University of Chicago Press.

———. 1998. "Heidegger and Foucault on the Subject, Agency and Practices." Unpublished paper.

Ferry, Luc, and Alain Renaut. 1990. *French Philosophy of the Sixties. An Essay on Antihumanism.* Trans. M. Cattani. Amherst: The University of Massachusetts Press.

———. 1991. *Pourquoi Nous ne Sommes pas Nietzschéens.* Paris: Éditions Grasset & Fasquelle.

———. 1997. "What Must First Be Proved Is Worth Little." In *Why We Are Not Nietzscheans,* ed. Luc Ferry, and Alain Renaut, A., trans. R. de Loaiza 92–109. Chicago and London: The University of Chicago Press.

———. eds. 1997. *Why We Are Not Nietzscheans.* Trans. R. de Loaiza. Chicago and London, The University of Chicago Press.

Hollingdale, R. J. 1968. "Introduction" to *Twilight of the Idols* and *The Anti-Christ,* Friedrich Nietzcshe, trans. R. J. Hollingdale. Harmondsworth, England: Penguin.

Large, Duncan. 1993. "Translator's Introduction" to Sarah Kofman, *Nietzsche and Metaphor,* vii–xl. London: The Athlone Press.

Leitch, Vincent. 1996. *Local Effects, Global Flows.* New York: State University of New York Press.

Lilla, Mark, ed., 1994. *New French Political Thought.* Princeton: Princeton University Press.

Macksey, Richard, and Eugenio Donato, eds. 1970. *The Structuralist Controversy: The Languages of Criticism and the Sciences of Man.* Baltimore and London: John Hopkins University Press.

Margolis, Joseph. 1994. "Deferring to Derrida's Difference." In *European Philosophy and the American Academy,* ed. Barry Smith, 195–226. La Salle, Ill.: The Hegeler Institute, Moinst Library of Philosophy.

Nancy, Jean-Luc. 1991. "Introduction." In *Who Comes After the Subject?*, ed. E. Cadava, P. O'Connor, and J.-L. Nancy, 1–8. London and New York: Routledge.

Nietzsche, Friedrich. 1968. # 490, Book Three, "Principles of a New Evaluation," *The Will To Power*. Trans. W. Kaufmann and R. J. Hollingdale, ed. W. Kaufmann, 270. New York: Vintage Books.

Peters, Michael. 1996. *Poststructuralism, Politics and Education*. Westport, Conn., and London: Bergin & Garvey.

———. 1998. "Introduction: Naming the Multiple." In *Naming the Multiple: Poststructralism and Education*, ed. M. Peters. Westport, Conn., and London: Bergin & Garvey.

———. 2001. "Humanism, Derrida, and the New Humanities." In *Derrida and Education*, ed. Gert Biesta and Denise Egéa-Kuehne, 209–231. London: Routledge.

Raynaud, Phillippe. 1997. "Nietzsche as Educator." In *Why We Are Not Nietzscheans*, ed. Luc Ferry and Alain Renaut, trans. R. de Loaiza, 141–57. Chicago and London: The University of Chicago Press.

Rorty, Richard. 1995. "Deconstruction." In *The Cambridge History of Literary Criticism*, Vol. 8, *From Formalism to Poststructralism*, ed. Raman Selden. Cambridge: Cambridge University Press.

Schrift, Alan 1995. *Nietzsche's French Legacy: A Genealogy of Poststructuralism*. New York and London: Routledge.

Smith, Barry, ed., 1994. *European Philosophy and the American Academy*. New York: Open Court Publishing Co.

———. 1996. "Nietzsche's French Legacy." In *The Cambridge Companion to Nietzsche*, ed. B. Magnus and K. Higgins, 323–55. Cambridge: Cambridge University Press.

Spivak, G. C. 1976. "Translator's Preface," to J. Derrida, *Of Grammatology*. Baltimore and London: The John Hopkins University Press.

Taylor, Charles, from *Multiculturalism*, A. Gutmann, ed. 1994. Princeton: Princeton University Press (1994).

Trifonas, Peter. 1998. "Jacques Derrida: The Ends of Pedagogy—From the Dialectic of Memory to the Deconstruction of the Institution." In *Naming the Multiple: Poststructuralism and Education*, ed. M. Peters, Westport, Conn., and London: Bergin and Garvey.

Ulmer, Gregory. 1985. *Applied Grammatology: Post(e)-Pedagogy from Jacques Derrida to Joseph Beuys*, Baltimore: John Hopkins University Press.

4

Pedagogies of Difference, Race, and Representation: Film as a Site of Translation and Politics

HENRY A. GIROUX

THE POLITICS OF ACADEMIC MULTICULTURALISM

Within the past decade a number of critical theorists have made a strong case for rethinking the political and pedagogical possibilities of multiculturalism within higher education.[1] Signaling a new understanding of how the mechanisms of domination and exclusion work to reproduce and legitimate the entrenched nature of class, race, gender, and sexual hierarchies in higher education, critical multiculturalists often combine the study of symbolic forms and signifying practices with a reinvigorated and necessary study of the relations between culture and politics.[2] For many critical multiculturalists the process of schooling is viewed as a terrain of struggle over the meaning and purpose of the humanities, the value of disciplinarity, the regulatory function of culture, the relationship between knowledge and authority, and who has ownership over the conditions for the production of knowledge.[3] Critical multiculturalists have also called into question the foundational categories that establish the canons of great works, the high and low culture divide, and the allegedly objective scholarship that marks the exclusions within and between various disciplines.[4] Similarly, they have fought bitter battles to establish academic programs that address the interests of various groups, including women's studies, Latino studies, and gay and lesbian programs.[5] In addition to challenging the content of curricula, they have successfully confronted the institutional distribution of power in higher education, in part, by expanding through affirmative action and other programs the opportunities for minority students to gain access to colleges and universities.

Critical academic multiculturalism has scored some of its greatest successes by significantly adding to the sum of public discourses available within the university that provide students with a range of pedagogical options in which they can invest, act, and speak in order to affirm their capacities for critical, social agency. Within progressive notions of multiculturalism old disciplinary and cultural boundaries have given way to new ones, regimes of the normal have been challenged, and the grip of monoculturalism has been significantly eased through a sustained emphasis on pluralized cultures in which various groups can now lay claim to the particularized identities and histories that inform and shape diverse cultural experiences.[6] Left multiculturalists, in particular, have made it clear that issues relating to gender, sexuality, age, and race are not trivial but central to how they understand their lives and relationships to others.

Arguing that cultural texts are inextricably related to broader social processes, critical academic multiculturalists have enhanced our understanding of how culture functions within higher education to construct knowledge, produce different social identities, and legitimate particular maps of meaning. By making visible the social construction of identities, left multiculturalists have performed an enormous theoretical service in opening up new ways of talking about how relations of power are deployed by the state, through the force of cultural apparatuses, and in everyday life in "maintaining the stakes of the already privileged."[7] Such insights have furthered our notion of cultural politics and the opportunity to make the pedagogical more political by linking the reading and writing of cultural texts to the acquisition of those skills and knowledges necessary to identify how power is deployed on and through cultural texts. Drawing upon various theories of deconstruction, poststructuralism, and postmodernism, academic multiculturalists have appropriated the critical turn toward language, particularly the emphasis on strategies of indeterminacy, uncertainty, and polyvocal meanings, in order to challenge Western logocentrism and reveal the racial codes that discursively construct "whiteness" as a mode of oppression and domination. Texts are now seen not only as objects of struggle in challenging dominant modes of racial and colonial authority but also as pedagogical resources to rewrite the possibilities for new narratives, identities, and cultural spaces. Focusing on the politics of representation to call attention to the ways in which texts mobilize meanings in order to suppress, silence, and contain marginalized histories, voices, and experiences, academic multiculturalists have reasserted the power of the symbolic as a pedagogical force in securing authority and as a pedagogical strategy for producing particular forms of contestation and resistance.

Subjectivity and representation constitute the core determinants in shaping cultural politics in the liberal and radical discourses of academic multiculturalism and serve to foreground pedagogical strategies that privilege the reading of texts and the related struggle over the control and production of identities.[8] Although academic multiculturalists have been attentive to the relationship between culture and systemic relations of power within the university, they have largely focused their efforts pedagogically on matters of language, negotiation, and cultural identity. Within these discourses, the political as a form of ideology critique defines literacy largely as the pedagogical imperative to read texts differently, "draw attention to discursive ambivalence,"[9] recognize different logics of signification, and unsettle the consensus of common sense that constitutes dominant public values, national identity, and the meaning of citizenship. Academic multiculturalism in its more radical strains has emphasized more than simply opening texts to a multiplicity of interpretations, an in-between space of translation where subaltern knowledge can be represented and heard. It has also insisted on the need for dominant intellectuals to work against the grain of their own embedded interests and privileges while "undoing the authority of the academy and knowledge centers at the same time that [they] continue to participate fully in them and to deploy their authority as teachers, researches, planners, and theorists."[10]

At its best, academic multiculturalism has reinvigorated the debate over the role the humanities and the university might play in creating a pluralized public culture essential for animating basic precepts of democratic public life. It has also worked to provide an institutionalized space for generating new bodies of knowledge, critical methods, and social relationships along side of the old, traditional, and familiar.[11] Academic multiculturalism has provided new discourses for contesting oppressive power within the university in order to produce the formation of new publics of difference. In pluralizing literacy, critical multiculturalists have redefined the pedagogical possibilities for teachers and students to engage their own historical locations and hybridized identities as formative rather than static, as part of a process of border crossing and mode of becoming in which the production of cultural differences is both ongoing and an invaluable asset to democratic public life.[12]

BEYOND THE TEXTUALIZATION OF POLITICS

As important as these developments have been within higher education, they have not gone far enough in taking seriously the role that academics might play as engaged intellectuals willing to link the imperatives of a radical multiculturalism or a politics of difference with struggles outside of the university. If the academy is to assume a meaningful role in contesting racial injustice, class hierarchies, and the politics of exclusion, progressive academics will have to do more than challenge right-wing assaults on the curriculum or the attempt by corporate centrists to reduce multicultural-ism to a market strategy, they will also have to challenge those poststruc-turalist and postmodern versions of multicultural textualism that reduce culture to the logic of signification. This suggests that critical multi-culturalism must overcome its insularity and reliance on textual strategies and address a cultural politics of difference that takes seriously the rela-tionship between culture and power, and the implications the latter has for connecting work within the university to broader struggles in the larger society. As Lawrence Grossberg points out, culture must not be equated exclusively with the domain of meaning and representation, but rather addressed as "both a form of discursive practice and an analysis of institu-tional conditions."[13] Moreover, multiculturalism in its most promising form must not only be equated with issues of justice and human rights but also with the need for the redistribution of resources, with its implicit "struggle against the huge accumulations of power and capital that so dis-tort human life."[14]

Although it is widely recognized that academic multiculturalism's emphasis on textuality has provided an important theoretical service in opening up institutional spaces that enable teachers and students to inter-rogate different readings of cultural texts and address critically the signi-fying power of such texts to create and affirm particular social identities, such work has often resulted in reductive pedagogical and political prac-tices. Removed from broader public discourses and analyzed outside of a whole assemblage of other cultural formations, texts either become the reified markers of a narrow version of identity politics or pedagogical resources for uncovering the attributes of specific identities.

Critical multiculturalists, especially those that inhabit literary the-ory programs, often focus inordinate attention on texts, signs, and dis-ciplinary turfs. Herman Gray, in response to the textualization of politics within the academy, rightfully insists that "By privileging cultural texts over practice as the site of the social and political, the social and histor-ical contexts that shape, situate, and structure cultural texts/products are largely ignored."[15] David Theo Goldberg reinforces Gray's criticism by arguing that cultural politics is not simply a signifying scheme through which identities are produced, but also a "mobilization around material resources regarding education, employment conditions, and political power."[16] Both of these theorists are correct in assuming that the textu-alization of multiculturalism, with its emphasis on expanding the cur-ricula, its uncritical endorsement of multiple readings, and its use of texts to recover and affirm marginalized identities offers a narrow version of cultural politics. The politics of textuality has little to say about the underlying political and economic forces that keep various social groups marginalized or how to address the often subtle ways in which cultural practices both deploy power and are deployed in material relations of power.[17]

Within many liberal and critical approaches to academic multiculturalism, the politics of meaning becomes relevant only to the degree that it is separated from a broader politics of engagement. Reading texts becomes a hermetic process, once removed from larger social and political contexts, and engaged in questions of power exclusively within a politics of representation. Such readings largely function to celebrate a textuality that has been diminished to a bloodless formalism and the nonthreatening, if not accommodating, affirmation of indeterminacy as a transgressive aesthetic. Lost here is any semblance of a radical political project that "grounds itself in the study of concrete cultural practices and . . . understands that struggles over meaning are inevitably struggles over resources."[18] By failing to connect the study of texts, identity politics, and the politics of difference to the interests of a project that expands the goals of the Civil Rights Movement, human rights campaigns against international tyranny, radical democratic feminist visions, and the opposition to antiwelfare and immigration policies, many critical multiculturalists conceive politics as largely representational or abstractly theoretical.[19]

Equally important to politically viable academic work is the recognition that the struggle over culture is not a substitute for some kind of real or concrete form of politics, but a crucial "site of the production and struggle over power—where power is understood not necessarily in the form of domination,"[20] but as a productive and mediating force for the making and remaking of diverse and interconnected social, political, and economic contexts that make up daily life.

As citizenship becomes increasingly privatized and students are relentlessly educated to become consuming subjects rather than critical social subjects, it becomes all the more imperative for critical educators to rethink how the educational force of the culture works to both secure and resist particular identities and values. In opposition to born-again multiculturalists such as Nathan Glazer (who declares that "we are all multiculturalists now"), critical educators can foreground the importance of progressive work in higher education as part of a broader radical democratic project to recover and rethink the ways in which culture is related to power and how and where it functions both symbolically and institutionally as an educational, political, and economic force that refuses to live with difference or simply manage it as part of the deadly logic of assimilation and control.

LINKING CULTURE AND POWER

As more and more young people face a world of increasing poverty, unemployment, and diminished social opportunities, those of us in education can struggle to vindicate the crucial connection between culture and politics in defending higher education as an essential democratic public sphere dedicated to providing students with the knowledge, skills, and values they will need to address some of the most urgent questions of our time. But if addressing multiculturalism as a form of cultural politics within the university is to become a meaningful pedagogical practice, critical academics will have to reevaluate the relationship between culture and power as a starting point for bearing witness to the ethical and political dilemmas that connect the university to other spheres within the broader social landscape. In doing so, educators need to become more attentive to how multicultural politics gets worked out in urban spaces and public spheres that are currently experiencing the full force of the right-wing attack on culture and racial difference. It is no longer possible for academics to make a claim to a radical politics of multiculturalism by defining it merely as a set of intellectual options and curriculum imperatives. Critical multiculturalism must also examine actual struggles taking place in the name of cultural difference within institutional sites and cultural formations that bear the brunt of dominant machineries of power designed to exclude, contain, or disadvantage the oppressed. The institutional and cultural spheres bearing the brunt of the racialization of the social order are increasingly located in the public schools, in the criminal justice system, in retrograde anti-immigrant policy legislation, and in the state's ongoing attempts to force welfare recipients into workfare programs.[21]

I am not suggesting that we redefine multiculturalism by moving away from issues of representation or that we shift our pedagogical efforts in the interests of a democratic politics of difference away from the university. On the contrary, we need to vitalize our efforts within the university by connecting the intellectual work we do there with a greater effort to pressing public problems and social responsibilities. This means engaging not only how culture deploys ideological meanings and representations, but engaging the latter as a resource for addressing the social gravity of the problems such representations either reinforce or challenge. A radical approach to multiculturalism must address how material relations of power work to sustain structures of inequality and exploitation in the current racialization of the social order. It must ask specific questions about the forms racial domination and subordination take within the broader public culture and how their organization, operation, and effects both implicate and affect the meaning and purpose of higher education. At stake here is the need for critical educators to give meaning to the belief that academic work matters in its relationship to broader public practices and policies, and that such work holds the possibility for understanding not just how power operates in particular contexts but also how such knowledge "will better enable people to change the context and hence the relations of power"[22] that inform the inequalities that undermine any viable notion of multiculturalism within spheres as crucial to democracy as the public schools and higher education.

In short, I want to insist that multiculturalism is not simply an educational problem. At its roots it is about the relationship between politics and power; it's about a historical past and a living present where racist exclusions appear "calculated, brutally rational, and profitable."[23] Embedded within a systemic history of black restriction, subjugation, and white privilege, the politics of multiculturalism is still, as Supreme Court Justice Ruth Bader Ginsburg puts it, "evident in our workplaces, markets, and neighborhoods."[24] David Shipler argues powerfully that race and class are the two most powerful determinants shaping American society. After interviewing hundreds of people over a five-year period, Shipler's book, *A Country of Strangers,* bears witness to a racism that "is a bit subtler in expression, more cleverly coded in public, but essentially unchanged as one of the 'deep abiding currents' in every day life, in both the simplest and the most complex interactions of whites and blacks."[25]

Although there can be little doubt that racial progress has been achieved in many areas in the past fifty years,[26] it is also true that such progress has not been sustained. This is particularly evident in the dramatic increase in black prisoners and the growth of the prison-industrial complex, crumbling city infrastructures, segregated housing, soaring black and Latino unemployment, exorbitant school drop out rates among black and Latino youth coupled with the realities of failing schools more generally, and deepening inequalities of incomes and wealth between blacks and whites.[27] Pushing against the grain of Civil Rights reform and racial justice are reactionary and moderate positions ranging from the extremism of right-wing skinheads and Jesse Helms-like conservatives to the moderate "color-blind" positions of liberals such as Randall Kennedy.[28]

Crucial to the reemergence of this new racism is a cultural politics that plays a determining role in how race shapes our popular unconscious. This is evident in the widespread articles, reviews, and commentaries in the dominant media that give inordinate amounts of time and space to mainstream conservative authors, film makers, and critics who rail against affirmative action, black welfare mothers, and the alleged threats black youth and rap artists pose to middle-class existence. Rather than dismiss such rampant conservatism as either indifferent to the realities of racism or deconstruct its racialized codes to see where such language falls in on itself, educators can engage these commentaries more constructively by analyzing how they function as public discourses, how their privileged meanings work intertextually to resonate with ideologies produced in other sites, and how they serve largely to construct and legitimate racially exclusive practices, policies, and social relations. Central to such a project is the need to produce a multicultural politics that offers students and teachers opportunities to critically engage how certain racialized meanings carried in cultural texts gain the force of commonsense in light of how racialized discourses are articulated in other public spheres and institutionalized sites.

In order to deepen the cultural politics of multiculturalism, educators can address questions of culture, power, identity, and representation as part of a broader discourse about public pedagogy and social policy. In this pedagogical approach, power becomes central to the study of cultural texts and practices and socially relevant problems can be explored through theoretical engagements with wider institutional contexts and public spaces in which multicultural discourses gain their political and economic force. If teaching students to interrogate, challenge, and transform those cultural practices that sustain racism is a central objective of multicultural education, such a pedagogy must be addressed in ways that link cultural texts to the major social problems that animate public life. Texts in this instance would be analyzed as part of a social vocabulary of culture that points to how power names, shapes, defines, and constrains relationships between the self and the other, constructs and disseminates what counts as knowledge, and produces representations that provide the context for identity formation.[29] Within this type of pedagogical approach, multiculturalism must find ways to acknowledge the political character of culture through strategies of understanding and engagement that link an antiracist and radically democratic rhetoric with strategies to transform racist institutionalized structures within and outside of the university.

At its best, critical multiculturalism should forge a connection between reading texts and reading public discourses in order to link the struggle for inclusion with relations of power in the broader society. It is precisely within the realm of a cultural politics that teachers and students develop pedagogical practices that close the gap between intellectual debate and public life not simply as a matter of relevance, but as a process through which students can learn the skills and knowledge to develop informed opinions, make critical choices, and function as citizen activists. Robin D. G. Kelley provides one direction such a project might take. He insightfully argues:

[Multiculturalism cannot ignore] how segregation strips communities of resources and reproduces inequality. The decline of decent-paying jobs and city services, erosion of public space, deterioration of housing stock and property values, and stark inequalities in education and health care are manifestations of investment strategies under de facto segregation. . . . [Progressives must address] dismantling racism, bringing oppressed populations into power and moving beyond a black/white binary that renders invisible the struggles of Latino, Asian Americans, Native Americas and other survivors of racist exclusion and exploitation.[30]

Implicit in Kelley's call for action is the recognition that any viable pedagogy and politics of representation needs to address the realities of historical processes, the actuality of economic power, and the range of public spaces and institutions that constitute the embattled terrain of racial difference and struggle. This suggests developing a critical vocabulary for viewing texts not only in relation to other modes of discourse "but also in relationship to contemporaneous social institutions and non-discursive practices."[31] Within this approach, cultural texts cannot be isolated from the social and political conditions of their production. Nor can the final explanation of such texts be found within the texts themselves. On the contrary, such texts become meaningful when viewed both in relation to other discursive practices and in terms of "the objective social field from which [they] derive."[32] Pedagogically, this suggests addressing how cultural texts in the classroom construct themselves in response to broader institutional arrangements, contexts of power, and the social relations that they both legitimate and help to sustain.

In what follows, I demonstrate the theoretical relevance for developing a multicultural pedagogical practice in which issues of representation and social transformation mutually inform each other. In doing so, I want to focus on a recent Hollywood film, *Baby Boy* (2001), in order to demonstrate how this film might be used as a both a public text and a form of public pedagogy designed to integrate representations of black masculinity and individual agency with broader relations of power and regimes of racial difference. In addition, I want to address how this text can be connected to the dynamics of racially exclusive practices and policies in sites that often appear too far removed from the privileged security of the university to be included in the discourse of an academicized multiculturalism.

RACIAL CODING IN THE HOLLYWOOD TEXT

During the past ten years, Hollywood has cashed in on a number of young, talented black directors such as Spike Lee, Allen and Albert

Hughes, Ernest Dickerson, and John Singleton. Films such as *New Jack City* (1991), *Boyz 'N the Hood* (1992), *New Jersey Drive* (1995), *Clockers* (1995), *Belly* (1999), and *Baby Boy* (2001) have not only appealed to a lucrative black audience but have crossed over and become successful with white audiences as well. Many of these films in varying degrees have offered up an image of the inner city ghetto as largely inhabited by illiterate, unmotivated, and violent urban youth who are economically and racially marginalized. The increasingly familiar script suggests a correlation between urban public space and rampant drug use, daily assaults, welfare fraud, teenage mothers, and young black men caught in the ritual behavior of thug life, prison, and moral irresponsibility. *Baby Boy* is a controversial addition to this genre, because it makes an attempt to both represent and critically engage the arrested development of black, male youth in the South-Central section of Los Angeles. Rather than address the economic, political, and social forces at work in the dehumanization, exploitation, and pathologizing of poor, urban youth of color, *Baby Boy* focuses on the refusal of such youth to grow up and assume the responsibility of getting jobs, taking care of their families, and becoming productive members of the community. *Baby Boy* is less interested in the broader forces that produce racism than it is in the way in which the effects of racism are experienced by those who bear the burden of its effects. This is not an unimportant project, but it is taken up through an ideological register that is all too characteristic of the 1990s. Social problems in this film become personal problems, and systemic issues are reduced to private considerations. Matters of personal commitment and character push aside broader considerations of how individual incapacities and misfortunes bear the burden of larger systemic forces. Private struggles replace social struggles, and collective solutions give way to individual responsibility. *Baby Boy* echoes the conservative call for black males to stop whining, pick themselves up, take personal responsibility for their behavior, and do themselves and the larger society a favor by exercising some self criticism for the infantile and irresponsible lives they lead. Needless to say, black conservatives such as Stanley Crouch and white liberals such as Roger Ebert closed ranks in praising *Baby Boy* as both an honest and deeply serious film. Crouch claims it is one of the few black films ever made that has the courage to "look at those strutting young Los Angeles black men who father children by various women and make little or no effort to support them."[33] Roger Ebert, the film critic for the *Chicago Sun-Times,* exalts in *Baby Boy's* "message to men like its hero: yes, racism has contributed to your situation, but do you have to give it so much help with your own attitude?"[34]

Written and directed by John Singleton, *Baby Boy* is the follow up to his 1991 hit *Boyz 'N the Hood.* Both films deal with the rite of passage young black men face in South-Central Los Angeles. Whereas *Boyz 'N the Hood* explores the connection between racism, violence, and militarized masculinity, *Baby Boy* narrows its focus and addresses the theory that racism and macho fantasy infantalize African-American males who cannot assume the responsibilities that come with being a mature adult. To prove his point Singleton explains his theme in the first few minutes of the film through a mix of spectacle and the alleged legitimacy of scientific rhetoric. The film opens with a surreal, dreamlike image of a fully grown, naked black man, the twenty-year old protagonist Jody (Tyrese Gibson), floating in his mother's womb. Jody is curled up in a fetal position and imagines that he is about to be aborted. Jody's imagined and yet infantile fears immediately become the backdrop for a voice over quoting a "lady psychiatrist," Dr. Frances Cress Welsing, author of the 1991 book *Isis Papers: the Keys to the Colors,* who asserts that African-American men both baby themselves and believe that they deserve to be treated with the indulgences accorded an infant. To support the claim that racism has made black men think of themselves as babies, Welsing offers the following: "What does a black man call his girlfriends?—Momma; his acquaintances?—boyz; and his place of residence?—crib." Far from rupturing this absurd reductionism, Jody's character seems to embody it to its fullest. Early on the film makes it clear that Jody has two young children, a boy and a girl, each of whom has a different mother. He lives at home with his own mother who is constantly telling him to grow up, watches cartoons on television, and builds and plays with model cars. When he is not sponging off his mother, he is taking advantage of his girlfriend, Yvette (Taraji Pl Henson), constantly borrowing her car and capitalizing on her love for him by fooling around with other women. When Yvette "steals" back her car, he ends up riding around the neighborhood on a ridiculously garish, childhood bicycle.

Once Jody leaves the womb, we find him outside of an abortion clinic waiting for Yvette, one of the two women with whom he has fathered children. Jody drives Yvette home and puts her to bed, but because she is in pain, distraught, and slightly drugged from the painkillers, she doesn't want to talk to Jody, whose irresponsibility appears as an uncomfortable reminder as to why she got the abortion in the first place. Lacking the compassion or sensitivity to stick around and offer some comfort, Jody borrows Yvette's car, and takes off in order to visit his other girlfriend, Peanut (Tamara Laseon Bass), the mother of his other baby. Compassion quickly turns to self-absorption and Jody begins his journey into an unremitting display of narcissism, selfishness, and grossly infantile behavior. Jody's rite of passage is marked by four significant events. First, Jody's domestic life is shattered when his mother brings home a boyfriend, Melvin (Ving Rhames), whose presence Jody bitterly resents. Melvin is an old style gangsta whose history of violence and ten years imprisonment is boldly displayed in the words "Thug" and "187" tattooed on his huge, muscular arms. Melvin is a painful reminder that Jody's mother, Juanita (A. J. John-son), a youthful thirty-six years old, has her own desires and needs a life of her own. But more is at stake than his mother's independent pleasures; there is also the possibility that Jody will be forced to leave the house once Melvin settles in. In fact, Melvin becomes a grim reminder of when Juanita allowed a former boyfriend to join the household and as a result Jody's brother was asked to leave the house, and eventually was killed while on the streets. Melvin's increasing presence around the house becomes more threatening when Jody wakes up one morning and finds Melvin stark-naked in the kitchen, scrambling eggs for his Juanita. Melvin now owns a landscaping business and has given up the thug life, but when dealing with Jody, whom he rightly resents, he quickly resorts to both the reasoning and violence of his past. Melvin may no longer kill people, but his sense of agency is still firmly rooted in a macho ebullience that appears removed from any kind of critical understanding that might question the allure of violence for men, and how it both infantilizes them and numbs them to the plight of others. Jody also fears that Melvin might eventually abuse his mother, a pattern he has seen in her relationships with other men, but while such a fear is legitimate, it simply becomes a rhetorical tool to try to convince his mother to get rid of Melvin. Jody's insincerity is echoed in his imperviousness to his own treatment of women as objects, which not only reproduces a particularly repugnant form of moral insensitivity, but makes it all the more predictable that he will engage in the very abuse that he believes Melvin is capable of producing.

Another turning point in Jody's life occurs while hanging out with Sweetpea (Omar Gooding), his unemployed childhood friend, in a liquor store parking lot. Observing various individuals engage in small time boosting, he realizes that he will never make it out of South Central until he can become, as he puts it to Sweetpea, the master of his destiny. Accord-ing to Jody, "Everybody moving is making money." And as far as Jody is concerned, the world can be divided into buyers and sellers. Noting that the world moves through commerce, Jody decides he wants to be a seller. But Jody doesn't want to sell drugs, the trade of choice in his neighbor-hood. To become a seller, Jody begins boosting women's clothes from the fashion district and sells them in neighborhood beauty parlors. Jody has a vague sense that his own sense of manhood depends on getting a job and becoming more independent, but he has no sense of the political and economic forces in his neighborhood that construct the problem as a social issue and not merely as a problem of individual initiative or character. Manhood for Jody is about making money, hardly an oppositional stance toward the system that punishes young black men like himself. Put differently, Jody's newfound sense of agency is entirely entrepreneurial and privatized, and offers little understanding of how the racialized stratification of power and opportunity that limits his own sense of possibility—not to mention the possibilities of the young men and women that populate his impoverished neighborhood. Jody recognizes that to be a consumer you have to be a producer, but has little sense of the economic and political dynamics at work in shaping the relations of the marketplace.

While Jody is able to take in some extra cash, his life takes a turn for the worse when he angrily confronts his mother and demands that she throw Melvin out of the house. At first Melvin lays back and says nothing, but he finally explodes and tells Jody to grow up and be a man, adding that he needs to stop blaming everyone else for his problems. To add insult to injury, Melvin suggests that Jody has an oedipal complex and at the root of his problem is the fact that he desires his own mother. Melvin then decks Jody, and Jody leaves the house for good. Jody not only has no place to go, he no longer has a car, which Yvette has taken back. Reduced to riding around the neighborhood on his childhood bike, Jody suffers another indignity when he is attacked by a group of neighborhood teens. Jody finds Sweetpea and they cruise the streets until they find the group of fourteen-year old punks out in a park. Sweetpea and Jody give all of them a beating that redeems Jody's manhood, but the violence makes him uncomfortable and serves as a marker for him to rethink his own relationship to violence and his notion of masculinity. The crisis of masculinity Jody faces soon faces another challenge when Rodney (Snoop Dogg), a dope-smoking gang-banger and former lover of Yvette's, comes to town after being released from jail.

Rodney ends up in Yvette's house and tries to pick up the relationship before Yvette got involved with Jody. Rodney is a menacing figure who settles in despite Yvette's desire to get him out of the apartment. Resentment soon turns to violence as Rodney tries to rape Yvette but gives up the attempt when Yvette's baby boy, JoJo, enters the room and pleads for Rodney to leave her alone. Rodney's resentment then turns on Jody as he gets some of his boyz together and drives over to Jody's house in order to shoot him. Jody and Sweetpea get caught in the line of fire but manage to escape unhurt. Jody and Sweetpea now have to face the indignity of both the failed rape attempt against Yvette and the attempt by

Rodney and his boyz against their own lives. Their identities, if not masculinity, are now on trial and though they hesitate about committing a violent act, they hunt Rodney down and murder him. Jody is completely shaken and learns about male responsibility through a street code that offers few rewards, except survival. He goes back to his mother's house, slumps in a corner, trembling while holding the gun he used to shoot Rodney. Melvin finds him in the room, takes the gun, wipes off the prints, and leaves the room. No words are exchanged between them. Melvin and Jody have now bonded through the ritual of excessive masculine violence, removed from either the sphere of moral responsibility or the necessity for argument. Violence is not renounced in this instance, but harnessed for the greater good of the family. Macho fantasy still feeds adult reality, but in the service of helping Jody overcome his immaturity and selfishness. The film ends with Jody leaving his mother and moving in with Yvette, with the implication that he is finally willing to try to live up to his responsibilities as a father and husband.

FILM AS PUBLIC PEDAGOGY

Pedagogically, films such as *Baby Boy* can be interrogated initially by analyzing both the common-sense assumptions that inform them as well as absences and exclusions that limit the range of meanings and information available to audiences. Analyzing such films as public discourses also provides pedagogical opportunities to engage complex institutional frameworks, which provide the conditions for the construction, legitimation, and meaning of such cultural texts. As public discourses, these cultural texts can be addressed in terms of how they are constituted as objects that gain their relevance through their relationship to other social institutions, resources, and nondiscursive practices. In this instance, *Baby Boy* could possibly be taken up as a discursive practice and public text whose pedagogical assumptions might be addressed in relation to struggles over race in related contexts where questions of meaning and representation are connected to the contest over power, social agency, and material resources. Some of these issues are illustrated below.

According to John Singleton, Jody, the main character in *Baby Boy*, is one of the most dangerous young men around "because he is hypersensitive," a young man who is trying to negotiate what it means to be a man, while laboring under a social code that says "you're not a man unless you are a killer."[35] Singleton rightly views this behavior as utterly dysfunctional and uses the film to explore the relationship between the crisis of masculinity and violence, on the one hand, and the politics of agency and responsibility, on the other. But the landscape used to frame these issues operates within a political register that almost completely ignores their broader historical, economic, racial, and political contexts. Moreover, the crisis of identity and masculinity that he constructs finds its resolution as a matter of integration into the existing social order rather than as a challenge that calls for its transformation.

Singleton wants to capture what it means for some young black men to grow up in poverty without fathers, how they are raised by mothers who do their best, and how both get by without the benefit of older role models. But against this seemingly severe deprivation is not only the presumption that women do not do enough to help these young men reach a state of maturity and independence; there is also the sense that the traditional, nuclear family is the normalizing space where these problems can be resolved. This is a deeply flawed and conservative position not only because it never confronts the misogyny and inequalities that structure such families, especially amid an unproblematic legacy of machismo and severe social problems, but also because it has no way of understanding how the family is connected to larger social forces that it alone cannot shape or control. All of these issues offer an opportunity for educators and students to take up this film as part of a broader understanding of the racial, economic, and political forces that both frame its major assumptions and connect it to those ideologies and public spheres that exist outside of the often isolated space of higher education.

Singleton's conservative ideology is most evident in his refusal to raise questions about the larger forces that bear down on Jody's sense of agency and possibility. What does it mean to be a man in a neighborhood marked by deep racial and economic inequalities? To what degree does self-responsibility become the marker of possibility when neighborhoods such as the one Jody lives in are burdened by concentrations of poverty, segregated housing, a lack of decent schools and neighborhood organizations, high unemployment, and usually a hostile police force? How does one talk about individual initiative in a system when the poverty rate for blacks is 28.3 percent, more than double what it is for whites (11.2 percent)? What role do biographical solutions play in dealing with systemic problems such as the ongoing discrimination against African-American youth in the workplace and schools? How does one theorize the concept of individual responsibility or character within a social order in which the national jobless rate is about 6 percent, but unemployment rates for young men of color in places such as South-Central Los Angeles have topped 30 percent? How does one ignore the fact that while it is widely recognized that a high school diploma is essential to getting a job, it is increasingly difficult for large numbers of African-American youth to even stay in school, especially with the advent of zero tolerance policies now driving school policy. In fact, as a result of such policies, the rate of expulsions and suspensions for such students is increasing at an alarming rate. For instance, Marilyn Elias reported in a recent issue of *USA Today* that "In 1998, the first year national expulsion figures were gathered, 31% of kids expelled were black, but blacks made up only 17% of the students in public schools."[36] Moreover, as many states invest more in prisons than in schools, more African Americans are dropping out of school and ending up under the control of some aspect of the criminal justice system. The figures on this are extraordinary. Of the two million people behind bars, 70 percent of the inmates are people of color with 50 percent being African Americans, while 17 percent are Latinos.[37] Law professor, David Cole, in his book *No Equal Justice,* points out that while "76 percent of illicit drug users were white, 14 percent black, and 8 percent Hispanic—figures which roughly match each group's share of the general population," African Americans constitute "35 percent of all drug arrests, 55 percent of all drug convictions, and 74 percent of all sentences for drug offences."[38] A Justice Department Report points out that on any give day in this country "more than a third of the young African-American men aged 18–34 in some of our major cities are either in prison or under some form of criminal justice supervision."[39] The same department reported in April of 2000 that "black youth are forty-eight times more likely than whites to be sentenced to juvenile prison for drug offenses."[40] Within such a context, the possibilities for treating young people of color with respect, dignity, and support vanishes and with it the hope of overcoming a racial abyss that makes a mockery out of justice and a travesty of democracy.

Rather than point to the weakness of Jody's character in addressing what it would mean for him to be a man, students might address the implications of what it would have meant for Singleton to point to the conditions that would offer Jody the resources to expand his capacities, knowledge, and skills to make informed choices. Singleton might have acknowledged the need for eliminating racism in the workplace, addressing the ongoing discrimination in the schools, and the growing violence and militarization waged against black youth by the state. He could have gone even further and brought attention to the need for the federal government to provide funds for a range of proven programs that improve the life of impoverished communities with limited jobs and institutional infrastructures. He might have pointed to the need for Head Start and drug prevention programs, youth centers, urban school reform, subsidizing of low-income housing, as well as child care and health care programs. Clearly, these are far more important in establishing the conditions for giving young men and women in the urban cities an opportunity to lead their lives as responsible adults and critical citizens. All of these considerations might be addressed by students and teachers as a starting point for not just acknowledging the absences in the film, but for engaging issues that link multicultural critiques with particular political projects.

Any attempt to address *Baby Boy* as a form of public pedagogy would have to analyze the largely privatized and individualized analysis that shapes this film and how it resonates with the ongoing privatization and depoliticization of the public sphere. As neoliberalism has gained momentum since the 1980s, one of its distinguishing features has been an assault on all those public spheres that are not regulated by the language of the market. Under the onslaught of neoliberal ideology and its turn toward free market as the basis for human interaction, there is an attempt to alter radically the very vocabulary we use in describing and appraising human interest, action, and behavior. Individuals are now defined largely as consumers, and self-interest appears to be the only factor capable of motivating people. Public spaces are increasingly displaced by commercial interests, and private utopias become the only way of understanding the meaning of the good life. It gets worse. As public life is emptied of its own separate concerns— importance of public goods, civic virtue, public debate, collective agency, and social provisions for the marginalized—it becomes increasingly more difficult to translate private concerns into public considerations. The Darwinian world of universal struggle pits individuals against each other while suggesting that the misfortunes and problems of others represent both a weakness of character and a social liability. Within such a system, the state gives up its obligations to provide collective safety nets for people and the ideology of going it alone furthers the myth that all social problems are the result of individual choices.

Unfortunately, *Baby Boy* not only refuses to challenge the myth of individual motivation and pathology as the source of unemployment, violence, welfare dependency, bad housing, inadequate schools, and crumbling infrastructures, it actually reinforces this well rehearsed stable of conservative ideology. It does so by suggesting that collective problems can only be addressed as tales of individual survival, coming of age stories that chronicle either selfishness, laziness, and lack of maturity or individual perseverance. By suggesting that Jody's life is colonized by the private, cut off from larger social, economic, and political issues, *Baby Boy* both renders hope private and suggests that communities in struggle can only share or be organized around the most private of intimacies, removed in large part from the capacity to struggle over broader issues. Dependency in this film is a dirty word, and seems to ignore the ways in which it resonates with right wing attacks on the welfare state and the alleged perils of big government. Granted, *Baby Boy* is supposedly about the refusal of immature

African-American youth to grow up, but the film's attack on dependency is so one-sided that it reinforces the myth that social safety nets simply weaken character, and it supports this ideology, in part, by refusing to acknowledge how dependency on the welfare state *has worked* for those millions for whom it has "made all the difference between wretched poverty and a decent life."[41] Similarly, if Jody's dreams are limited to the demands of the traditional family structure and the successes associated with the market ideology, there is no room in *Baby Boy* to recognize democracy, not the market, as a force of dissent and a relentless critique of institutions, as a source of civic engagement, or as a discourse for expanding and deepening the possibilities of critical citizenship and social transformation. In the end, *Baby Boy* fails to offer a space for translating how the private and public mutually inform each other; consequently, it reinforces rather than ruptures those racially oppressive trends in American society that disfigure the possibility of racial justice, democratic politics, and responsible citizenship.

AGENCY AND MASCULINITY AS THE POLITICS OF PATHOLOGY

Questions of identity are central to *Baby Boy* and to Jody's development as a character. Identities are neither fixed nor unified but are about an ongoing process of becoming. Identities are constructed through the differences and exclusions, mediated within disparate and often unequal relations of power, which largely determine the range of resources—history, values, language, and experiences—available through which individuals and groups experience their relationship to themselves and others. While the link between agency and identity is a complex one, agency precisely registers the connection between the private and the social, the individual and the public sphere both as a matter of politics and power. Agency, as Lawrence Grossberg observes,

> involves the possibilities of action as interventions into the processes by which reality is continually being transformed and power enacted. That is, in Marx's terms, the problem of agency is the problem of understanding how people make history in conditions not of their own making. Who gets to make history? That is, agency involves relations of participation and access, the possibilities of moving into particular sites of activity and power, and of belonging to them in such a way as to be able to enact their powers.[42]

Identity in *Baby Boy* is shaped outside of the discourse of political power, and as a result enacts a notion of agency for Jody that is defined primarily through the discourse of immaturity and self-inflicted injury. Identity in this instance does not become a site of social contestation, but collapses into a static notion of masculinity in which the body occupies a limited sense of agency defined primarily through discourses of violence, crime, dependency, pleasure, and social pathology.[43] Within this commonplace Hollywood stereotype, black male power is removed from the realm of critical thought and plays itself out in a display of excessive machismo, lurid sexuality, exoticized athleticism, and patriarchical masculinity. Trapped within a discourse of identity and agency mediated through a form of masculinity that is reduced to affirming and negotiating the dynamics of violence, Jody has no tools for either negotiating how power actually works in society or what it would mean to favor "negotiation over violence and the will to justice over the will to dominate."[44] *Baby Boy* presents its viewers with a "flattened moral landscape bereft of difficult choices," one in which limited visions are matched by a cynical politics that parades as part of a naturalized morality.[45]

Violence in this film operates as both a constant threat and a medium for men to express their masculinity. Jody is haunted by the death of his brother and harbors fears in his dreams of being murdered in the streets. At one point, he tells Yvette that he wanted their child so something would be left behind once he is killed. Jody is also ambivalent about committing violence and this becomes clear when he participates in beating up the young punks who robbed him and when he hunts Rodney down and murders him for attempting to rape Yvette and kill both him and Sweetpea. There is also the sense that Melvin while still a tough guy no longer resorts to the kind of brutalizing violence that defined his life in the past. But in all of these cases, violence is still the only terrain on which these men move, define themselves, and work out their problems. This is violence packaged as a representation of masculine crisis, but it is a decontextualized violence more intent on an aesthetics of posturing than on disrupting conventional stereotypes that portray black youth and men in the image of Bigger Thomas. In the end, *Baby Boy* falls prey, regardless of how it attempts to complicate masculinity, to constructing black men through the performance of violence, and in doing so it both infantilizes them and numbs them to the plight of others. Similarly, by decontextualizing the violence in their lives, it mystifies the sources and real nature of violence that assaults the minds and bodies of black men throughout the United States in the form of poverty-ridden schools, low teacher expectations, racist profiling, housing discrimination, employment block outs, and police brutality.

Masculinity in *Baby Boy* is not only defined through the posture of the tough menace, the high pleasure quotient of promiscuity, and the infantilization of the black male psyche, it also works to preserve male power while legitimating inequality and power relations between men and women. All of the major female characters in this film are defined largely as props for men's pleasures and as integral to maintaining some semblance of family values. Jody's lovers and his mother, even when they display some insight about the difficult nature of their lives, never rise to the occasion of challenging the wider misogynist structures in which they live out their daily existence. All of these women are caught within a violence that carries an erotic charge, all of them experience the pain and suffering that comes with the submission to male power, but none of them can imagine themselves outside of its dominating influence. At most, they try to do the best they can to control its worse excesses. Singleton not only defines women as the binary opposite of masculinity in this film, he goes a step further and suggests that "African-American men are systematically prevented from assuming adult responsibilities by their mothers, who insist on smothering them with affection."[46] Given the film's view of the relationship between masculinity and women, this seems to be a predictable response to a dreadful form of misogynist logic. In the end, *Baby Boy* through its representations of masculinity, violence, and women dissolves politics into pathology and agency into narcissistic modes of self-absorption. Under such circumstances, public politics becomes difficult to imagine as issues of agency, vision, and transformation collapse into the realm of the personal and the psychological as opposed to the collective and social.

CONCLUSION

Baby Boy is an important film for addressing both the stereotypes and the conservative ideology that construct its particular notions of race, agency, masculinity, violence, and politics. In this instance, *Baby Boy* represents more than a text that portrays a particularly offensive image of black men and women; it also functions as a form of public pedagogy in enabling, legitimizing, and reinforcing discursive practices that offer neither a context for moral considerations nor a language for defending those vital social institutions that oppose racist values and practices. As a public text, *Baby Boy* provides little opposition to those social, economic, cultural, and political forces in American society that condemn minorities of color and class to the most debilitating and exploitative aspects of racism.

Clearly, if the dominant codes at work in such a film are to be questioned, it is imperative for students to address how the absences in such a film become meaningful when understood within a broader struggle over issues of racial identity, power, representation, and everyday life. Depictions of urban youth as dangerous, pathological, and violent, in turn, must be addressed as part of a larger examination of their use and effects in shaping the contexts of everyday life, and how such depictions might register sites of struggle for racial justice in sites other than in the university. For example, the depictions of youth in *Baby Boy* resonate powerfully with the growth of social policies and highly visible criminal justice system whose get-tough policies fall disproportionately on poor black and brown youth. Students might be asked to weigh what the potential effect of a film such as *Baby Boy* might be in addressing the political, racial, and economic conditions that threaten to wipe out a whole generation of young black males who are increasingly incarcerated in prisons and jails, and whose populations are growing at the rate of about seven percent a year and costs more than 30 billion annually to operate?[47] And what might it mean to shift the analysis and concern for multicultural justice from the reading of a film to a struggle against the rise of the prison-industrial complex? How might a cultural text such as *Baby Boy* be used to address the increasing perception of black men as lazy, the ongoing attack on the welfare state, the dismantling of affirmative action policies in higher education, and the plight caused by industrial downscaling and rising unemployment among young black men across America's inner cities at the beginning of the new century? What might it mean for students to address their own responses to the moral panics concerning crime and race that have swept across the middle classes in the last decade, made manifest in strong electoral support for harsh crime laws and massive increases in prison growth.[48] At the very least, educators can address *Baby Boy* not merely in terms of what such a text might mean but how it functions within a set of complex social reactions that create the conditions of which it is a part and from which it stems. Lawrence Grossberg insightfully argues that such a pedagogy would:

> involve the broader exploration of the way in which discursive practices construct and participate in the machinery by which the ways people live their lives are themselves produced and controlled. Rather than looking for the 'said' or trying to derive the saying from the said, rather than asking what texts mean or what people do with texts, [a critical pedagogy] would be concerned with what discursive practices do in the world.[49]

Films such as *Baby Boy* become important as part of a public pedagogy of difference because they play a powerful role in mobilizing racial ideologies, investments, and identifications. They produce and reflect important considerations of how race functions as a structuring principle in shaping and organizing diverse sets of relations in a wide variety of social spheres. At the same time, if we are to read films such as *Baby Boy* as social and political allegories articulating deeply rooted fears, desires, and visions—they have to be understood within a broader network of cultural spheres and institutional formations rather than as isolated texts. The pedagogical and political character of such films resides in the ways in which they align with broader social, sexual, economic, class, and institutional configurations.

Needless to say, *Baby Boy* as well (as any other cultural text) can be read differently by different audiences, and this suggests the necessity to take up such texts in the specificity of the contexts in which they are received. But at the same time, educators, social critics, and others can shed critical light on how such texts work pedagogically to legitimate some meanings, invite particular desires, and exclude others. Acknowledging the educational role of such films requires that educators and others find ways to make the political more pedagogical. One approach would be to develop a pedagogy of disruption. Such a pedagogy would raise questions regarding how certain meanings under particular historical conditions become more legitimate as representations of the real than others, or how certain meanings take on the force of commonsense assumptions and go relatively unchallenged in shaping a broader set of discourses and social configurations. Such a pedagogy would raise questions about how *Baby Boy*, for instance, resonates with the ongoing social locations and conditions of racial fear that are mobilized through a wide variety of representations in the media and popular culture, as well as in a number of other institutional sites. More specifically, a pedagogy of disruption would engage a film's attempts to shift the discourse of politics away from issues of justice and equality to a focus on violence and individual freedom as part of a broader neoliberal backlash against equity, social citizenship, and human rights. Such an approach would not only critically engage the dominant ideologies of black masculinity, violence, and dependency that give *Baby Boy* so much power in the public imagination, but also work to expose the ideological contradictions and political absences that characterize the film by challenging it as symptomatic of the growing reaction against multiculturalism, the right-wing assault on the welfare state, and the increasing use of violence to keep in check marginalized groups such as young black males who are now viewed as a threat to order and stability.

Engaging the potential discursive effects of films such as *Baby Boy* might mean discussing why this Hollywood film received such popular praise in a largely white-owned, dominant press, or equally important, why it did not receive much criticism given its extremely conservative message. Such a film also raises questions about how it functions as a public text that rationalizes both the demonization of minority youth and the defunding of public and higher education at a time when black youth are in desperate need of jobs, education, and resources to be able to participate in shaping public life. Pedagogically, this suggests raising questions about a public text that moves from understanding it as a form of public pedagogy to redefine the relationship critical understanding and the more concrete act of social intervention in a public issue.

The popularity of such films as *Baby Boy* in the heyday of academic multiculturalism points to the need, in light of such representations, for educators to expand their understanding of politics as part of a broader project designed to address major social issues in the name of a multiracial democracy. This suggests getting beyond reducing multiculturalism to simply the study of texts or discourse, and addressing multicultural politics as part of the struggle over power and resources in a variety of public spheres. This might mean engaging and fighting to change how the "economics of school funding and school policy [work to] sustain segregation in American public education [through] inhuman fiscal policies that have ensured the continuous impoverishment of schools attended wholly by black or Hispanic schoolchildren."[50] Or what it might mean for students to engage in a politics of multiculturalism aimed at reforming a criminal justice system that disproportionately incarcerates and punishes minorities of class and color. Issues of representation and identity in this case offer the opportunity for multicultural educators to explore and challenge both the strengths and limits of cultural texts. This suggests developing a pedagogy that promotes a social vocabulary of cultural difference that links strategies of understanding to strategies of transformation that recognize the limits of the university as a site for social engagement, and refuse to reduce politics to matters of language and meaning that erase broader issues of systemic political power, institutional control, economic ownership, and the distribution of cultural and intellectual resources in wide variety of public spaces.

If academic multiculturalism is not going to abandon the world of public politics and take seriously the link between culture and power, progressive educators will have to rethink collectively what it means to link the struggle for change within the university to struggles for change in the broader society. Combining theoretical rigor with social relevance may be risky politically and pedagogically, but the promise of a multicultural democracy far outweighs the security and benefits that accompany a retreat into academic irrelevance and color-blind professionalism.

NOTES

1. Multiculturalism covers an extraordinary range of views about the central issues of culture, diversity, identity, nationalism, and politics. Moreover, the theoretical and political slipperiness of the term immediately makes suspect any analysis that moves from the specific to the general in engaging a topic as diverse as multiculturalism. And yet the arbitrary nature of such an analysis seems necessary if certain general tendencies that characterize a field are to be addressed and critically engaged, in spite of the presence of marginal discourses that are sometimes at odds with such tendencies. Some important recent books that address the multiple meanings of multiculturalism include: Henry A. Giroux, 1993, *Living Dangerously: Multiculturalism and the Politics of Culture* (New York: Peter Lang); Henry A. Giroux, 1992, *Border Crossings* (New York: Routledge); David Theo Goldberg, ed., 1994, *Multiculturalism: A Critical Reader* (Cambridge: Basil Blackwell); Avery Gordon and Christopher Newfield, eds., 1996, *Mapping Multiculturalism* (Minneapolis: University of Minnesota Press); David Bennett, ed., 1998, *Multicultural States* (New York: Routledge); Donaldo Macedo and Lilia I. Bartolome, 1999, *Dancing with Bigotry: Beyond the Politics of Tolerance* (New York: St. Martin's Press).
2. One important example of this work can be found in Joe L. Kincheloe and Shirley R. Steinberg, 1997, *Changing Multiculturalism* (New York: Open University Press).
3. A classic example of this type of work is Becky W. Thompson and Sangeeta Tyagi, eds., 1993, *Beyond a Dream Deferred: Multicultural Education and Politics* (Minneapolis: University of Minnesota Press).
4. A classic example of this work can be found in Lawrence Levine, 1996, *The Opening of the American Mind* (Boston: Beacon Press).
5. On the reforms in general education that have been enacted under the banner of multiculturalism, see Michael Geyer, 1993, "Multiculturalism and the Politics of General Education," *Critical Inquiry* 19: 499–533.
6. One important text in this genre is Gloria Ansaldua, ed., 1990, *Making Face, Making Soul: Haciendo Caras: Creative and Critical Perspectives by Women of Color* (San Francisco: Aunt Lute Foundation). I would include here the emergence of critical scholarship on whiteness studies. The literature is too extensive to cite but some recent work includes: Richard Delgardo and Jean Stefanic, eds., 1997, *Critical Whiteness Studies* (Philadelphia: Temple University Press); Ruth Frankenberg, ed., 1997, *Displacing Whiteness* (Durham: Duke University Press); Mike Hill, ed., 1997, *Whiteness: A Critical Reader* (New York: New York University Press); Annalee Newitz and Matthew Wray, eds., 1997, *White Trash* (New York: Routledge); David R. Roediger, ed., 1998, *Black on White: Black Writers on What It Means to Be White* (New York: Schocken Books); Abby L. Ferber, 1998, *White Man Falling* (Boulder: Rowman & Littlefield); George Lipsitz, 1988, *The Possessive Investment in Whiteness* (Philadelphia: Temple University Press).
7. Martin Duberman, 1994, "In Defense of Identity Politics," in *These Times.com*, www.inthesetimes.com/web2516/duberman2516.html. Cambridge: Basil Blackwell, p. 13–14. Of course, there are many exceptions to this rule, but they are marginal to the multiculturalist discourses within the university. See, for example, many of the essays in Cameron McCarthy and Warren Crichlow, eds., 1993, *Race, Identity, and Representation in Education* (New York: Routledge), as well as William V. Flores and Rina Benmayor, 1997, *Latino Cultural Citizenship* (Boston: Beacon Press); E. San Juan Jr., 1992, *Articulations of Power in Ethnic and Racial Studies in the United States* (New Jersey: Humanities Press); Peter McLaren, 1997, *Revolutionary Multiculturalism* (Boulder: Westview Press); Slavoj Zizek, 1997, "Multiculturalism, or, the Cultural Logic of Multinational Capitalism," in *The New Left Review* 225: 28–51; George Lipsitz, 1990, "Listening to Learn and Learning to Listen: Popular Culture, Cultural Theory, and American Studies," in *American Quarterly* 42(4): 621. Larry Grossberg argues that Edward Said's *Orientalism* is a classic example of a text that focuses on questions of difference almost entirely in terms of identity and subjectivity while ignoring the related issues of materialism and power. See Lawrence Grossberg, 1996, "Identity and Cultural Studies. Is That All There Is?" in Stuart Hall and Paul Du Gay, eds., *Questions of Cultural Identity* (Thousand Oaks, Calif.: Sage), 87–107; Grossberg, 1996, "Cultural Studies: What's In a Name?" in Stuart Hall and Paul DuGay, eds., *Questions of Cultural Identity* (Thousand Okas, Calif.: Sage) 248. Manning Marable, 1998,

"Beyond Color-Blindness," *The Nation* (December 14) 31. Lawrence Grossberg, 1997, "Cultural Studies: What's in a Name?" in *Bringing It All Back Home: Essays on Cultural Studies* (Durham: Duke University Press), 252–253. David Theo Goldberg, 1993, *Racist Culture* (Cambridge: Basil Blackwell), 105; Ginsburg cited in editorial, 1997, "Race On Screen and Off," *The Nation* (December 29), 6; Shipler summarized in Jack H. Geiger, 1998, "The Real World of Race," *The Nation* (December 1), 27. See also David Shipler, 1998, "Reflections on Race," *Tikkun* 13(1): 59, 78; David Shipler, 1998, *A Country of Strangers: Blacks and Whites in America* (New York: Vintage). African Americans made up almost half of the U.S. prison population, and about one in four young black males in their twenties were either in jail, on parole, or on probation (compared to only 6 percent for white males). Cited in Jimmie L. Reeves and Richard Campbell, 1994, *Cracked Coverage: Television News, the Anti-cocaine Crusade, and the Reagan Legacy* (Durham: Duke University Press), 41. Dave Kehr, 2001, "Mother Love, Too Little Or Too Much," *The New York Times* Late Edition (July 29), 2. These issues are taken up in David Theo Goldberg, in press, "Surplus Value: The Political Economy of Prisons," in Joy James, ed., *Police, Detention, Prisons* (New York: St. Martin's Press), 3–25.

8. See, for example, Michael Awkward, 1995, *Negotiating Difference* (Chicago: University of Chicago Press).

9. This notion of breaking into common sense is taken from Homi Bhabha in Gary Olson and Lynn Worsham, 1998, "Staging the Politics of Difference: Homi Bhabha's Critical Literacy—an Interview," *Journal of Composition Theory* 18(3): 367.

10. John Beverly, 1996, "Pedagogy and Subalternity: Mapping the Limits of Academic Knowledge," in Rolland G. Paulston, ed., *Social Cartography* (New York: Garland), 351–52.

11. For a selection of articles that address these issues, see David Theo Goldberg, ed., 1994, *Multiculturalism: A Critical Reader* (Boston: Basil Blackwell).

12. On the issue of multiculturalism and border crossing, see Henry A. Giroux, 1992, *Border Crossings* (New York: Routledge).

13. Lawrence Grossberg, 1997, "Cultural Studies: What's in a Name?" *Bringing It All Back Home: Essays on Cultural Studies* (Durham: Duke University Press), 268.

14. Edward W. Said, 2001, "The Public Role of Writers and Intellectuals," *The Nation* 273(9) (October 1): 6.

15. Herman Gray, 1996, "Is Cultural Studies Inflated?" in Cary Nelson and Dilip Parameshway Goankar, eds., *Disciplinarity and Dissent in Cultural Studies* (New York: Routledge), 211.

16. David Theo Goldberg, 1994, "Introduction—Multicultural Conditions," in David Theo Goldberg, ed., *Multiculturalism: A Critical Reader* (Cambridge: Basil Blackwell), 13–14.

17. Of course, there are many exceptions to this rule, but they are marginal to the multiculturalist discourses within the university. See, for example, many of the essays in Cameron McCarthy and Warren Crichlow, eds., 1993, *Race, Identity, and Representation in Education* (New York: Routledge) as well as William V. Flores and Rina Benmayor, 1997, *Latino Cultural Citizenship* (Boston: Beacon Press); E. San Juan Jr., 1992, *Articulations of Power in Ethnic and Racial Studies in the United States* (New Jersey: Humanities Press); Peter McLaren, 1997, *Revolutionary Multiculturalism* (Boulder: Westview Press); Slavoj Zizek, 1997, "Multiculturalism, or, the Cultural Logic of Multinational Capitalism," *The New Left Review* 225 (September/October): 28–51.

18. George Lipsitz, 1990, "Listening to Learn and Learning to Listen: Popular Culture, Cultural Theory, and American Studies," *American Quarterly* 42(4) (December): 621.

19. Larry Grossberg argues that Edward Said's *Orientalism* is a classic example of a text that focuses on questions of difference almost entirely in terms of identity and subjectivity while ignoring the related issues of materialism and power. See Lawrence Grossberg, 1996, "Identity and Cultural Studies. Is That All There Is?" in Stuart Hall and Paul Du Gay, ed. *Questions of Cultural Identity* (Thousand Oak, Calif.: Sage), 87–107.

20. Grossberg, 1996, "Cultural Studies: What's In a Name?" ibid., 248.

21. Manning Marable, 1998, "Beyond Color-Blindness," *The Nation* (December 14), 31.

22. Lawrence Grossberg, 1997, "Cultural Studies: What's in a Name?" in *Bringing It All Back Home: Essays on Cultural Studies* (Durham: Duke University Press), 252–253.

23. David Theo Goldberg, 1993, *Racist Culture* (Cambridge: Basil Blackwell), 105.

24. Ginsburg cited in editorial, 1997, "Race On Screen and Off," *The Nation* (December 29), 6.

25. Shipler summarized in Jack H. Geiger, 1998, "The Real World of Race," *The Nation* (December 1) 27. See also, David Shipler, 1998, "Reflections on Race," *Tikkun* 13(1): 59, 78; David Shipler, 1998, *A Country of Strangers: Blacks and Whites in America* (New York: Vintage).

26. Ellen Willis argues that the two major upheavals to America's racial hierarchy have been the destruction of the Southern caste system and the subversion of whiteness as an unquestioned norm. She also argues rightly that to dismiss these achievements as having done little to change racist power relations insults people who have engaged in these struggles. See Ellen Willis, 1998, "The Up and Up: On the Limits of Optimism," *Transition* 7(2): 44–61.

27. For a compilation of figures suggesting the ongoing presence of racism in American society, see Ronald Walters, 1996, "The Criticality of Racism," *Black Scholar* 26(1) (Winter): 2–8; A Report from the Children's Defense Fund, Yearbook 1998, 1998, *The State of America's Children* (Boston: Beacon Press).

28. For a devastating critique of Randall Kennedy's move to the right, see Derrick Bell, 1998, "The Strange Career of Randall Kennedy," *New Politics* 7(1) (Summer): 55–69.

29. Katya Gibel Azoulay, 1997, "Experience, Empathy and Strategic Essentialism," *Cultural Studies* 11(1): 91.

30. Robin D. G. Kelley, 1998, "Integration: What's Left?" *The Nation* (December 14), 18.

31. Cited in Randall Johnson, "Editor's Introduction: Pierre Bourdieu onto Make Learning Part of the Process of Social Change Itself. Art, Literature and Culture," in Pierre Bourdieu, 1993, *The Field of Cultural Production* (New York: Columbia University Press), 19.

32. Randall Johnson, 1993, "Editor's Introduction: Pierre Bourdieu onto Make Learning Part of the Process of Social Change Itself." Art, Literature and Culture, in Pierre Bourdieu, *The Field of Cultural Production* (New York: Columbia University Press), 17.

33. Stanley Crouch, 2001, "A Lost Generation and its Exploiters," *The New York Times* (August 26), AR, 8.

34. Roger Ebert, 2001, "Baby Boy," *Chicago Sun-Times*, www.suntimes.com (June 27), 1.

35. Cindy Fuchs, 2001, "All Grown Up: John Singleton on the Mature Baby Boy," http:citypaper.net/articles/062801/mov.singleton.shtml (June 28–July 5), 2.

36. Marilyn Elias, 2000, "Disparity in Black and White?" *USA Today* (December 11), 9D.

37. Cited in David Barsamian, 2001, "Interview with Angela Davis," *The Progressive* (February), 35.

38. David Cole, 1999, *No Equal Justice: Race and Class in the American Criminal Justice System* (New York: The New Press), 144.

39. Donziger, 1999, Ibid., 101.

40. Cited in Eyal Press, 2000, "The Color Test," *Lingua Franca* (October), 55.

41. Zygmunt Bauman, 2001, *The Individualized Society* (London: Polity Press), 73.

42. Lawrence Grossberg, 1996, "Identity and Cultural Studies; Is That All There Is?" in Stuart Hall and Paul Du Gay, eds., *Questions of Cultural Identity* (Thousand Oaks, Calif.: Sage), 99–100.

43. This theme is extensively explored in Paul Gilroy, 2000, *Against Race* (Cambridge: Harvard University Press).

44. Gilroy, 2000, Ibid., 230.

45. Gilroy, 2000, Ibid., 231.

46. Dave Kehr, 2001, "Mother Love, Too Little Or Too Much," *The New York Times* Late Edition (July 29), 2.

47. These figures are cited in Fox Butterfield, 1997, "Crime Keeps on Fall, But Prisons Keep on Filling," *The New York Times* (Sunday, September 28), 1. Jimmie Reeves and Richard Campbell provide a more extensive picture prison growth in the United States: "During the Reagan era, in fact, the U.S. prison population nearly doubled (from 329,821 in 1980 to 627,402 in 1989) as the number of drug arrests nationwide increased from 471,000 in 1980 to 1,247,000 in 1989. By 1990 the United States had the highest incarceration rate in the world: 9,426 per 100,000 compared to 333 per 100,000 in South Africa, its closest competitor). In that same year—when about half the inmates in federal prisons were there on drug offenses—African Americans made up almost half of the U.S. prison population, and about one in four young black males in their twenties were either in jail, on parole, or on probation (compared to only 6 percent for white males)." Cited in Jimmie L. Reeves and Richard Campbell, 1994, *Cracked*

Coverage: Television News, the Anti-Cocaine Crusade, and the Reagan Legacy (Durham: Duke University Press), 41.

48. These issues are taken up in David Theo Goldberg, in press, "Surplus Value: The Political Economy of Prisons," in Joy James, ed., *Police, Detention, Prisons* (New York: St. Martin's Press), 3–25.

49. Cited in Lawrence Grossberg, 1998, "The Victory of Culture, Part I," University of North Carolina at Chapel Hill, unpublished manuscript (February), 27.

50. Both quotes are from Michael Berube, 1993, "Disuniting America Again," *The Journal of the Midwest Modern Language Association* 26(1) (Spring): 41.

5

Discomforting Truths: The Emotional Terrain of Understanding Difference

MEGAN BOLER AND MICHALINOS ZEMBYLAS

According to the myth of liberal individualism, difference is not an obstacle to achieving the American dream. In the land of equal opportunity, everyone competes on a level playing field. If you work hard, you'll succeed; whoever reaps the benefits of the American dream deserves the rewards so rightly earned. In the land of the free, difference is either overlooked, tolerated, or celebrated as a flavorful ingredient for the melting pot.

Those who challenge these cherished myths face an uphill battle and often a thankless task. Equal opportunity, the virtues of hard work, just desserts—these beliefs are as pervasive and taken for granted as the air we breathe. It is a painstaking process to develop a critical and conscious awareness of something as omnipresent as oxygen. One of our students wrote a note describing her reaction to being asked to question critically the media's portrayal of these familiar myths:

> Also wanted to let you know that I am really coming to understand why "easy in the harness" is just that "easy." I have always thought that I maintained an open mind and open eyes. I don't usually accept things at face value, and while I'm not a rebel, I do ask questions when things don't feel/sound right.
>
> I've always thought of myself as a critical thinker.
>
> The combination of the events that have taken place in our nation and this class have caused me some discomfort . . . to be unsettled . . . to definitely not be easy in the harness. At almost 44 years old, there are some things that I have always accepted—patriotism, the American way . . .

I've really struggled the past week when hearing news reports and reading articles about the recent attack about hidden agendas and what the American public doesn't know. There's part of me that is angry—this is not the time that I would question "patriotism", etc. Part of me is also sad . . . maybe a loss of innocence—Ha! at 44??! Easy in the harness does have definite advantages!

To engage in critical inquiry often means asking students to radically reevaluate their worldviews. This process can incur feelings of anger, grief, disappointment, and resistance, but the process also offers students new windows on the world: to develop the capacity for critical inquiry regarding the production and construction of differences gives people a tool that will be useful over their lifetime. In short, this pedagogy of discomfort[1] requires not only cognitive but emotional labor.

In this essay, we outline a pedagogy of discomfort as an educational approach to understanding the production of norms and differences. As its name suggests, this pedagogy emphasizes the need for both the educator and students to move outside of their comfort zones. By comfort zone we mean the inscribed cultural and emotional terrains that we occupy less by choice and more by virtue of hegemony: "Hegemony refers to the maintenance of domination not by the sheer exercise of force but primarily through consensual social practices, social forms, and social structures produced in specific sites such as the church, the state, the school, the mass media, the political system, and the family" (McLaren 1998: 182). The comfort zone reflects emotional investments that by and large remain unexamined because they have been woven into the everyday fabric of what is considered common sense.

A pedagogy of discomfort recognizes and problematizes the deeply embedded emotional dimensions that frame and shape daily habits, routines, and unconscious complicity with hegemony. The purpose of attending to emotional habits as part of radical education is to draw attention to the ways in which we enact and embody dominant values and assumptions in our daily habits and routines. By closely examining emotional reactions and responses—what we call emotional stances—one begins to identify unconscious privileges as well as invisible ways in which one complies with dominant ideology.

We begin this chapter by outlining how the rhetoric and culture of liberal individualism conceptualizes difference. We outline several critical theories of difference, ranging from Audre Lorde to Michel Foucault, examining the power of binary oppositions and offering an overview of key philosophical conceptions of difference. We then argue for the importance of a pedagogy that embraces ambiguity in its critical conceptualization of identities. Our aim is to question some of our contemporary certainties about the kinds of identities we take for granted and the common normativity that is often at work in all diverse practices of individuals. Through this discussion, we illustrate the importance of a pedagogy of discomfort, which aims to encourage critical inquiry at a cognitive as well as an emotional level. In particular, we explore the concept of a pedagogy of discomfort to address how "inscribed habits of emotional attention"[2] limit, constrain, and/or open possibilities in the process of constructing difference. For this purpose, we use Dewey's ideas to analyze habits as patterns of emotional salience, and Nikolas Rose's views on the construction of self to theorize about the emotional labor involved in the process. In this discussion we attempt to show how emotional labor is part of the pedagogy of discomfort, which actively anticipates subsequent mutations in the habits themselves. Our hope is that, in rendering the importance of a pedagogy of discomfort for making habits more visible, it may help open these up for interrogation and transformation and subvert prevailing emotional rules that assert regulative ideals about difference. In short, pedagogy of discomfort is quite specifically counterhegemonic.

CHALLENGING THE MYTHS OF LIBERAL INDIVIDUALISM

Hegemony takes different forms in different national and cultural contexts. As suggested in our introduction, in the United States hegemony is closely tied to liberal individualism. The dominant cultural myths such as equal opportunity and meritocracy depend rhetorically on several "acceptable" views of difference.

The following are three examples of reductive conceptions of difference regularly encountered by educators who embrace critical inquiry and radical educational practices as foundations in the work of social justice. These three models of difference represent a partial map of the American dream. Despite any contradictions between the models, they often coexist within an individual's belief system.

THE CELEBRATION/TOLERANCE MODEL

"Every individual is different. We should respect and honor everyone's difference equally." Those who teach issues of race, class, gender, and sexual orientation in the field of education are familiar with the problem of difference being understood as benign. For example, our pre-service teachers are likely to embrace a philosophy that celebrates difference as neutral flavors of food: you eat beans and rice, I eat Jell-O molds, she eats spaghetti. This

benign multiculturalism, however, fails to address power. To celebrate differences as so many flavors overlooks the fact that those who eat beans and rice are also likely to have experienced systematic institutional, educational, and economic discrimination. However, although this conception of difference claims to celebrate all differences equally, certain differences are merely tolerated on this view. For example, teachers who subscribe to the celebration/tolerance model are very likely to say that they will not address lesbian or gay inclusive curriculum, because those issues are a private family matter. Thus, "don't ask, don't tell" applies to certain differences in this model. The celebration/tolerance model of difference is extremely palatable within neoliberal societies. On this view, one finds legislation that protects individuals' privacy and right to expression of difference as long as it "doesn't hurt others." Ironically, those differences that reflect the norms of the dominant culture do not require protection and are not seen as possibly hurting others. In other words, public displays of heterosexual affection are so deeply normalized that they do not fall beneath the policing gaze of liberal and individual rights.

THE DENIAL/SAMENESS MODEL

"We are all the same underneath the skin. Why do we have to pay so much attention to difference?" Liberal individualism also encourages a philosophy of difference that simply wants to deny or erase difference. Those who subscribe to "we are all the same" embrace—however unconsciously—a commitment to assimilation. This approach reflects the dominant culture's privileged capacity to decide when and why differences are important. One is likely to hear a person of the dominant culture say to a person of color "I don't see you as [Japanese]." This statement is meant as a compliment, and is meant to include this person as a member of the majority group "one of us,"—Such utterances offensively deny to those who are not white, Anglo-Saxon Protestants the significance of cultural heritage. In sum, the "we are all the same underneath the skin" philosophy is a version of liberal humanism that also denies the ways in which power shapes and seeks to erase difference.

THE NATURAL RESPONSE/BIOLOGICAL MODEL

"Some differences are innate. Some fears of difference are innate. Fear of difference is a natural response." A third conception of difference encouraged by liberal individualism is to justify xenophobia by explaining fear of differences as a natural emotion, a fear that should be understood as a fundamental feature of being human. This embrace of biological explanation

denies a more sophisticated understanding of the ways in which power allows certain groups to use their fear as justification for the oppression of other groups. For example, white man's fear of being emasculated by black men has historically been used to justify lynching in the United States.

Each of these models of difference can be said to reflect a parallel emotional stance regarding difference. One emotional response to differences is easy tolerance: the celebratory stance that assumes that differences are benign. A second emotional stance is denial: we are all the same, can we just move on? A third is to retreat to the safety of biology or "that's just how God made us," thereby excusing oneself from engaging in the difficult emotional terrain of difference as social and political.

A common denominator in each of these emotional stances is a tendency to abdicate responsibility for how differences are produced and perpetuated by individual beliefs and through psycho-social relations. Common to all of these emotional stances is an unwillingness to engage the difficult work of (re)constructing one's own beliefs, values, and assumptions. There is understandable reluctance to encounter one's fears, and instead one may cling to particular safety zones. Indeed, we believe that educators face profound ethical questions regarding the emotional effects of critical pedagogy when they engage students in deconstructing identity, worldviews, and ethical beliefs.

THE THANKLESS TASK

The educator encounters a further irony in attempting to dissect entrenched emotional investments in liberal individualism. Even if an educator entices students to recognize the construction of differences, and to recognize that the playing field is not level, students understandably want to believe in their own agency and free choice. No one wants to be told that the choices they believe they have made are not in fact a result of free will but rather determined by powerful ideological forces. Thus for the educator to suggest that we are all victims of hegemony runs counter to individualism on multiple levels.

Educators who seek to challenge these notions of difference are also likely to encounter the stubborn myth that education can be fully objective, neutral, apolitical. As common as the myth of objective journalism is the myth that education does not have a political agenda. This myth takes the form of such statements as "educators should simply present both sides, and students should be allowed to make up their mind according to their own free will." On this view, education does not seek to change individuals. To the contrary, we believe that education explicitly and implicitly, through overt as well as hidden curriculum, shapes and changes individuals to adapt them to dominant cultural values, to the work force needs—in short, that education fundamentally shapes and changes every student.

However, radical education—education that works for social justice, that challenges the myths of the dominant culture—is inevitably seen as political propaganda. To engage students in sophisticated critiques of difference requires unlearning the myth of neutral education. As Macedo (2000) writes in his introduction to *Chomsky on MisEducation*, "Given the tendency for humans to construct satisfying and often self-deceptive stories, stories that often damage themselves and their groups, particularly when these deceptive stories are rewarded by the dominant social order, the development of a critical comprehension between the meaning of words and a more coherent understanding of the meaning of the world is a prerequisite to achieving clarity of reality. As Freire (1990) suggests, it is only 'through political practice that the less coherent sensibility of the world begins to be surpassed and the more regulated rigorous intellectual pursuits give rise to a more coherent comprehension of the world' " (10–11). To gain a clarity of reality requires particularly close attention to those stories that naturalize themselves through common sense or familiar cultural myth.

NO ONE ESCAPES HEGEMONY: WE ARE ALL DISCOMFORTED

Those born in the United States as well as those who immigrate to this nation absorb—consciously or not—common sense beliefs about what it means to be an American. One should not make the mistake of assuming that a pedagogy of discomfort seeks only to destabilize members of the dominant group. A pedagogy of discomfort invites not only members of the dominant culture but also members of marginalized cultures to re-examine the hegemonic values inevitably internalized in the process of being exposed to curriculum and media that serve the interests of the ruling class. No one escapes hegemony. Of course, every individual will have his or her own idiosyncratic experiences of discomfort. Heterosexuals, for example, may as a group tend to experience discomfort when asked to think carefully about their views toward lesbian and gay people. White people may be more uncomfortable discussing racism than people of color are. However, there are moments in which it is uncomfortable for a gay person to consider his or her own internalized homophobia—similarly, for a person of color to reflect on their own internalized racism. The point is that no one escapes internalizing dominant cultural values, even though these values take different forms in different individuals.

One obvious example of how compliance with assumed norms creates hegemony is the compulsory public educational practice of pledging allegiance to the flag—and at this historical moment, rallying around the flag, which in the United States currently connotes an overwhelmingly singular and dominant meaning. In this instance, the power of the dominant culture to appropriate a national symbol and define the emotional and political means of that symbol in an extremely narrow way defines difference by its absence. "The dominant culture tries to 'fix' the meaning of signs, symbols, and representations to provide a 'common' worldview, disguising relations of power and privilege through the organs of mass media and state apparatus such as schools" (McLaren 1988: 183). Particularly after September 11, the American flag does not symbolize a wide array of different possible meanings; the narrowed beliefs and values that constitute "being American" do not allow for difference in the construction of the flag-saluting citizen. "Within the hegemonic process, established meanings are often laundered of contradiction, contestation, and ambiguity" (McLaren 1998: 183).

One of Megan's students poignantly illustrates the discomforting emotional labor involved in critical thinking. In her essay, written a few weeks after September 11, she reflects:

> The myth of the liberal media really opened my eyes to the media and I was really shocked by some of the things that were mentioned. I immediately started viewing the evening news with a critical eye and caught myself questioning everything that was said. In the article "The Construction of Reality in Television News,"[3] the author talks about news stories and states that "once reported, there is a further threshold of drama: the bigger this story, the more added drama is needed to keep it going" and "the events, which in themselves would normally not reach the threshold of a news worthiness, were made into dramatic stories in order to keep the pot boiling." This is especially true when you think about the media's initial coverage of the bombings last week. There were dramatic stories about the victims of the tragedies on the news every morning and evening, which otherwise would never have made the news although I realize, after thinking critically, why the media continually broadcasted those stories, watching those stories actually helped me grieve for those that are missing or dead and I felt compelled to watch them. I actually started feeling guilty when the news would come on and I would start thinking critically about what was being broadcasted.

This student expresses the discomfort of simultaneously viewing the media critically while feeling at the same time that she should participate uncritically in the patriotic emotions being demanded of her by the news broadcast. Her comments nonetheless reflect what we will call in this chapter *emotional labor*. Her reflection is precisely what critical educators would hope for: "In order to go beyond a mere word-level reading of reality (i.e., humanitarian intervention), we must develop a critical comprehension of psychological entities such as 'memories, beliefs, values, meanings, and so forth . . . which are actually out in the social world of action and inter-action.' We must first read the world—the cultural, social, and political practices that constitute it—before we can make sense of the word level description of reality" (Macedo in Chomsky 2000: 11).

The next example illustrates how a pedagogy of discomfort directly conflicts with the internalized emotional processes of hegemony. In the following instance, liberal individualism's emphasis on agency and equal opportunity effectively hides oppression even from those who likely experience it.

When Megan's class was discussing gender and sexism, several women whose ages ranged from twenty-two to forty-five insisted that they had never experienced sexism; that their fathers wanted them to be engineers; that they chose the profession of teaching for reasons that have nothing to do with culturally constructed gender roles. One woman kept reiterating that while growing up she never saw herself as different from the boys. Megan finally asked her how she knew she was a girl. She replied, after some hesitation, that she guessed she knew she was a girl because she wore dresses and had an Easy Bake Oven. The invisibility of gender to these women reflects simultaneously the success of hegemony, in the sense that these women have been so powerfully steeped in liberal individualism that they cannot recognize gender differences at all. However, we would also argue that one witnesses hegemony at work in the emotional resistance of these women, in their desire not to see sexism as a social force that touches their lives. Complicating this picture even more, to be told by feminism that their experience and identity is not authentic, that their lives do not represent truly free choice, makes them angry and in fact discounts their sense of agency.

In sum, we wish to underscore: (1) Pedagogy of discomfort asks not only members of the dominant culture but also members of marginalized cultures to reexamine the hegemonic values inevitably internalized in the process of being exposed to curriculum and media that serve the interests of the ruling class; (2) Hegemony and liberal individualism will encourage people not to recognize how institutionalized sexism, racism, homophobia, and the like has affected oneself or others. In the next section, we illustrate how the process of hegemony and the discourses of naturalization work alongside the desire not to see difference.

DIFFERENCE AND THE PROCESS OF HEGEMONY

Hegemony masks itself as common sense, as natural: "That's just how things are!" Dominant ideology relies on the processes of naturalizing what are in fact culturally constructed values. For instance, the idea that women are naturally better child rearers than men or that certain ethnic groups are naturally less intelligent than other groups are examples of ideologies made to seem normal or natural. In Western and modern cultures, the discourses of science, objectivity, and "facts" neatly function to hide socially constructed differences.

We absorb the values of the dominant culture through what might be called popular history. In an essay written in 1950, Jacques Barzun argues that

> We must distinguish between history as it exists in the minds of men and history as it exists on the shelves of libraries; we must mark a difference between popular history and what I shall not blush to call Unpopular History. Popular history is the living room of tradition in the minds of the majority. It is a commonplace that this spirit of nationality which characterizes the modern age is based on the possession of a common language, common customs, and common historical traditions. However stupid or uneducated, the most indifferent citizen will remember and respond to certain ideas connected with his country's past. It may be a picture of Abraham Lincoln's log cabin or it may be the two words Monroe Doctrine—these symbols are popular history in this sense that they call up at once a series of compelling beliefs about the past. . . . *The sources of popular history are two in number: the textbooks used in the schools and popular literature. In this latter category, I include newspapers and periodicals—especially the photographic-historical and other novels, "readable" biographies and histories, and moving pictures.* (32, emphasis added)

This definition of popular history illustrates one of the challenges of engaging a pedagogy that is not reductive and that does not oversimplify the complexity of how meanings and identities are produced. To critically analyze the production of meanings and identities, it is useful to look at critical media literacy as a theoretical and pedagogical approach especially essential during a time of increased uncritical patriotism. Increasingly, we find as educators that we turn to critical theories concerned with the politics of representation and media as some of the most useful intellectual tools for analyzing ideological production.

The combination of the use of reductive binaries in the production of meaning, with the stereotyped use of simplistic symbols in the media, with people's general discomfort with ambiguity makes it very challenging to deconstruct differences.

The desire to deny racism is illustrated by students' responses to the following essay. This semester in a class called "Schooling and Diversity," one of us (Megan) shared with students Robert Moore's article on stereotyping in language in which he analyzes the use of the term "black." Moore's essay contains a startling catalog of the extent to which the signifier "black" has accrued, over historical time, a host of negative and pejorative connotations. The following is a one sentence excerpt from a very long paragraph that reveals some thirty examples: "I may become a black sheep (one who causes shame or embarrassment because of deviation from the accepted standards), who will be blackballed (ostracized) by being placed on a blacklist (list of undesirables) in an attempt to blackmail (to force or coerce into a particular action) me to retract my words" (in Hill Collins: 323). Part of what makes this catalog powerful is its illustration of the extent to which racism is imbedded in language in ways that many English-speaking persons would not consciously have recognized. Nonetheless, despite the historical and cultural evidence that racism and other differences are in fact social constructions—indeed, embedded in language that is surely a social construction—in both of Megan's graduate seminars several students strongly disagreed on how to interpret the list. Discussions of the paragraph led to three different explanations: (1) use of the term "black" is merely coincidence—i.e., that the above examples are not necessarily racist but rather a linguistic coincidence; (2) negative association with darkness comes from the days of pre-electricity, when one *should* fear the dark; (3) fear of difference is natural—everyone fears that which is strange or foreign to them.

Discussions of difference often lead to the question: isn't the fear of difference natural? Are perceptions of difference—xenophobia—innate aspects of our cognitive and perceptual experience? On the one hand, this is a valid question. Bowker and Starr's (1999) recent book suggests some interesting ways that the human mind tends to categorize and organize differences in order to make sense of the world. Yet to assume that because when we were once Cavemen living without the benefit of electricity we learned to fear the dark, and that because of this primordial fear we can thereby explain the negative connotations surrounding the term black, is to conflate two strands of cultural history that must be untangled.[4] To insist that they are the same strand is to enact privilege—in this case white privilege—in the form of an explicit desire to attribute fear of difference to social Darwinism.

There is much to be explored in all of these complex responses, but we want to underscore the curious emotional stance common to all three: a desire to deny the possible racism embedded in language. The claims above were not made only by white students but by students of diverse ethnicities. In short, there is a significant desire to deny the culturally constructed, ideologically invested significance of differences.

DIFFERENCE AS PRODUCED THROUGH SILENCE AND ABSENCE

Difference is produced not only through an explicit naming but also through the power of silence and absence. In the above instance, "black" is used explicitly to identify and name that which is deviant, different than, that which is not the norm. Identities are also produced through normalized assumptions and the active process of *not* naming silence itself as a productive practice. One of the primary contributions of poststructural philosopher Michel Foucault is his analysis of "technologies of the self." The self—rather than being a taken for granted or pre-given identity—is produced through a variety of discourses, languages shaped by authoritative communities and voices. Examples of discourse communities include the medical profession or the legal system. These discourses can be thought as "technological" in the sense that "they seek the calculated orchestration of the activities of humans under a practical rationality directed toward certain goals. They attempt to simultaneously maximize certain capacities of individuals and constrain others in accordance with particular knowledges (medical, psychological, pedagogic) and toward particular ends (responsibility, discipline, diligence, etc.)" (Rose 1998: 153). However, in addition to the explicit discursive technologies of this self, identities are also shaped by silence and by ignorance.

From Foucault's point of view, discourse is a form of power that circulates in the social and political terrain and can attach to strategies of domination as well as to those of resistance (Sawicki 1991). Consequently, from a Foucauldian perspective, no discourse is inherently liberating or oppressive. Further, "discourse is constituted by the difference between what one could say correctly at one period . . . and what is actually said. The discursive field is, at a specific moment, the law of this difference" (Foucault as cited in Johannesson 1998: 305). Discourses, then, are not limited to words; rather discourses refer to the ways in which they become social and political practices with material effects. This means that discourses include the silences as much as they include the spoken and written words (see also Britzman 1991). For instance, in the organization of the subject matter what is *not* included in the school curriculum can be as telling as that which is included (Britzman 1991: 189). The ways in which such absences create knowledge (or lack of knowledge) shape teachers and students' identities and define the present knowledges as normal while the absent knowledges are deemed deviant (Zembylas in press).

The ways in which ignorance can actually create knowledge and identities is often illustrated by "the epistemology of the closet." Drawing on the work of Michel Foucault, Eve Sedgwick (1990) writes: "If ignorance is not . . . a single . . . aboriginal maw of darkness . . . perhaps there exists instead a plethora of ignorances, and we may begin to ask questions about the labor, and erotics, and economics of their human production and distribution. In so far as ignorance is ignorance *of* a knowledge—a knowledge that may itself, it goes without saying, be seen as either true or false under some other regime of truth—this ignorance is, far from being pieces of the originary dark, are produced by and correspond to particular knowledges and circulate as part of particular regimes of truth" (8).

Thus, differences are produced visibly and explicitly, as well as invisibly. "There is no binary division to be made between what one says and what one does not say; we must try to determine the different ways of not saying such things . . . there is not one but many silences, and they are an integral part of the strategies that underlie and permeate discourses" (Foucault quoted in Sedgwick 1990: 3). Sedgwick explains how, for lesbian and gay people, "closetedness itself is a performance initiated as such by the speech act of a silence—not a particular silence, but a silence that accrues particularity by fits and starts, in relation to the discourse that surrounds and differentially constitutes it." (1990: 3)

The challenge in understanding how a difference is produced is to get beyond simplistic binary understandings. One of the unfortunate effects of popular history, of oversimplified and reductive understandings of difference, is that we are prevented from seeing contradictions, and from inhabiting more ambiguous and less rigid, identities and relations to the world. In short, differences are often coded by the dominant culture through simplistic systems of binary, either/or, black/white meanings. The absence of space for contradiction and ambiguity makes resistance to dominant meanings very difficult. This is especially visible in terms of the sex/gender system that imposes the either/or identities of male/female, heterosexual/homosexual on all persons, excluding even the biological reality of hermaphrodites, and most certainly excluding transgender identities and the possibility of gender fluidity or ambiguity.

THE POWER OF BINARIES

Theorists across a range of disciplines echo the following concise summary offered by Audre Lorde (1984): "Much of Western European history conditions just to see human differences in simplistic opposition to each other: dominant/subordinate, good/bad, up/down, Superior/inferior. In a society where the good is defined in terms of profit rather than in terms of human need, there must always be some group of people who, through systematized oppression, can be made to feel surplus, to occupy the place of the dehumanized inferior" (114). Lorde emphasizes the ways in which binary oppositions lay the foundation for constructions of what counts as normal, or as highly valued, verses what counts as deviant and less valued.

One result of the power of binaries in defining identity is that—consciously as well as unconsciously—these values and norms are internalized. Lorde (1984) continues: "Somewhere, on the edge of consciousness, there is what I call a *mythical norm,* which each one of us within our hearts knows 'that is not me.' In America, this norm is usually defined as white, thin, male, Young, heterosexual, Christian, and financially secure. . . . Those of us who stand outside that power often identify one way in which we are different, and we assume that to be the primary cause of all oppression, forgetting other distortions around difference, some of which we ourselves may be practicing" (116; author's emphasis).

The end result of restrictive binary oppositions is to preclude the possibility of the ambiguous identities. Ambiguity is feared; it is a source of discomfort to those forced to live in a culture defined by simple binary oppositions. For example, the binary of biological sex is imposed systematically by the medical profession on to newborn babies. Many infants are born with ambiguous gender—known as hermaphrodites. A recent documentary series titled *Sex Unknown* illustrates the ways in which the medical profession and science disallow individuals from occupying ambiguous gender categories. Most often, when a child is born a hermaphrodite, the doctor urges the parents to permit surgery that will assign the child a certain sex. In one instance, even when the parents told the doctor that they did not want their child to undergo surgery, the doctor conducted this surgery without the parents' consent. The fear of ambiguity is not only abstract and emotional, but is a fear that polices the construction of identities and individuals in painfully material ways.

RELATIONS OF SELF AND OTHER

Difference depends both on systems of understanding and meaning, as well as the everyday social interactions between people. To understand how a difference is created and enacted in social relationships and networks has required theorists and philosophers to analyze self/other relationships. The relationship of self and other is a central preoccupation of such philosophers as Hegel; contemporary French philosophers such as Levinas, Irigaray, and Derrida; existential philosophers such as Sartre and de Beauvoir; Marxist humanists such as Freire; and postcolonial theorists such as Fanon and Memmi. Finally, psychoanalysis ranging from the work of Freud to object relations theory to Lacan struggles most centrally with the self and other relation. Jessica Benjamin (1988), the author of *The Bonds of Love* is renowned for having posited a theory of intersubjectivity. Intersubjectivity is contrasted with the Hegelian relation of self and other in which the self must negate the other and make the other into an object that exists solely to boost one's own sense of identity. Instead, intersubjectivity is defined as a form of mutual recognition, one in which self and the other are both recognized as autonomous subjects that may be in some ways similar, in some ways different.

In an essay titled "Not You/Like You: Post-Colonial Women and the Interlocking Questions of Identity and Difference," Trinh Minh-Ha (1990) states, "To raise the question of identity is to reopen again the discussion on this self other relationship in its enactment of power relations. Identity as understood in the context of a certain ideology of dominance . . . that requires the elimination of all that is considered foreign or not true to this self, that is to say, not I, either" (371).

She goes on to point out that "differences do not only exist between outsider and insider—two entities. They're also within the outsider herself, within the insider herself—a single entity" (Minh-Ha 1990: 371). Echoing Lorde's comments above, Trinh continues "she who knows she cannot speak of them without speaking of herself, of history without involving her story, also knows that she cannot make a gesture with that activating the to and fro movement of life" (371).

Difference is produced through dominant cultural meanings, and it is also produced significantly in the relationship of self and other—in short, through the social relations that constitute the lived and everyday experience of culture. Without a doubt, a critical inquiry into hegemony needs to examine closely how individuals internalize dominant meanings and reproduce these both in the dynamic of relationships, but also within one's self: as Trinh Minh-Ha writes, "differences also work within the outsider herself, within the insider herself" (371).

The success of hegemony relies on individuals internalizing dominant values, and relies as well on these values shaping intersubjective relationships between individuals. For these reasons, theoretical accounts of power require not only critical analyses of how culture shapes and determines individuals (for example Marxist economic determinism), but also accounts of a psychological nature: why do individuals comply with hegemony, even when it goes against their best interests? This has been the perplexing question in many ways still unanswered, represented by the dilemma of Marxist notion of "false consciousness" or the existentialist notion of "bad faith."

There is significant resonance, rather surprisingly, between psychoanalytic accounts of subjectivity and Marxist humanist accounts. For example, Paolo Freire and Jessica Benjamin speak in very similar language about the ways in which the oppressed identifies with the oppressor, so that often when seeking freedom and liberation, the oppressed simply reverses the binary and take on the qualities of the oppressor. This phenomenon is significantly a psychological one. It is closely related to the example we discuss earlier in this chapter in which we describe the views of some young women who claim not to have been affected by sexism, instead embracing what they claim to be free choice and agency that has determined their actions and identity. As Freire suggests, "men and women rarely admit their fear of freedom openly, however, tending rather to camouflage it—sometimes unconsciously—by presenting themselves as defenders of freedom. But they confuse freedom with the maintenance of the status quo; so that if conscientizacao threatens to place that status quo in question, it thereby seems to constitute a threat to freedom itself" (360). Both a psychoanalytic account and a critical theory account would likely argue that such individuals have affectively internalized and identified with the oppressor.

Benjamin writes, "the subjugated whose acts and integrity are granted no recognition, may, even in the very act of emancipation, remain in love with the ideal of power that has been denied to them" (220). Freire similarly points out, "The fear of freedom which afflicts the oppressed, a fear which may equally well lead them to desire the role of oppressor or bind them to the role of depressed, should be examined" (46). Notice the use of the terms "love" and "fear" in the above descriptions of the relationship of oppressed and oppressor. Benjamin's title *The Bonds of Love* and Freire's emphasis on "the fear of freedom" indicates the extent to which domination and constructions of difference are rooted in emotional habits and perceptions. We find it striking that the critical traditions that inform radical pedagogies rarely analyze the educational importance of attending to the emotional habits that accompany values, beliefs, and knowledge. We turn now to an analysis of these habits using John Dewey and Nikolas Rose's ideas to help us think about the emotional labor involved both in constructing identities as well as in a pedagogy of discomfort.

EMBRACING "AMBIGUITY" IN THE CONSTRUCTION OF IDENTITIES

One of us (Michalinos) has been recently forced unwillingly to return to his "home country" (somewhere in the Middle East) after spending eight years studying and working in the United States. The classic questions he was facing while being in the United States as a migrant were: "Why are you here?" and "When are you going back to your home country?" He never knew the answer to either question (no migrant ever knows the answers to such questions, says Stuart Hall). To try to define oneself intellectually, emotionally, and politically after returning to one's home country—willingly or unwillingly—is not an easy task. "It is an un-settled and unsettling identity," as Uma Narayan (1997: 3) asserts, espe-cially when one feels an exile, a foreigner in one's own home country, like in this case. Of course, who among us, after all—Western or non-Western, white or nonwhite—is not always caught in the space between the narratives of traditions, of history, of a culture and the "unspeakable" stories of subjectivity (as Hall 1987 calls them) after spending years being "Westernized"? Identity, according to Stuart Hall, is formed at the unstable point between the cultured narratives and the self constituted in some kind of absent-present contestation with something else, which is and isn't there. In a sense, one is always "somewhere else": an exile is "doubly marginalized, displaced always other than where he or she is, or is able to speak from" (Hall 1987: 44). As such, the self is in continuous construction, never completed, never fully coherent, never completely centered securely in experience.

"The trouble is that the instant one learns to be 'an immigrant' one recognizes one can't be an immigrant any longer" (Hall 1987: 45). The same holds for someone who returns back home. There is no home to go back to: it isn't a tenable place to be. In a sense, the self is always a fiction and identities are kinds of closures—national, ethnic, family, sexual, and others—arbitrary closures. The arbitrary nature in constructing identities implies plenty of space for ambiguity.

The discourses of displacement have always depended on one's *dif-ference* from the rest. This ambiguity is "an immensely important gain when one recognizes that all identity is constructed across difference and begins to live with the politics of difference" (Hall 1987: 45). Inhabit-ing this ambiguity "enables one to see, with humility, and gratitude, and pain, how much one has been shaped by one's contexts, to sense both the extent and the boundaries of one's vision, to see how circumstances can circumscribe as well as inspire, and to become self-aware to some extent of one's perspectives on things" (Narayan 1997: 3). For instance, in Michalinos's case when he says that his attempts to define himself emerge from pain and suffering for being an exile in his own country, he refers to the personal struggle to name the location from which he constructs his voice. Simultaneously, embracing the emotional labor associated with this ambiguity maximizes his capacity to shape his knowledges, emotions, and habits and subverts the practices and discourses that aim at bringing closure in the name of nature, freedom, or culture revealing the deceptions and self-deceptions inherent in these attempts. The alternative is a fully closed narrative of the self—a politics of identity as a hegemonic project.

Nikolas Rose (1998, 1999) argues that identity and emotions are understood as properties, not of mental mechanisms but of conversations and practices. These discourses and practices are both producing people assumed to be subjects and produced by people assumed to be subjects. In this sense, subjects *do* emotions; emotions do not just happen to passive actors. Such analyses are more instructive when they focus not on what emotional utterances *mean* but on what they *do*: what aspects of subjectivities they connect up, what connections they do not permit, what enables individuals to feel, to desire, to be afraid of, to have disappointments and fulfillments. Thoughts, emotions, beliefs, desires, and actions may appear as the very fabric and constitution of a coherent identity, but they are socially organized and governed. This is precisely why we argue that attending to the emotions associated with these beliefs and values one is able to begin to problematize the complex of practices and assemblages within which identities are fabricated, and which presuppose and enjoin particular privileges and emotional habits. The earlier example with the student who wrote the essay reflects her willingness to examine what she is and is not able to hear in the news and why she chooses a path that considers the complexity of how we are "taught" to see and hear in historically specific ways. Further, she describes in clear terms how her emotions change as a result of embracing ambiguity and learning to see differently.

Ultimately, the goal is to inhabit a more ambiguous sense of self not reduced to the binary positions of good and evil. "In this process one acknowledges profound interconnections with others, and how emotions, beliefs, and actions are collaboratively co-implicated" (Boler 1999: 187). Beyond good and evil lie possibilities to embrace ambiguity and question the techniques for understanding and improving one's self in relation to that which is considered true, permitted, and desirable. For example, instilling patriotism within schools creates particular relations governed by feelings of superiority, inferiority, anger, and guilt. Relations between teacher and student depend on shared allegiance to the flag, governing who can express a feeling to whom, and a climate of superiority and respect of state. A critical ontology of one's self in this context is about interrogating what one (a teacher, a student) has become, the nature of that present in which one is and the refusal to submit to the categories, explanatory schemes, and norms according to which we should think and judge ourselves. This ambiguity implies a decentered, multiple, nomadic process of constructing identities. The nomadic character of this process can produce resistance, transformation, and transgression (e.g., in the example above, alternative views about patriotism) because the self is not obliged any more to succumb to the norms and techniques by which freedom (the freedom of liberal individualism) is supposed to be achieved.

John Dewey asserts that by being actively engaged in something suggests that interest and emotions are build into truth, into the practice of doing so, namely searching for truth. Emotional selectivity is found in every belief and action. This is what takes place in the example with several women who claim that they have never experienced sexism in their lives. Their collectively produced emotional habits describe the selectivity that is embedded in their beliefs. These habits refine the ways they feel about sexism in relation to their selves. The inability to express and name particular emotions is in part a consequence of habits, "inscribed habits of attention."

Inscribed habits of attention acknowledge the importance of a collectively produced habit and describe the selectivity of attention as a result of cultural and political patterns. These habits often limit and constrain possibilities of inhabiting ambiguity in constructing identities through disciplining differences, "individualizing humans through classifying them, calibrating their capacities and conducts, inscribing and recording their attributes and deficiencies, managing and utilizing their individuality and variability" (Rose: 1998). For example, the power of the dominant culture to define patriotism in narrow terms does not allow for difference in the construction of the meaning of patriotism, in the sense of exploring its horizons and its condition of possibility. Its aim is to predetermine judgment and "discipline" alternative views (e.g., the idea of an international patriotism). Through classifying individuals into patriots and nonpatriots (or perhaps traitors) using emotional and political means, the dominant culture manages to establish meanings that marginalize ambiguity and difference. Patriotic beliefs and emotional habits create certain conditions of identity construction.

For Dewey (1985) beliefs are habits, not simply cognitive statements. In fact he fused belief, body, and emotion into a single construct—habit (see Garrison 1997). In this sense, habits refine our emotions. The discussion of habits, then, is ultimately a discussion upon the nature of our selves. As Dewey writes, "Habit reaches . . . down into the very structure of the self; it signifies a building up and solidifying of certain desires; an increased sensitiveness and responsiveness . . . or an impaired capacity to attend to and think about certain things" (1985: 171). Habit means a disposition to act and, therefore, it involves desires, interests, choices, and emotions. In other words, Dewey's argument is that altering one's beliefs means altering one's habits. His view makes more clear the notion that a pedagogy of discomfort involves considerable emotional labor—changing one's habits demands emotional labor; it is much easier to hold back to these habits and the comfort they offer than uprooting them.

Habits are formed in a particular social and historical context in which some customs are held. Jim Garrison (1997) writes, "To acknowledge oneself as controlled by habits and conditioned by social customs is simply to recognize that one's values, beliefs, interests, perceptions, and so on are largely predetermined by scripts and plot lines that comprise the social context, including dominant cultural texts, of a given historical epoch" (140). Various discourses and practices have established arrays of norms (e.g., emotional rules) according to which the capacities and conduct of self have been determined. These norms enable all complexities of social interactions to be coded in terms of conformity and deviation. However, discourses and practices do not simply identify emotions or work exclusively by repressing them but rather constitute them and, according to Foucault, in the practice of doing so conceal their own invention. The example with the women who claim that they have not experienced sexism in their lives is a classic case that shows how the practice of learning to think that sexism is absent conceals its own presence in everyday practices. Such habits—which often are disguised as ethical codes, (e.g., that "men and women are equal, everyone accepts this")—instill particular aspirations to these women and no space is left to question what is taken for granted.

At the same time, Dewey rejects a teleological account and argues that the habits we have acquired through prior experiences provide useful resources for our responses in future similar situations. Future situations, however, imply that new circumstances arise every time in a changing environment. If our habits are not modified to meet the new challenges (a continuous struggle for adjustment) there will be disappointments, tensions, and failures. Everyday tensions are like this—when something is disturbing us and challenging "the way we are used to doing things." The desire to settle the tensions propel alternative possibilities for action within a context of ongoing activity. Discomfort, then, impels critical thinking and inquiry. Conscious critical thinking for Dewey is the center of re-thinking our habits. Dewey's account raises interesting questions about the real possibilities of change. This is precisely why we argue that to change emotionally we need experiences of working through (i.e., emotional labor) and some history of success (e.g., subversion of emotional rules). Pedagogy of discomfort opens possibilities for both. On this view, it is not surprising that individuals often find themselves resisting the forms of identity that they are forced to adopt.

Such an analysis of the relations with ourselves interrogates and subverts. It reveals the fragility of that which seems coherent and the contingency of that which seems essential. The ambiguity, thus, becomes empowering in the sense that it forces us to produce new narratives that erode the biases we so often ascribe to others, and to ourselves not least. As Rose (1998) contends: "Human beings are not the unified subjects of some coherent regime of government that produces persons in the form in which it dreams. On the contrary, they live their lives in a constant movement across different practices that subjectify them in different ways" (35). Through learning how such positionalities shift in complex and often unpredictable ways, through embracing ambiguity in how these positionalities shift, one is able to explore the diversity of strategies and tactics of subjectification that have taken place in relation to different classifications and differentiations of persons. Through learning to see how and when particular emotional investments become inscribed habits of attention, one can explore various understandings of difference. In the earlier example of the student who wrote the essay on the news, the change in her emotional stance came as a result of learning to see differently and beginning to explore that there might be alternative perspectives. What does it mean to be "taught" that there is a particular way of expressing patriotism? What are the emotional investments attached to the particular ways with which one should express patriotism? These questions create spaces that examine how these emotional investments shape one's actions, and evaluate how one's actions affect others.

Inhabiting this ambiguity can be very discomforting and demands substantial negative emotional labor such as vulnerability, anger, and suffering. To tolerate this ambiguity, one has to dismantle old habits and replace them with new ones and this involves considerable emotional and intellectual risk. However, emotional labor in the context of inhabiting ambiguity can produce favorable results, including self-discovery, hope, passion and a sense of community. For example, issues of oppression (racial, gender, sexual, or otherwise) are frequently dealt with by silence and omission that stem from ignorance and feelings of discomfort for what is different. The reductive binary model of innocence vs. guilt is the one in which many of us might subscribe. This model constrains plenty of possibilities. However, through learning to see how one is emotionally involved in such issues, one is likely to develop accountability for how he or she sees one's self and question cherished beliefs and habits. If this takes place in an emotionally open and safe environment—that nurtures emotions of anger or guilt but challenges them with compassion and courage—there will be possibilities for mutual exploration that also nurture hope and a sense of community for initiating change. Even the response we often hear—"I will not change"—is successful in the sense that the process of self-discovery has been somehow enriched. Also, in doing so one gains a new sense of interconnection with others. Thus, it would be simplistic to claim that ambiguity produces only vulnerability—it is rather a matter of how assemblages of vulnerability *and* hope, labor *and* passion, anger *and* self-discovery trace the "lines of flight" with which habits, claims to truth, and systems of norms participate in the construction of identities and regulation (or creation) of difference.

This call for ambiguity and vulnerability must apply as much to the educator as to the students. An example perhaps illustrates what we mean: following the instance in which the female students claimed both publicly in the classroom as well as privately during office hours with the professor, that they had not experienced sexism, the professor experienced a deep frustration. This frustration calls for extensive self reflection about useful pedagogical approaches as well as considerable reflection about what these women were trying to say. In this instance, the professor discussed the frustration with colleagues and with friends. She realized that people will only see what they are ready and willing to see, and that an adversarial approach—for example, "let me tell you how you are oppressed or let me give you some more examples of how women are oppressed"—was not appropriate. Instead, the next week she began the class by acknowledging what the women had said: she reflected back to them their experience that they had never experienced sexism.

The emotional work involved here included a willingness to recognize the other person's experience without judgment. The educator also reflected back to the class that quite a number of the students had mentioned to her during office hours that the experience of critical thinking was affecting personal relationships. The educator asked the class to talk about how the educational experience was impacting students' personal lives. This process of consciously recognizing the subjectivities at work created a refreshing and productive openness in the conversation. In the process of recognizing her own limits, the educator created "space" in the classroom (Zembylas 2001).

Peter Trifonas suggests that "it would not be possible to adhere to the democratic spirit of the principle of educational equity by arbitrarily choosing among differences of race, class, gender, or sexuality so as to privilege a pedagogy that appeals to some aspects of difference while marginalizing or rejecting others." The critical theories and traditions that inform radical pedagogies all recognize differences as culturally and ideologically produced. Each pedagogical tradition—critical pedagogy, feminist pedagogy, queer pedagogy, and media literacy—tends to privilege or emphasize certain differences over others. While it is true to say that certain pedagogies privilege one difference over another, in practice we would suggest that it is the educators' own habits of attention and in some cases unexamined privilege that accounts for overlooking certain differences.

Further, while the idea of pedagogy of difference that does not privilege one social category over another is appealing, we suggest that pedagogy of discomfort extends pedagogy of difference to include the inscribed unemotional patterns of salience. These emotional stances, as we have pointed out earlier, describe what John Dewey calls "habits of mind." Growth, in pedagogy of discomfort, requires challenging the emotional accumulations that constitute the embedded nature of etiology in our embodied life.

Pedagogy of discomfort urges students as well as educators to move outside of their comfort zones. Pedagogy of discomfort invites critical inquiry regarding cherished beliefs and assumptions, and also calls for students and educators to take responsibility and even action in the collective struggle for social justice. Pedagogy of discomfort is similar to pedagogy of difference, but distinct in its emphasis on the necessity of emotional labor as part of the radical work of changing social relationships. In the next section, we theorize the relation between difference and our call for a pedagogy of discomfort arguing for the catalytic role of emotional labor both in its positive and its negative formation.

DIFFERENCE AND PEDAGOGY OF DISCOMFORT: THE CHALLENGE OF "CRITICAL THINKING"

A pedagogy of discomfort invites educators and students to engage in *critical thinking* and explore the multitude of habits, relations of power, knowledge, and ethics through which the conduct of educators and students is shaped by others and by themselves. Within this culture of critical thinking (which is not separated from feeling), a central focus is the recognition of the multiple, heterogeneous, and messy realities of power relations as they are enacted and resisted in localities, subverting the comfort offered by the endorsement of particular norms.

The use of binaries and stereotypes takes the form of rationalizing an array of certainties and thus avoids the problem spaces between such binaries and stereotypes. Of course, discourses and practices do not have the systematic and closed character of binaries and stereotypes. The naming of what is absent and salient through the problematization of what is given to educators and students as necessary to think, feel, and do is a primary ethical aim of a pedagogy of discomfort. This aim enhances the contestability of that which has been invented for educators and students, and inspires them to start inventing themselves differently. It is partly through the analysis of the practices of control of educators and students' thoughts, emotions, and actions that educators and students can identify the price that is paid by them—that is to say, for what they have come to think, feel, and do—for their current regimes of self-identity construction, in particular, that of self-management.

It is in this context that a pedagogy of discomfort creates both its critical effect (making it more difficult and perhaps discomforting for educators and students to think, feel, and act in accustomed ways) and its positive emotional labor (clearing a space for a collective process of thinking otherwise and considering the conditions for a transformation of what individuals are supposed to be). For example, the educator and the students are now placed at the origin of all the activities of laboring—this is a pedagogy that invites as many new fears as it inspires projects of inventions. In the story with the student who wrote the essay on the news, she begins to critically trace out the ways in which claims to truth and systems of authority have participated in the elaboration of appropriate emotional habits consonant with the rationalities of liberal individualism. Pedagogy of discomfort invites her to experience positive emotional labor because critical thinking, passion, and self-discovery are deployed to construct a new conception of engaging with others and with herself. Its ethical aim, therefore, is to reshape and expand the terms of discourses and practices in education, enabling different thoughts and feelings to be experienced, enlarging the space of discourses and practices, "modifying the relations of the *different* participants to the truths in the name of which they govern or are governed" (Rose 1999: 277; emphasis added).

On the other hand, such pedagogy produces—or rather invites—an array of emotions that accompany discomfort and provide some comfort. Without resurrecting new binaries, pedagogy of discomfort becomes an approach to understanding the ways in which something new is created, how difference is introduced into history. A greater sense of comfort and positive emotional labor comes with examining the ways in which this creativity and invention arise out of how educators and students engage in discourses and practices that open new possibilities.

This is not an argument about encouraging a sense of lost agency within the context of a radical pedagogy. Pedagogy of discomfort is concerned with the present, not with the transcendental or with a utopian future. It arises in "cramped spaces within a set of relations that are intolerable, where movement is impossible, where change is blocked and voice is strangulated. And, in relation to these little territories of the everyday, [it] seek[s] to engender a small reworking of [its] spaces of action" (Rose 1999: 280).

This is not about proposing a radical pedagogy because it is all too well known that even radical trajectories often become organized and systematized. Following Nikolas Rose (1999) we argue that the role of a pedagogy of discomfort is to help maximize the capacity of educators and students (both individually and collectively) to shape their habits, knowledges, and emotions and to "configure the practices that govern them in the name of their nature, their freedom, and their identity . . . revealing the lies, falsehoods, deceptions and self-deceptions which are inherent within these attempts to govern us for our own good" (282). This capacity is comforting because it embodies a certain vitalism that operates under a minimum normativity: "each person's life should be its own telos . . . we should oppose all that which stands in the way of life being its own telos" (283). Also, such capacity is comforting because despite the entailed ambiguity, it makes it possible to encourage vitalism, critical thinking, and the invention of new ways of being in the world. Above all, pedagogy of discomfort seeks to open the space within which educators and students can exercise their ethical responsibilities to oppose all that subverts their capacity to assert for themselves their own vitalism, their own will to shape their lives. In doing so, one is able to gain a new sense of interconnection with others and expand the borders of comfort zones.

CONCLUSION: DIFFERENCE AS CREATIVITY

In her famous essay "The Master's Tools Will Never Dismantle the Master's House" Audre Lorde writes, "Difference must be not merely tolerated, but seen as a *fund* of necessary polarities between which our *creativity* can spark elected dialectic. Only then does the necessity for interdependency become threatening" (1994: 111; emphasis added). The idea that difference functions as a creative energy is also echoed in the works of Cornel West. West argues that "the new cultural politics of difference are neither simply oppositional in contesting the mainstream (or malestream) for inclusion, nor transgressive in the avant-gardist sense of shocking conventional bourgeois audiences. Rather, they are distinct articulations of talented (and usually privileged) contributors to culture who desire to align themselves with demoralized, demobilized, the politicized and disorganized people in order to empower and enable social action and, if possible, to enlist collective insurgency for the expansion of freedom, democracy and individuality." (1990: 19–20)

This means that one has to leave the confines of convention and privilege to see how differences can be used to create collective situations that don't feature the aspired selfhood. In the context of pedagogy, the question is not so much how one can break these conventions and replace them with new ones but how much risk, emotional labor one can take in allowing one's practices and discourses to modify and be modified by the world. It means that such pedagogy looks for the sources of invention and creativity that have been missed while being attuned to the best that previous conventions have to offer. The idea is simple, although very hard to carry out: no risk, no creativity, no good invention, thus no difference that makes difference.

Cornel West (1990) reflects this idea and asserts the importance of being a critical catalyst who affirms the creative power of difference: "The most desirable option for people of color who promote the new cultural politics of difference is to be a critical organic catalyst. By this I mean a person who stays attuned to the best of what the mainstream has to offer—its paradigm, viewpoints and methods—yet maintains a grounding in affirming and enabling subcultures of criticism. Prophetic critics and artists of color should be exemplars of what it means to be intellectual freedom fighters, that is, cultural workers who simultaneously position themselves within (or alongside) the mainstream while clearly aligned with groups who vowed to keep alive potent traditions of critique and resistance" (33).

In showing us that difference can be seen as a fund and that our creativity can spark passion and interconnection, Audre Lorde, Cornel West—as well as our own proposition for a pedagogy of discomfort—open possibilities for challenging and extending the safety and security of our personal comfort zones; it is possible to act upon these borders in the name of such creativity and the practice of each life as its own telos. It is true that there might be criticisms that to destabilize and denaturalize the emotional stances we internalize requires considerable suffering and vulnerability and thus, the ethical responsibility of the educator becomes a complex issue. We agree but we also ask: why should educational processes necessarily be comforting? How could we create a public sphere that enables educators and students to take responsibility or demand justice without expecting that considerable emotional labor be involved? Abandoning ourselves to a mute acceptance of "fate" or "common sense" about differences might be less discomforting, but why should someone privilege comfort anyway? Besides, if identity is seen to be nomadic rather than unified, the process of understanding difference and creativity is already imbued with its own comforting trajectory. It is in this sense that educators and students are called to exercise their ethical responsibilities.

NOTES

1. In the final chapter of *Feeling Power: Emotions and Education* (1999), "A Pedagogy of Discomfort: Witnessing and the Politics of Anger and Fear," Boler outlines her conception of this pedagogy and analyzes how students of a dominant culture in particular experience discomfort when asked to examine history through a lens of social responsibility.
2. In the first chapter of *Feeling Power,* Boler defines "inscribed habits of inattention" as a description of how emotions are a site of social control. She suggests this approach of examining the habituated selectivity of our attention as an alternative view to that of "repression" and the "unconscious." See pages 16–17, 20, 172, and 180.
3. Mark Peace, http://www.aber.ac.uk/media/Students/mbp9701.html.
4. Engaging Toni Morrison's arguments regarding "whiteness and the literary imagination" (1992) is useful at such junctures.

REFERENCES

Barzun, Jacques. 1950. *The Interpretation of History.* New York: Peter Smith.

Benjamin, Jessica. 1988. *The Bonds of Love: Psychoanalysis, Feminism, and the Problem of Domination.* New York: Pantheon Books.

Boler, Megan. 1999. *Feeling Power: Emotions and Education.* New York and London: Routledge.

Bowker, Geoffrey, and Susan Leigh Starr. 1999. *Sorting Things Out: Classification and its Consequences.* Cambridge: MIT Press.

Britzman, Deborah. 1991. *Practice Makes Practice: A Critical Study of Learning to Teach.* Albany: State University of New York Press.

Chomsky, Noam. 2000. *Chomsky On Miseducation.* Ed. and introduction by Donaldo Macedo. Lanham, Md.: Rowman & Littlefield.

Dewey, John. [1932]. 1985. "Ethics." In *John Dewey: The Later Works, Vol. 7,* ed. J. A. Boydston. Carbondale, Ill.: Southern Illinois University Press.

Freire, Paolo. 1970. *Pedagogy of the Oppressed.* New York: Continuum.

Garrison, Jim. 1997. *Dewey and Eros: Wisdom and Desire in the Art of Teaching.* New York: Teachers College Press.

Hall, Stuart. 1987. "Minimal Selves." In *Identity,* ed. Lisa Appignanesi, 44–46. London: Institute of Contemporary Arts.

Johannesson, Ingolfur. 1998. "Genealogy and Progressive Politics: Reflections on the Notion of Usefulness." In *Foucault's Challenge: Discourse, Knowledge, and Power in Education,* ed. Thomas Popkewitz and Marie Brennan, 297–315. New York: Teachers College Press.

Lorde, Audre. 1984. *Sister/Outsider.* New York: Crossing Press.

McLaren, Peter. 1998. *Life in Schools: An Introduction to Critical Pedagogy in the Foundations of Education.* New York: Longman.

Minh-Ha, Trinh T. 1990. "Not You/Like You: Post-Colonial Women and the Interlocking Questions of Identity and Difference." In *Making Face, Making Soul: Haciendo Caras,* ed. Gloria Anzaldua. San Francisco: Aunt Lute Foundation Books.

Moore, Robert. 2000. "Racist Stereotyping in the English Language." In *Race Class and Gender: An Anthology,* ed. Margaret Andersen and Patricia Hill Collins. New York: Wadsworth.

Morrison, Toni. 1992. *Playing in the Dark.* New York: Vintage.

Narayan, Uma. 1997. *Dislocating Cultures: Identities, Traditions, and Third-World Feminism.* New York and London: Routledge.

Rose, Nikolas. 1998. *Inventing Ourselves: Psychology, Power, and Personhood.* Cambridge: Cambridge University Press.

————. 1999. *Powers of Freedom: Reframing Political Thought.* Cambridge: Cambridge University Press.

Sawicki, Jana. 1991. *Disciplining Foucault. Feminism, Power, and the Body.* New York: Routledge.

Sedwick, Eve Kosofsky. 1990. *The Epistemology of the Closet.* Berkeley: University of California Press.

West, Cornel. 1990. "The New Cultural Politics of Difference." In *Out There: Marginalization and Contemporary Cultures,* ed. Russell Ferguson et al. Cambridge: MIT Press.

Zembylas, M. 2001. "A Paralogical Affirmation of Emotion's Discourse in Science Teaching." In *Teaching Science in Diverse Settings: Marginalized Discourses and Classroom Practice,* ed. A. Barton and M. Osborne, 99–128. New York: Peter Lang.

————. In press. "Emotions and Teacher Identity: A Poststructural Perspective." *Teachers and Teaching: Theory and Practice.*

6

The Struggle for Happiness: Commodified Black Masculinities, Vernacular Culture, and Homoerotic Desires

RINALDO WALCOTT

For Brett Cemer

The Capitalist conception of sport is fundamentally different from that which should exist in an underdeveloped country. The African politician should not be preoccupied with turning out sportsmen, but with turning out fully conscious men, who play games as well. If games are not integrated into the national life, that is to say in the building of the nation, and if you turn out national sportsmen and not fully conscious men, you will very quickly see sport rotted by professionalism and commercialism.

—Frantz Fanon

It is still true, alas, that to be an American Negro male is also to be a kind of walking phallic symbol: which means that one pays, in one's own personality, for the sexual insecurity of others. The relationship of a black boy to a white boy is a very complex thing.

—James Baldwin

Nothing could be worse, for the work of mourning, than confusion or doubt: one has to know *who is buried where—and* it is necessary *(to know—to make certain) that, in what remains of him,* he remains there. *Let him stay there and move no more!*

Let us call it a hauntology.

—Jacques Derrida

. . . cultural forms such as rap and hip hop are not just brilliant and haunting political aesthetics rising from the ruins of deindustrialized cities, they are also global communicative forms. Culture may be commodification but it is also communication.

—Angela McRobbie

In the winter of 2000 one of my students brought me a copy of *Notorious*—Sean "Puffy" Combs' then-new magazine named in honor of the late Notorious BIG, or Biggie Smalls. She wanted to share with me an interview with the artist now known again as Prince. She told me of a comment Prince had made about being emancipated from his record contract with Warner Brothers—a fight that took seven years. Prince said in the interview that "Contracts don't work. Now that I'm free I can make an album with Lenny Kravitz, but he can't. He's still on the plantation. He's down south, I'm up north." I was entirely intrigued by the ways in which Prince's economy of speech called to attention a range of haunting historiographic metaphors to map the tensions, contradictions, and banalities of black commercial musicians in the contemporary era. The haunting of slavery and segregated U.S. racial politics marked his speech. But as I skipped through the magazine I came to the back cover and the advertisement on it and could not move on—I could not put the magazine down. The Nike ad caught my attention and immediately called to mind the savage beating of Abner Luima in New York City. The ad was a plunger and a blue and white AirGarnett sneaker set on a full page; between the Air-Garnett and the plunger were the words "ALWAYS GETS THE JOB DONE." The Nike ad shocked me because those of you who followed the Luima case will remember that it was alleged that Luima was homophobically sodomized with a plunger. It was later revealed to be a broom. The Nike ad called to mind for me all the violent ways in which black male bodies are inserted into late modernism, even when those bodies remain absented. In this particular case the absented presence of black male bodies both victimized and spectacularized as pitchmen for Nike bore down heavily on me as I responded to the ad psychically and emotionally—not to mention ethicopolitically.

In this chapter I want to elliptically think through or think about the relation of violence as a behavior-orienting practice of the relations between the black man and the whi\te man. I am therefore suggesting that violence appears to be the foundational site for the enactment of the racialized and sexualized relations between white and black men. This violence finds itself played out in the brutal sexuality of capitalism and is reproduced in the haunting vernacular cultures of the black Atlantic in late modern capital as black men unconsciously evoke the disappointment and the pleasures of their location within late modern capitalist behavior-orienting practices. This violence is partially lived out through the complex relations of both the practices and artifacts of late modern capitalism. This chapter takes up the problematic of the popular spectacularization of the hard black male body as both desire and threat vis-à-vis its relation to the white male body. In particular, I probe representations and representations of black popular culture for this archetypical black hard body, but I also look to alternate renditions of black male bodies, less popular but politically and intellectually engaging, to ascertain the continuing yet changing dynamic relations of black masculinities. I suggest that the life/death axis of slavery in a postslavery world continues to haunt our contemporary cultural moment.

The salability and bankability of blackness—and therefore its commodification—is currently unquestionable. It is evident whether we are talking about clothing, music, or prisons. Such an observation can serve as a place for the production of a melancholic response. I'm going to try to avoid such a response. The commodified conditions of representations of blackness, specifically black maleness, in late modern capitalist cultural practices leaves much to be desired and this conundrum of race, masculinity, and capital has often expressed itself as melancholic—in fact, one might read the Nation of Islam's Million Man March as a symptom of melancholia. Whether we are talking about Oprah Winfrey, Michael Jordan, Vince Carter, bell hooks, Henry Louis Gates Jr., Spike Lee, or Bruny Surin, specific markers of blackness have been coded, possibly patented, trademarked, and solidified as a commodity. The marked and marketed body of the slave is the flesh of early modern capital that haunts our contemporary consumerist culture. In my reading, at least for this instance, I am going to call on what Paul Gilroy has recently termed in a signifying gesture, or at least a trace to Gayatri Spivak, as "strategic universalism." This strategic universalism, one which for the moment wraps us all into the infectious dragnet of blackness[1] does so with a desire that recognition of our complicity might allow those of us opposed to the regimes of late modern capitalism to formulate ethico-political responses that allow for imagining a different present–future.

In Gilroy's *Against Race: Imagining Political Culture Beyond the Color Line* and David Scott's *Refashioning Futures: Criticism after Postcoloniality* both theorize of what Scott calls the "changing present" and turn to the disappointments of our "post" society (postcolonial, postmodern, post-civil rights, etc.) to require us to at least force the question of reimagining—and therefore, articulating—a different political present–future than the one we presently inhabit. Their demand is a politically inflected demand, largely built on the foundationality of Frantz Fanon's critique of a colonial world system. The recent return to Fanon by those who as Stuart Hall says, "work on and work with"[2] him and those who have established orthodoxies concerning "the correct" Fanon has opened up a moment for thinking about the stakes of (and it will be clear which side I come down on) working over theorists and thinkers for our postcolonial present–future. In such a regard, I invoke C. L. R. James in the title of this chapter to signal what will be an implicit working through of his thesis in *American Civilization*. In that text, James suggests that what the people want at all cost is happiness. But lest I suggest that James is offering us some abstract notion of happiness let me hasten to say that James means liberty, leisure, and sustaining material conditions of life by happiness.[3] In essence then, James's notion of happiness sits at odds with capitalist regimes of socioeconomic organization. Happiness can't be bought—so cancel your trips to Disney World and remember that the sensation of buying those Armani pants will only last as long as it takes to make the transaction.

Happiness is not exchange value and it ain't Prozac—it is use value. I work through the notion of a struggle for happiness to arrive at a place where thinking the complexities of black manhood (and I deliberately placed it in the singular here), might occasion both a sustaining critique of some of its various articulations and utterances, and point us somewhere else as well. Calling into question the complex architectures of black masculinities and manhood requires a "hauntological" approach following Derrida's re-reading of Marx in a post-communist world. The postslavery world in which black Atlantic manhood comes to be requires that we think about black masculinities contrapuntally within and against the various transformations of capitalist reordering. Frederick Douglass's experiences of manhood have come to be the *de rigeur* founding text (here I mean to signal what has come to be marked as the pivotal fight between Douglass and Covey) for discussing the symbolic formations of black manhood and the hauntological conditions of black manhood in the postslavery and postmodern era. A brutal sexuality as constitutive of capitalism is revealed in the slave narratives often as heterosexual dominance. However, along with the insights of Darieck Scott, I want to insist that we also need to account for the homosocial and pathological homophobic homosexuality of early capitalism as it is premised on the slave economy.[4] So let me transgress, then, and suggest that no longer is Frederick Douglass's schema of how a man is made a slave and a slave a man an immediately useful intervention for thinking about the formations of black manhood in late capitalism.

Therefore, the hauntology that I offer is one that seeks to map not a linear and unbroken narrative of the shadow of slavery flashing up in contemporary associations and affiliations of black masculinities, but rather one that is informed by the ways in which trans-Atlantic slavery offers us the lens through which to constitute a deciphering of black masculinities that might point us in ethico-political directions useful for articulating a possible politics of rupture of our present episteme. Such a rupture would require that we follow Sylvia Wynter's call for "a practice of decipherment" (240).[5] Wynter's notion of decipherment takes its tenor from ethnocriticism, deconstruction, and a challenge to unitary ways of knowing as constituting meaning. Wynter writes: "a deciphering turn seeks to decipher what the process of rhetorical mystification does. It seeks to identify not what texts and their signifying practices can be interpreted to mean but what they can be deciphered to do, and it also seeks to evaluate the "illocutionary force" and procedures with which they do what they *do*" (266–67).[6] It is with this insight of Wynter's in mind that I bring a number of different black Atlantic theorists into association and affiliation and offer a reading of the black male body in its material substance, its imaginary fantasmatic qualities, its "hardness," its desires and disappointments, and its "genitalization" into conversation.

But I do so because I want to write against masculinity—that is against masculinity studies[7] as it repeatedly constructs the white male body and its body politics as the continued ground of its address. In short, I want to enter into the debate of masculinity studies—which is at least some fifteen years old now—to ask what is at stake when men—black or white, not to mention all the others—formalize the study of themselves in relation to the fields constituted in some registers as feminist studies, women's studies, and gender studies? This is no doubt an old question, but one that bears repetition in the aftermath of the various "million marches" after the Nation of Islam's Million Man March. For example, in the 2000 Million Mother's March on Washington, D.C., on Mothers' Day, most of the TV news clips I saw focussed on mothers speaking about the gun deaths of boys as though girls don't die by guns too—what an irony! A certain kind of evasion is occurring that has important consequences for social, cultural, and political reorderings. What about daughters killed by the guns of abusive husbands and partners—one wants to ask?

In "Pecs and Reps: Muscling in on Race and the Subject of Masculinities" the afterword to *Race and the Subject of Masculinities,* Deborah McDowell calls into question the study of masculinity when the study does not shift from what she identifies as "those who study and those who are the objects of study. Non-white men dominate the latter camp" (366).[8] McDowell's demand for a shift from white maleness and its constitutive powers is important, and yet it raises an interesting dilemma for those of us— black—who seek to turn the gaze on ourselves and by so doing to reveal what she calls "the psychic architecture of white masculinity" (367).[9] This is a disturbing dilemma, if as Fanon pointed out, now almost fifty years ago, "not only must the black man be black; he must be black in relation to the white man" (110).[10] Thus McDowell's suspicion of masculinity studies is well founded when the study of the man of color might only be yet another way of reproducing the father figure of us all—the Great White Daddy. The white man's burden never ends, even when it is in a black mask. Yet I want to resist what Gamal Abdel Shehid calls "good-boy feminism" and not entirely endorse McDowell's argument, even though I see my concerns as affiliated with those cogently and critically articulated by her—especially her skepticism that masculinity studies holds, at least an ambivalent and ambiguous relation to feminist studies. I am concerned to extricate black manhood from the wretched phantasm of masculinity as we currently know and experience it. Therefore, my project is steeped in a self-conscious method of renovation of masculinities so that different present–futures might be imagined and possibly achieved without an attempt to render women an absented presence and more importantly, to undermine feminists politics of all kinds.

The decade of the 1990s produced a bevy of black masculinities in a range of representational apparatuses.[11] However, it might be too simplistic to say—but I'll risk it anyway—that one particular performance of black manhood has been consolidated, at least, in the popular imaginary— the one of hardness. The sporting world has continued to be one of the most salient places for the spectacularization of black manhood. Everyone from Joe Louis to Paul Robeson to Muhammad Ali, to Magic Johnson to Michael Jordan to Dennis Rodman, to Mike Tyson to Ben Johnson to Tiger Woods stand in as some kind of representation of black manhood across historical time. However, most of the contemporary representations of black manhood have been contextualized in popular film, music, and music videos. Much of this popular cultural representation harkens back to an identifiable tradition of the blues and prison literatures of previous decades, but not with the same panache—and need I say, not with the same intellectual rigor. For example, can you conceive of Chester Himes in conversation with Dr. Dre or Ice Cube? And what of Tupac with Assata? One needs only to visit the impossible conversation between Angela Davis and Dr. Dre in *Transition* in 1992[12] to encounter the relative unsophisticated and importantly, conservative utterances of contemporary prison articulations among its popular cultural representatives as expressed in gangsta rap.

The consolidation of a hard black masculinity sits alongside the "endangered black man" thesis and if critically read reveals at least one irony: If black men are indeed "the hardest of the hard," they also seem to be the easiest victims in North Atlantic society—thus the discourse of endangered. Where does their hardness disappear to? This irony of hard, yet victim and therefore endangered, flashes up I believe because black men suffer from the crises of the undermining of patriarchy in postliberation society in ways that continually reference the haunting of slavery. bell hooks writes of the relations between black men and white men, "The discourse of black resistance has almost always equated freedom with manhood, the economic and material domination of black men with castration, emasculation. Accepting these sexual metaphors forged a bond between oppressed black men and white male oppressors. They shared the patriarchal belief that revolutionary struggle was really about the erect phallus, the ability of men to establish political dominance that could correspond to sexual dominance" (58).[13] While postslavery society has provided avenues for black men to partake more fruitfully of the patriarchal pie, black men's access to full patriarchal participation has continually been limited.

The endangered black man discourse juxtaposed with his hardness is really about the inability of the black man to resignify masculinities in ways that might produce a different kind of economy of masculinity— and thus community. For as Spike Lee, John Singleton, the Hughes brothers, the Hudlin brothers, and a bevy of sports stars and popular musicians made public and consumable a variety of versions of black masculinity— all of them in one way or another hard—other less popular versions have been offered up as well. What about RuPaul? Isaac Julien, Marlon Riggs, Essex Hemphill, Joseph Beam, Samuel Delany, Dennis Rodman, Keith Piper, Lyle and Thomas Harris, and a host of artists working across a range of genres offered and continue to offer representations of black masculinities that force ethico-political questions on those who engage their work. That much of this work is only viewed, read, and engaged in other ways by relatively small groups—often academic and activist/intellectual communities—means that the struggle to produce forms of masculinity that utter different performances resonate within small and relatively privilege communities that might have the luxury to think otherwise about performing masculinity. I raise such as a concern, in its apparent naiveté and simplicity, as an intellectual caution and not as an excuse for the lack of a broader engagement for resignifying masculinities in black Atlantic communities more generally. Black masculinities are conceived so very much along an axis of life and death that throughout the 1990s representations of black male death continually crossed the hetero/homo divide, culminating and consolidating I believe in the death of rapper Eazy E.[14]

The death of former NWA rapper Eazy E from AIDS was reported as being caused by a previous drug habit. His death occasioned a moment of reflection in the largely patriarchal conservative hip hop world whereby rappers stopped to consider AIDS and its consequences. But I often can't help wondering: What would it mean to have imagined that Eazy E died of AIDS contracted through male on male sex? What would have happened to the hardness of hip hop in the late 1990s had Eazy E's death been connected to male on male sex? Would this have been the moment when some reflection on the regime of black male hardness would have occurred? How would hip hop resignify itself as "real" had Eazy E contracted AIDS from male on male sex? I ask these questions because life and death issues have been so central to the production of 1990s black pop culture—but most of the deaths of black men in those venues were deaths that looped back to the black man as victim and endangered. A dangerous discourse for black feminisms. It might well be argued that 1990s hip hop represented the pinnacle of necrophilic responses in pop culture to-date. This necrophilic impulse in what we short handedly called gangsta rap cannot and should not be minimized. If anything would have caused a sustained reengagement with Fanon's thesis in *Wretched of the Earth,* "Concerning Violence," it could have been the continued fantasmatic representations of violence in the lyrics and music videos of gangsta rap. Fanon wrote "The native who decides to put the program into practice, and to become its moving force, is ready for violence at all times. From birth on it is clear to him that this narrow world, strewn with prohibitions, can only be called in question by absolute violence" (37).[15] It is not difficult to read Fanon's thesis in relation to post-Reagan ghetto culture with its helicopter surveillance, barricade-like policing, and other forms of surveilling poor and working class communities alongside the rise of the crack economy, AIDS and other forms of devastation like the disappearance of jobs and service opportunities (the pulling out from these neighborhoods of banks, stores, etc.) unleashed on mainly black and Latino/a urban communities. Life and death issues characterized the decade of the 1990s for urban communities.

But there is also a possible other accounting for hip hop's necrophilic desires. Fucking the dead in hip hop is largely a homoerotic activity. This homoerotic relation to the dead plays out not only in revenge fantasies or homeboy love, but I would suggest as well in the potential erotic charge that taking another's life might offer. New World slavery might be understood as at least one script for that desire. In effect, I am suggesting to you that one of the affects of hardness as the substance of a black manhood is the erotic charge of violence in its relation to the violence that white males inflict on black manhood, reducing black men to, in the language of gangsta rap, "pussies." It would not be too simplistic to suggest that part of Fanon's thesis on violence has in part something to do with the relationship between the fractured mirror of the (mis)recognition of the black man to the white man and vice versa. The misrecognitions are in effect forms of violence.

The difficult queer writings of Gary Fisher highlight this relation of violence and its erotics for black/white relations.[16] Because Fisher can acknowledge his homoerotic pleasures and thus perform without guilt or shame, he is able to reveal for us the primal nature of the black man's attachment to the white man and their self-constituting practices—it is often a practice of violence, desired and disavowed. For performances of black male heterosexuality, Fisher's cross-racial erotics are refracted as a kind of plutonic homeboy love. But this homeboy love is revealed as something more in the moment of death. Trauma reveals the hints of a homeboy love that must fashion a hardness to resist the potential of sexual encounter, sexual pleasure.

One only needs to encounter the "love and loss" songs in honor of Tupac, and especially The Notorious BIG, to at least recognize the workings of an erotics and a politics of necrophilia in black popular cultures, especially gangsta rap. The "I am missing" genre thematizes the homeboy love and allows for its outlet in publicly affirmative ways. In the tribute to Notorious BIG the track "We'll Always Love Big Poppa" publicly announces homeboy love but in its repetitions of "we'll always love big poppa" I hear—or rather, I detect—a kind of love that exceeds platonic tones. Loving "big poppa" can easily shift into loving the lost/loss father of us all—the Big White Daddy—which is McDowell's concern. The open-endedness of the genre allows its listeners/readers to substitute just whatever it might be they are missing. It could be a range of things. But lest we forget, academics like to fuck the dead too; we share necrophilic textual relationships, and there in might be the link between the downbeat of hip hop and its attraction to academics like myself.

The deaths of Tupac and Biggie Smalls, like the retirement of Michael Jordan from the National Basket Ball Association (NBA) signaled an end of a particular era in black Atlantic popular culture. I like to think of it as the post-NBA era, for the link between basketball and hip hop while indelible and enduring no longer holds any real mystique in relation to some notion of an authentic black community. It is now clearly exposed as all consumption. And, the number of black pop personalities who want to be seen at basketball games as a part of constituting a public black authenticity evidences this (Spike Lee, Whoopi Goldberg, etc.). But most importantly, this post-NBA era highlights, I believe, the crisis of masculinity in North America, at the least. But let's encounter the obvious once again: masculinities of all sorts are in crisis and the crisis of masculinity in North America exists for both homosexual and heterosexual men. The crisis is one whereby the struggle to be happy is experienced through a relation to a possibly commodified masculinity—we are all required to figure out which one or which ones, we will try on, living with it and adjusting as necessary. That men in North America find it difficult to figure masculinity outside of commercial interests should not be surprising.

As Fanon cautioned in a discussion of the making of national culture, "if you turn out national sportsmen and not fully conscious men, you will very quickly see sport rotted by professionalism and commercialism" (196).[17] While Fanon seems to suggest that there exist some pristine elements before professionalism and commercialism, what is important here is the emphasis that national sport once inserted into the regimes of capitalist organization does not bring with it any ethico-political consciousness. We need only engage the politics of Jordan, Charles Barkley, or Rodman to ascertain such.[18] So what is at stake, then, is the way in which these men work symbolically to render possible particular forms of masculinity.

The symbolic work of sporting figures and other popular cultural figures, like musicians and movie actors, as the scuffling that commodified masculinities are built on rests on the scopic nature of late modern capitalist conformist-fashionings. The look is central to commercial masculinities. This is particularly evident as ESPN launched its new fashion magazine *The Life* on *Fashion TV*.[19] The first issue featured basketball players, mainly black, dressing each other. Vince Carter and Charles Oakley were featured in the television story. While it was briefly mentioned that Oakley designed and made all his own clothes because of his size, the new magazine had no intention of using that as the basis for the kind of masculinity it sought to erect. Instead, the spokesperson, when asked, by *Fashion TV's* Genie Becker to comment on why ESPN was getting into the fashion business, made statements like: "it is [that is clothing and style] [which is] something straight average guys can feel good about" and "athletes are living every fifteen-year-old boy's fantasy life, are you going to tell them that's girly?" as a way to justify ESPN's penetration into the fashion and style market. (But to be rhetorical, I always thought it was girly-men, otherwised called gay, who revealed the pleasures of shopping for other men). Black male bodies were called to labor once more, in yet another echo of the postmodern plantation, but to retain the complexities of our moment, these sporting/laboring bodies are transcendental in the contemporary market place—they are black and something more.

These mainly black figures, at least in the narrative I am constructing here, represent bodies in labor for capital. Again let us take note of the hauntological qualities of this late modern capitalist practice as it raises the specter of slavery and postslavery permutations of the exploitation of black male bodies given release in service of capital.

However, in postmodern and postcolonial society the complexities of black male insertions into late modern capitalism are far more complex than merely raising the specter of slavery would suggest. Black men as producers, artists, and consumers are implicated in a conservative "biopolitics"[20] to use a Paul Gilroy term, which marks and markets the black male body in ways that cannot be merely read as white racist projections and insertions of black male bodies as the victimized lack and excess of racist capital. For example, Suge Knight's record company, Death Row Records, specifically cites the relationship between life and death that I discussed earlier. As one of the major producers of gangsta rap in the 1990s, and the recording and others kinds of home for Tupac, at the time of his death, Suge Knight and Death Row Records played a pivotal role in cementing the hard image of black manhood. But it is not a long stretch to metaphorize the hardness of black manhood to the hardness of the black man's genitalia. In many ways gangsta rap reproduced and reduced black manhood down to "a dick thing."

But if the black man is both only a penis and its opposite—a pussy—simultaneously, the black man might embody the fantasmatic representations of not only the spectacularization of one aspect of colonial gender ordering but more pointedly, as McDowell suggest, the black man might be the best example of "masculinity [as] incoherent, unstable, and in a state of utter convulsion" (369).[21] The black man's manhood might be in many ways the clearest example of the crisis of masculinity. There is probably no better recent example of the crisis of masculinity than for example this: Bert Archer, a white man announces the "end of gay"[22] while another white man—Eric Brandt, articulating an antiracist queer positionality—edits a book devoted to addressing the tensions between blacks, gays, and the struggle for equality.[23] Those two texts speak to the instability and incoherence of masculinity in its queer appearances and its impossible performances in post-liberation movement North America. That at least one white boy can mobilize academic queer theory to announce the end of gay; as yet another white boy attempts to make space in queer politics and sociality for black queers, leaves much for consideration. Added to all this, the ways in which some black queer men struggle to find space within the fraternity of sexual practice and consumer niche marketing of postmodern urban gay life is, to say the least, ironic. For that niche market is significantly marked as white. However, once the socio-political consequences of what currently constitutes queerness in North America is approached the ethicality of the end of gay recedes into the place of how the architecture of whiteness, even in its "weaker, feminized" male queer forms holds such potential to shape how the world might be represented and even possibly lived in certain contexts (just encounter *Queer as Folk, Friends,* or *Will and Grace* as examples of this white architecture).

So let me read against the grain, but not in contention with some folks that I don't normally conceptually disagree with. Contrary to Richard Dyer, Fred Pfeil, and some others of the whiteness school, who have given us the language of white invisibility as constitutive of a marked whiteness, I want to suggest something else. I want to suggest that in contemporary queer culture whiteness is not at all invisible, but highly spectacularized. Whiteness and in particular white masculinities are spectacularly performed as "white" (see *Queer as Folk* and *Will and Grace*). That is, in contemporary post–Stone Wall gay male culture whiteness is not invisible, but whiteness is an assumed quality and qualifier of gayness, thus Eric Brandt's anthology *Black, Gays and the Struggle for Equality* (an attempt to place blacks within the rubric of queer—still) and the absence of any consideration of the cross-cutting complexities of queerness in Bert Archer's contribution to queer debates. But this marked and marketed whiteness in everything from ads for circuit parties to boat cruises, to bathhouses to furniture and booze elides a complex sexual politics that, as Baldwin wrote, makes "the relationship of the black boy to the white boy a very complex thing" (217).[24] What is this complex thing that we are to see? I want to suggest, along with a number of other theorists, that it is a scopic relation—that is, it is about the "look," the place, the site, and desire of the "look." In contemporary queer culture the "look" is white and it is not invisible; it is the quality and colour actively sought after and desired. And one of the best places to see it at work is in a place where the etiquette "look" is more central than the word—that is the bathhouse.

The bathhouse is a site where despite being populated by the weaker and feminized forms of masculinity, patriarchal regimes are unleashed to the fullest. The "look" and the touch in the space of the bathhouse are the appeal to relations of power and performances and practices of power that are deeply gender racialized and obviously sexually racialized. The space of the bathhouse is the place where the unveiling of the complex thing between the black boy and white boy reveals itself. Each of them performing or relinquishing an exterior structure of behavior-orienting practices in favor of a desire and pleasure that is entirely scripted and rescripted on the basis of the economy of stereotype and a public all-male privacy. But the bathhouse is also the place were white is adamantly visible in an economy of sexual desires and practices were men otherwise formed and fashioned by more complex narratives of racial positioning relieve themselves of those ethical considerations and turn to a sexually racialized practice that ordains the white body as that which is most desirable.

Now some might ask, "what makes this different from the norm outside of the bathhouse?" Well, the point I am trying to make is that in the context of the bathhouse patriarchal relations reveal the ways in which the scopic pleasures of, for my purposes, being constituted the Negro as in Fanon's famous scene might be and can be—and often is—lived out as a very pleasurable thing. To enjoy being constituted as the Negro (either brute or passive) is to open up the disturbing pleasures of a post-liberation society haunted by the constitutive degradations of the erotic economy of slavery. So to be the Negro in the bathhouse can also be the imagined body of continued rejection, in a manner that would be contested ethically and politically in any other circumstance outside the bathhouse as racist. But this contradiction of love/hate dynamics between white men and black men is one of the primary self-constituting practices of at least North Atlantic black masculinities—both homo and hetero. In the space of the bathhouse black and white men demonstrate that the black man "is black in relation to the white man"—and importantly vice versa—and that it might be pleasurable, as Isaac Julien provokes us to think in his short film *The Attendant.* This revelation within the context of the practice of male-on-male sex opens up the mutual self-constituting nature of sexually racialized practices, which have enormous consequences for outside the bathhouse where these performances revert to the "real thing" of black and white—that is, the contemporary moral regime of simple notions of racism. In the "real thing" the antagonisms and tensions that exist can lead to extremes, including death, but in their more mundane everyday world these are played out at the level of black and white patriarchal struggles over the authority to speak on behalf of respective imagined communities. We are left wondering about the silences of patriarchal collusion, even when it is an unequal patriarchal union.

Let me move toward a conclusion with—or at least on—a more hopeful note. I want to think about and think with at least one of the artists that I mentioned earlier who I believe offers a different "look" and register of black masculinity. In particular, I want to concentrate my concluding comments on the work of Lyle Ashton Harris, who is a photographer and performance artist. I first encountered Lyle Ashton Harris's photography in the summer issue of the now defunct *Outlook: National Lesbian and Gay Quarterly* in 1991. An image of Harris's irreverent self-portraiture adorned the cover. But I did not purchase the magazine for his images. In fact, I thought that the image was an accompaniment to the Essex Hemphill article—the reason I had bought the magazine in the first place. When I read the magazine I encountered Harris's self-portraiture and his accompanying article "Revenge of a Snow Queen," in which he wrote: "For me transgression begins not by going beyond, but by inhabiting that racially and sexually fetishized space, and by exploring our relationship to it." His art then takes up the dilemma that I tried to describe above, but without sentiment and fully conscious of the risks involved, so that something else might happen—possibly a shift in our consciousness? This is ethico-political art inflected by post-liberation movement disappointments and pleasures that engage a critical intellectual tradition.

The self-portraiture of Harris is a site where a practice of decipherment and a hauntology collide in terms of reading practices, and the ethics required to do justice to reading the work. Harris's work forces us to confront the gendered, racialized, and sexualized work of the "look." This is not a look that can be commodified, for its does not have market qualities. In fact, the "look" that Harris's work engenders is one that seeks to call attention to the ways in which looking is ideologically and psychically constituted. Harris's work in *Outlook* engaged explicitly with Fanon; in fact, one image even resignified Fanon by quoting him: "In the world through which I travel, I am endlessly creating myself." This engagement with black skin/white mask and white mask/black skin, as it reverses in Harris's work, places a number of very important issues on the table concerning race, whiteness, blackness, gender, masculinity, femininity, sexuality, homosexuality, and heterosexuality. I want to focus more specifically on a reading of Harris's work for questions of masculinity.

Harris's work highlights the genitalization of the black male body. The black male body reduced to a penis, Harris attempts to resignify the penis as something more. In fact, it might be suggested that the explicit engagement of the economy of stereotype to call attention to gendered and racialized sexual looks in the work of Harris opens up "what has come to be called the scopic drive—the eroticisation of the pleasure in looking" (16), as Stuart Hall puts it in discussion of Fanon's use of the look as a central theme in his writing. In the photography of Harris the look is both autobiographical and autoethnographic in that his performative self-portraiture draws on cultural fragment as evidence of the constitutive elements of discriminatory practices. Stuart Hall puts it this way: "The principal counterstrategy here has been to bring to the surface—into representation—that which has sustained the regimes of representation unacknowledged: to subvert the structures of 'othering' in language and representation, image, sound and discourse, and thus to turn the mechanisms of fixed racial signification against themselves, in order to begin to constitute new subjectivities, new positions of enunciation and identification . . ." (19). Hall is writing of the black British contexts, reading it through the work of Fanon, but he could have been writing of Harris.

Harris thematizes these "new subjectivities, new positions of enunciation and identification" by revealing the process of genitalization. Because his self-portraiture embodies being both the pussy and the dick the ambivalent relations of taking pleasure in the relations of domination and subordination in all its racial, sexual, and gendered connotations are at the least opened up. His resignifying of black manhood, for example, opens up the "spectacular matrix of intelligibility" (20) in which "the loss of social power by substituting an aggressively phallo-centred 'black manhood' " (30) is deconstructed in favor not of a resolution, but rather for the possibility of talk to occur—here then enters the talking cure. Harris's work is not about cracking the mirror, or that mimesis can become possible—we all already know that it can not—rather reflected in Harris's mirror are the little bits that we all share in each other. His cross-resonant photography highlights a practice, one which speaks to the indelible cross-cutting of identities and identifications in the post-Enlightenment world, a strategic universalism.

Thus central to Harris's art is the pose and how the pose informs our look. In the essay "Posing" Craig Owens suggests that the pose cut at least two ways, especially in photographs: "[F]or that matter, in any photograph—is the figuration of a gaze which objectifies and masters, of course, but only by immobilizing its objects, turning them to stone" (207). But photography—or rather posing for the photograph—is "a form of mimicry" (212) and "posing has everything to do with sexual difference" (212), Owens tells us in parenthesis. Finally, Owens tells us that "to *pose* is, in fact neither entirely active nor entirely passive" (214) but rather "the subject in the scopic field, insofar as it is the subject of desire, is neither seer nor seen; *it makes itself seen*. The subject poses as an object *in order to be a subject*" (215). Owens's contribution to thinking psychoanalytically about the pose is useful because it refuses to allow for a reading of the work of artists like Harris as only constituted through a crass notion of the social. And yet we must still insist on the social, but as a Fanonian sociogeny in which the collective unconscious might be accounted for. Lyle Ashton Harris's work invokes and provokes the Fanonian project of sociogeny cogently articulated by Fanon in the opening pages of *Black Skin, White Masks*. I have produced art here as a kind of savior and a kind of last resort for at least opening up new places for different kinds of identifications that might occasion a more ethico-political response in the world.

But lest I leave you with the idea that art always holds some possibility for offering us a way out of ethico-political conundrums, a few words about the much acclaimed *Boys Don't Cry*. An otherwise quite interesting and provocative fictionalization of the documentary *The Brandon Teena Story* and the chronicling of a life cut short, *Boys Don't Cry* creators made the decision to excise the murder of Philip Devine from the fictionalized version. I don't know their reasons for excising Devine, but what remains a pressing concern is the life and death axis that engenders a patriarchal discourse of endangered black male and is given partial credence by such choices. Devine's clearly sexualized-racialized murder adds to the complex picture of Brandon's death, for Devine's death also points to the anxieties that our culture holds about sexual and racial difference and the price that is exacted on some as representative of that difference. To have excised Devine from the fictional version, for whatever reasons, is to reproduce the notion that these things do not cross-cut each other. Such is the furthest from the truth. Is there a correspondence between *Boys Don't Cry* and the Nike ad that I began with? And how might we think about the ways in which we cross-cut each other? Is it still possible to approach identity and its behavior-orienting practices as exclusive performances or do we require methods for thinking about our cross-cutting resonances? How does late modern capitalist consumption and commodification cross-cut and implicate us all in its complex webs and circuits?

Finally, in Lee Edelman's reading of James Baldwin's *Just Above My Head*, Edelman argues that Baldwin's commitment is to "dismantling the armored identities that keep self and other, inside and outside, resolutely, if arbitrarily distinct" (73). Baldwin's project, then, was to reveal the ways in which we cross-cut each other as a way of moving us toward a more ethico-political orientation to the world we inhabit. His ethico-political demand suggests that identity-orienting practices required a move from identities as foundational to processes of identification that would allow for the acknowledgement of our cross-cutting resonances, a different universalism. Edelman points us to the concluding words of Baldwin in the essay "Here Be Dragons," in which Baldwin's project of hope and possibility is partially revealed, and I conclude with them: "Each of us, helplessly and forever, contains the other—male in female, female in male, white in black and black in white. We are part of each other. Many of my countrymen appear to find this fact exceedingly inconvenient and even unfair, and so, very often, do I. But none of us can do anything about it" (74).[25]

NOTES

1. See Barbara Browning, 1998, *Infectious Rhythm: Metaphors of Contagion and the Spread of African Culture.* New York: Routledge.
2. Stuart Hall, 1996, "The After-Life of Frantz Fanon: Why Fanon? Why Now? Why Black Skin, White Masks?" In *The Fact of Blackness: Frantz Fanon and Visual Representation,* ed. Alan Reed. Seattle: Bay Press.
3. See chapter 6 in particular C.L.R. James, 1993, "The Struggle for Happiness." *American Civilization.* Cambridge: Blackwell.
4. See D. Scott, 2000. "More Man than You'll Ever Be: Antonio Fargus, Eldridge Cleaver and Toni Morrison's *Beloved.*" In *Dangerous Liaisons: Blacks, Gays, and the Struggle for Equality,* ed. Eric Brandt. New York: The New Press.
5. Sylvia Wynter, 1992, "Rethinking "Aesthetics": Notes Towards a Deciphering Practice." In *Ex-Iles: Essays on Caribbean Cinema,* ed. Mbye Cham. Trenton, N.J.: African World Press, Inc.
6. Wynter, 1992.
7. For examples, see R. W. Connell; Lynne Segal; Brian Pronger; Fred Pfeil.
8. See 1997, *Race and the Subject of Masculinities,* ed. Harry Stecopoulos and Michael Uebel. Durham: Duke University Press.
9. Deborah McDowell, 1997, "Pecs and Reps: Muscling in on Race and the Subject of Masculinities." *Race and the Subject of Masculinities,* ed. Harry Stecopoulos and Michael Uebel. Durham: Duke University Press.
10. Frantz Fanon, 1967, *Black Skin, White Masks.* New York: Grove Press.
11. See for example: 1996, *Representing Black Men,* ed. Marcellus Blount and George P. Cunningham. New York: Routledge; 1996, *Are We Not Men?: Masculine Anxiety and the Problem of African-American Identity,* Phillip Brian Harper. New York: Oxford; 1997, *Race and the Subject of Masculinities,* ed. Harry Stecopoulos and Michael Uebel. Durham: Duke University Press.
12. Angela Davis and Dr. Dre, "Nappy Happy," *Transition,* Issue 58.
13. bell hooks, 1990, "Reflections on Race and Sex." In *Yearning: Race, Gender, and Cultural Politics.* Toronto: Between the Lines Press.
14. See Rinaldo Walcott, 1998, "Queer Texts and Performativity: Zora, Rap and Community." In *Queer Theory in Education,* ed. William F. Pinar. Mahwah, N.J.: Lawrence Erlbaum Associates, Publishers.
15. Frantz Fanon, 1968, *The Wretched of the Earth.* New York: Grove Press.
16. Gary Fisher, 2000. See *Gary in your Pocket: Stories and Notebooks of Gary Fisher.* Ed. Eve Kosofsky Sedgwick. Durham: Duke University Press; Robert Reid-Pharr, "The Shock of Gary Fisher." In *Dangerous Liaisons: Blacks, Gays, and the Struggle for Equality,* ed. Eric Brandt. New York: The New Press.
17. Frantz Fanon, *The Wretched of the Earth.*
18. See bell hooks on Michael Jordan's politics, "Representing the Black Male Body." In *Art on My Mind: Visual Politics.* New York: The New Press.
19. The show aired on May 13, 2000, on CityTV, Toronto, Canada.
20. Paul Gilroy, 2000, *Against Race: Imagining Political Culture Beyond the Color Line.* Cambridge: Harvard University Press.
21. McDowell, 1997.

22. Bert Archer, 2000, *The End of Gay: (And the Death of Heterosexuality)*. Toronto: Doubleday Canada.

23. Eric Brant, *Dangerous Liaisons: Blacks, Gays, and the Struggle for Equality*, ed. Eric Brandt. New York: The New Press.

24. 1993, "The Black Boy Looks at the White Boy." In *Nobody Knows My Name*. New York: Vintage.

25. Lee Edelman, 1994, "The Part for the (W)hole: Baldwin, Homophobia, and the Fastasmastics of 'Race.' " In *Homographesis: Essays in Gay Literary and Cultural Theory*. New York: Routledge.

7

Inside Noah's Tent:
The Sodomitical Genesis of Race
in the Christian Imagination

WILLIAM F. PINAR

[A] historical perspective is needed to help break into the contemporary codes of race and gender.

—Vron Ware[1]

A sodomitical impulse was an inherent potential of all fallen male descendants of Eve and Adam.

—Jonathan Katz[2]

The field of education—especially in the United States—is so very reluctant to abandon social engineering. If only we can find the right technique, the right modification of classroom organization (small groups, collaborative learning) or teach in the right way, if only students could learn to self-reflect or if only we develop standards—or, simply, focus on excellence—then students will learn what we teach them. The promise of "if only" rings repeatedly in research and teaching in the field of education, including teacher education and multiculturalism. Conceiving curriculum as "social psychoanalysis"[3] suggests understanding, not social engineering. While understanding is likely to transform the present, although probably not in predictable ways, it seeks the truth of the present state of affairs, not the manipulation of them for—in education—higher test scores. Higher test scores may well result, but they are hardly the motive for a curriculum of social psychoanalysis.

The project on which I am now working (and which this chapter anticipates) continues the theorization of curriculum as social psycho-analysis, here focused on the conflations of race and sex in the Christian imagination (no monolithic phenomenon, to be sure). I bring scholarship from several disciplines, including queer theory, to our understanding of multiculturalism, and, more broadly, of curriculum as racial text. If completed, the book would become the second in a multi-volume study of the autobiographical method of *currere,* the infinitive form of curriculum, meaning to run, a form which emphasizes the subjectivity of educational experience, a subjectivity inseparable from the social, in this instance the gendered, the historical, and the racialized: after Leigh Gilmore, an autobiographics of alterity. I also hope to make a contribution to teacher education. Many prospective teachers become too well acquainted with the "if only" tradition of social engineering in education; they need, I believe, to become aware of those profound psycho-cultural cross currents that function to undermine even their best intentions. What I hope to write is simultaneously a multiculturalism textbook, an instance of curriculum theory, an argument in cultural studies, and a primer for prospective and practicing teachers.[4]

There is a gendered myth of innocence in our profession[5] related to a myth of childhood[6] that keeps sexuality out of many U.S. classrooms,[7] while conceptualizing the problem of race as one of inclusion, the acceptance of diversity a problem of tolerance, sometimes even an appreciation of difference. This myth of innocence—connected to the invisibility and unselfconsciousness of "whiteness" and, specifically, hegemonic white masculinity—fails to appreciate how sex is interwoven with race, and how both together—intertwined in what too often seems a death embrace—are central to understanding the American identity. Whether or not black bodies are visible on the street—as they are not in segregated communities and regions—they are everywhere in film, on television, and this spectatorial politics of racial representation reproduces, in general, the sexual politics of race in the United States. As I expect to argue in the book, specularity and alterity follow from the denial of lack (or castration) in hegemonic white masculinity.[8]

In the previous volume I argued, focusing on lynching and prison rape, that white racism had circulating within it a mangled, disavowed homoerotic that was expressed in the castration of many black men in lynchings and in the rape and emasculation of many white men in prison.[9] I argued that the white man's hatred of the black contained (via denial and sublimation) his love, more precisely his desire, for the black male body, fetishized in an obsession with the black male phallus. The disavowal of desire sublimates into forms of white self-dissociation, black commodification and objectification, the white erasure of black subjectivity, and a racial politics of emasculation. In its gendered and specifically masculinized structures, white racism mistakes its own fantasies for reality, substituting stereotypes and skin color for concrete subjectivities.

I hope to portray one aspect of how this convoluted and ongoing racial crisis came to be. It is, for sure, a complicated (perhaps, finally, indecipherable) mix of cultural legacy and historical necessity. To start, I return to what was for many was the beginning, the "founding" and "imprinting" moment of "race" in the Christian imagination. For many—including for many slaveholders and racial segregationists—the genesis of race (and, for them, its implications of racial inferiority) is to be found in one line of that canonical Christian text, the Bible.

In this chapter I recite that verse (Gen. 9:24), recall a popular play based on it, review one telling instance of biblical scholarship concerning the passage, and conclude with an initial sketch of the pieces of the puzzle I hope to fit together later in the book. It is a puzzle locating the origin of race in an apparent homosexual incestuous assault, a mythic event that, we might say, reverberates for centuries, up through nineteenth-century lynching, twentieth-century prison rape, and in American schools today.

Some will argue that our students—often middle-class and white, and, especially, at the elementary level, mostly female—cannot bear to study such topics, indeed, that we must protect our daughters from such vulgar subjects. Surely such paternalism is no longer credible; surely it is clear that such gendered idealization and sentimentalization are misogynist. The innocence with which some teach courses in teacher education not only infantilizes our students, it leaves them unprepared for the often contestory character of many public school classrooms, microcosms of what sometimes seems an increasingly predatory American capitalist culture. In doing so it contributes to the reproduction of white racism, in institutional and specifically curricular forms, not to mention through the myriad of everyday, sometimes subtle, sometimes not, racialized interactions that occur, including those in all-white schools.

Because most prospective and practicing teachers in the United States are white and often subjected to a racialized curriculum that segregates black history and culture to one winter month, there is an urgent need to introduce our (especially white) students to black culture and history. In the United States all teachers are well-advised to take courses in African-American history and culture. Studying African-American history and culture is also labor for curriculum scholars. As I argued in volume one:

> Employing research completed in other disciplines as well as our own, let us construct textbooks . . . which enable public school teachers to reoccupy a vacated "public" domain, not simply as "consumers" of knowledge, but as active participants in conversations they themselves will lead. In drawing—promiscuously but critically—from various academic disciplines

and popular culture, [let us] work to create a conceptual montage for the teacher who understands that positionality as aspiring to create a "public" space.[10]

While the volume this chapter anticipates will hardly constitute a comprehensive introduction to African-American culture, it does instruct students in the conflations among race and (homo)sexuality in the Christian imagination. Especially after such instruction, European-American teachers dare not imagine they now "know" or can "see" their black students, dare not imagine that they can now teach European-American students to "deconstruct their own whiteness and decolonize their Eurocentrism in order to abolish or transcend their racial significance."[11] Whiteness is too pervasive, too complex, too unconscious for European Americans to be confident at all. The self-understanding to which I hope this volume contributes is not another "only if" that education-as-social-engineering expects and demands. But as those who value "holy sparks"[12] appreciate, the truth must be told, for its own sake.

I am a curriculum theorist, not a historian. There is no archival research in this study. As a curriculum scholar, I work from the academic disciplines to create curriculum for teachers, in this instance, an introduction to certain sexualized racial legacies that circulate still in American classrooms, in the textbooks American teachers teach, and inside themselves. It is, maybe, a step toward a "queer multiculturalism." A queer multiculturalism, as I conceive it, is "lesbigay"[13] affirmative action, feminist, and in solidarity with the political struggles of African Americans. That's as they say a tall order, and I am sure this book will fail to deliver it. But it places the order and by its presence asks that others take up where it ends, correct its mistakes, continue working despite its failures, animated perhaps by those failures.

There is, of course, a problem in a white man undertaking such a project, a problem serious enough to warrant a sustained meditation. In volume one I turned to the lyrical analysis of Saidiya V. Hartman.[14] In her brilliant analysis of abolitionist John Rankin's fantasies of empathy with a black male slave being beaten, Hartman underlines how nineteenth-century whites occupied the black body, not only legally but psychologically as well, even in the name of empathy and political solidarity. There was, in Rankin's case and, I worried, possibly in my own narration of the research on lynching and prison rape, a queer politics of empathy. When Rankin imagined himself inside the black male body of the tortured young slave, not only was he effacing that individual's subjectivity in his own heroic narcissistic gesture, he was also getting off.

Here I raise the issue in the context of feminist theory; it is to that literature I go to think about what is involved in cross-addressing issues of race.[15]

CROSS-ADDRESSING "RACE"

I do not mean to suggest that we can or should police each other, but I wonder about the possibilities of what my colleague Sharon Holland calls "complementary theorizing."

—Ann duCille[16]

In a thoughtful, perceptive, and widely cited essay, Ann duCille discusses a number of important issues in cross-addressing race. While opposed to territoriality, against racial, cultural, and gender essentialism, against treating African-American studies as the private property of those Spivak (1989) called "black blacks," duCille finds that questions of turf and territoriality, appropriation and cooptation persist "within my own black feminist consciousness."[17] She recalls that such questions are not new, that they represent, in one sense, an ancient argument over ownership of text, a term if expansively defined includes bodies, in this instance white ownership of black bodies. She recalls white anthropologists Melville and Frances Herskovits who worked during the 1920s and 1930s, and specifically the controversy that erupted in 1941 with the publication of their *The Myth of the Negro Past,* a study of African culture scorned by many black intellectuals.[18]

It was not until the 1950s that white scholars began to play a significant role in the fields of black historiography and literary criticism. It would be another forty years before white scholars would take up racial subjects in education. Black scholars would watch, duCille reports, as whites received attention and academic credibility that pioneering black historians and literary critics had not. This trend continued, so that, in 1980, African-American historian Darlene Clark Hine observed that "most of the highly-acclaimed historical works were, with few exceptions, written by white scholars." In her judgment, the legitimation of black history as a field had not benefited black scholars as much as it had whites, turning out to be a "bonanza for the [white] professional historians already in positions (as university professors and/or recognized scholars] to capitalize from the movement."[19]

The problem posed by often well-meaning whites who want to be of service in the struggle for racial justice is not new. One hundred thirty years ago, duCille remembers, the autobiography of former slave Harriet Jacobs was able to be published only with the aid of the well-known white abolitionist Lydia Maria Child (as editor and copyright holder). "I have signed and sealed the contract with Thayer and Eldridge, in my name, and told them to take out the copyright in my name," Child wrote in a letter to Jacobs in 1860. "Under the circumstances *your* name could not be used, you know."[20] The circumstances to which Child alluded but did not feel she had to name were those "circumstances" of slavery in which Jacobs had lived for most of her life and from which she had not fully escaped. Still today, duCille laments, too often it seems to take the interest and intervention of white scholars to legitimate and institutionalize African-American history and literature as well as other marginalized discourses such as postcolonialism and multiculturalism. That fact is, of course, a marker of institutional racism, and is, unfortunately, the case in the field of education as well.

Despite continuing racist conditions within the academy and within American intellectual life generally, conditions that privilege white scholarship over black, there have always been, despite the odds, black pioneers. Often unnoticed and unacknowledged by white scholars and readers, these racial and intellectual activists have made the formation of a black canon possible. Toni Cade Bambara's *The Black Woman* has been acknowledge by black feminist critic Gloria Wade-Gayles as "the first book that pulled together black women's views on black womanhood" and Jeanne Noble's *Beautiful, Also, Are the Souls of My Black Sisters* was the "first history of black women in America written by a black woman."[21] In curriculum studies, one might cite the groundbreaking scholarship of Horace Mann Bond, and, in my generation, James Banks, Louis A. Castenell Jr., Beverly Gordon, Patricia Hill Collins, Cameron McCarthy, Warren Crichlow, and William Watkins.[22]

Despite the absolute importance of Bambara, Noble, Joyce Ladner, and other black women intellectuals who performed the groundbreaking scholarly labor in the 1970s, it was, duCille complains, white feminist historian Gerda Lerner whom the academy recognized as the pioneer in reconstructing the history of African-American women. Lerner's documentary anthology *Black Women in White America* was published in 1972, making her, many declared, the first historian to produce a book-length study of African-American women. As indicated in her preface, Lerner's aspiration was to call attention to such "unused sources" as black women's own records of their experiences and "to bring another forgotten aspect of the black past to life." By publishing such first-person accounts as diaries, narrative, testimonies, and organizational records and reports, Lerner endeavored in her volume "to let black women speak for themselves."[23]

Lerner's notion of letting someone speak for herself is, duCille observes, "surely problematic," but duCille is less interested in the racial paternalism of the idea than in pointing out that Lerner was not, in fact, the first to draw upon what she implied were unexamined resources.[24] Black artists, activists, and intellectuals have made use of these unexamined resources for one hundred years and more. Former slave William Wells Brown is one example; duCille reports that he drew on such sources in the many novels, narratives, and histories he published between 1847 and his death in 1884. N. F. Mossell's *The Work of the Afro-American Woman,* first published in 1894, is another example; duCille cites of African-American women's commitment to acknowledge the accomplishments and contributions of "her black sisters."[25] There is the case of activist, educator, and "race woman" Anna Julia Cooper who wrote of the "long, dull pain" of the "open-eyed but hitherto voiceless" black women of America in *A Voice from the South,* published in 1892. The longevity of the debate over who gets to represent whom is, duCille points out, reflected in Cooper's one-hundred-year-old pronouncement: "Only the *BLACK WOMAN* can say 'when and where I enter, in the quiet, undisputed dignity of my womanhood, without violence and without suing or special patronage, then and there the whole Negro race enters with me.' "[26]

As well, duCille points to the intellectual labor of black literary scholar Charles Nichols, whose *Many Thousand Gone: The Ex-Slaves' Account of Their Bondage and Freedom* directed two generations of slave historians to a significant source: the "forgotten testimony of its victims."[27] In fact, duCille notes, it was Nichols's idea that Gerda Lerner employed a decade later in *Black Women in White America.* Black sources are not only important for black representation but for representations of American life generally. Speaking at a socialist conference in 1917, James Weldon Johnson, whom black historian of the Harlem Renaissance David Levering Lewis deemed the "dean of Afro-American letters" asserted that " 'the only things artistic in America that have sprung from American soil, permeated American life, and been universally acknowledged as distinctively American' were the creations of the Afro-American."[28] Acidly, duCille comments:

> [B]lack culture is more easily intellectualized (and canonized) when transferred from the danger of lived black experience to the safety of white metaphor, when you can have that "signifying black difference" without the

difference of significant blackness. . . . Lerner's [work] is undeniably important, but it does not stand alone as revolutionary. . . . [B]lack women had been speaking for themselves and on behalf of each other long before Gerda Lerner endeavored "to let" them do so.[29]

As duCille's analysis makes clear, the question of who speaks for whom is as "emotionally and politically charged as it is enduring and controversial."[30] While I speak for no one, perhaps not even myself,[31] what I say cannot stay within "whiteness," given how "whiteness" is interwoven with, dependent upon, and in disavowal of "blackness." While my intention is to contribute to the destruction of white racism and misogyny—interdependent as they are—there is, I suspect, no surgical precision possible. Moreover, my own racism will surface, however faintly (I hope) and in whatever convoluted fashion. The educational point is to learn from these surfacings. It is unlikely that my generation of European Americans will ever rid itself of internalized racism; the point is to be forever working on it, and not only for the political sake of African Americans, but for one's own spiritual sake. As James Weldon Johnson remarked once in reference to lynching: "lynching in the United States has resolved itself into a problem of saving black America's body and white America's soul."[32] Substitute "racism" for "lynching" and Johnson's formulation of the problem remains compelling.

Works on whiteness, especially when produced by white scholars, cannot substitute for texts about race written by black scholars. One's positionality matters. While duCille acknowledges that racial subjects can be taken up by those not occupying black subject positions, it is clear that the best of (white) intentions does not bleach out white tendencies toward colonization, territorialization, and occupation—all three of which are too often animated by intellectual imperialism and a pervasive, narcissistic careerism. Still, it is imperative—despite our necessarily convoluted motives—for whites to become "race traitors," to challenge white presumptions, especially when gendered, in my case amplified by internalized senses of masculine prerogative and privilege. Consequently, I do not presume to speak for or to African Americans in this project.

The students I have in mind as I write this antiracist curriculum textbook are European Americans, especially those straight and gay white men identified with hegemonic forms of white masculinity. Such masculinity is constituted by alterity, specularity, and the denial of lack (or castration), intersecting, interdependent elements of gendered and racialized self-structure.[33] In effect, I am asking men to return to that "founding moment" of "race," and there labor to dispel the curse. That curse is the infamous "curse of Ham," and that tent is both literal, in the sense of a specific biblical verse, and metaphoric, in the sense that to go inside Noah's tent today is to return to that intrapsychic space from which all men, black and white, are, in mythic terms, descended. In Freud's schema, it is to reexperience the moment of the "negative" oedipal complex, in which the love between father and son has not yet been disavowed, sublimated, and, for centuries of Christians, racialized. In this moment before the curse, we might imagine a different fate.

INSIDE NOAH'S TENT

And Noah awoke from his wine, and knew what his younger son had done unto him.

—(Gen. 9:24)

Bawdy songs fill the valley of Ararat in a one-act play, entitled *The First One,* published in New York in 1927. The play dramatizes the origin of black skin color within the dynamics of an extended family. Ham is a character reminiscent of Bacchus and Pan, singing that he feels like a young goat in the spring. Ham drinks and dances, arriving late at his father Noah's tent. Enormously relieved that the flood has receded, Noah enjoys the dance of Ham and his wife Eve. He drinks heavily with them from a goatskin of wine: "Pour again, Eve, and Ham sing on and dance and drink—drown out the waters of the flood if you can. . . . Drink wine, forget water—it means death, *death*!" Not long afterward Ham is heard "laughing raucously" inside Noah's tent. Then he emerges, laughing: "Our father has stripped himself, showing all his wrinkles. Ha! Ha! He's no young goat in the spring. . . . The old Ram, Ha! Ha! Ha! He has had no spring for years."[34]

This scandalous event prompts the scheming of Mrs. Shem, who insists to her husband that his own honor has been compromised as well. In order to "regain his birthright" he must cover Noah's nakedness: "Oh (she beats her breast) that I should live to see a father so mocked and shamed by his son to whom he has given all his vineyards!" Mrs. Japheth sends her husband along with Shem; the two men cover up their naked father, then awaken him. All the while Mrs. Shem and Japheth are weeping loudly. Mrs. Shem informs Noah that he has been humiliated, but not by them, but by Ham. Shem asks Noah: "Shall the one who has done this thing hold part of thy goods after thee?"[35]

The question works. Prompted by Shem, Noah excludes the guilty one from his share of the inheritance. Still somewhat drunk, Noah is not finished: "He shall be accursed. His skin shall be black! Black as the nights, when the waters brooded over the Earth!" Everyone is stunned. Mrs. Noah attempts to intervene in the curse, but to no avail. All now try to undo the curse by begging Noah to "unsay it all." Shem then accuses his wife of causing all the trouble, which prompts Noah to comment, misogynistically, that "Shem's wife is but a woman." Mrs. Shem feels remorse: "We coveted his vineyard, but the curse is too awful for him." Despite their prayers, Jehovah does not send another rainbow sign; the curse cannot be unspoken. Shem and Mrs. Shem have manipulated the patriarch to their own ends.[36] The price of capital accumulation is, however, higher than anyone imagined.

The price is the creation of the black race, a price to be paid by Africans and African Americans and others of African lineage. When the singing Ham reappears "they see that he is black. They shrink back terrified. He is laughing happily. Eve approaches him timidly. . . . She touches his hand, then his face: 'Look at thy hands, thy feet. Thou art cursed black by thy Father.' " Shem does not want to be touched by Ham; even his mother looks away from him. When Eve brings their boy in her arms, he has also turned black; the other children jeer and pelt him. Noah—still enraged—expels the pleading Ham: "Thou art black. Arise and go out from among us that we may see thy face no more, lest by lingering the curse of thy blackness come upon my seed forever." The play concludes as Eve and a somewhat cynical Ham leave in order to go to "the end of the Earth" "where the sun shines forever." Sobbing, Mrs. Noah continues to pray, but the worst has happened: the "black race" has been born.[37]

The curse on Ham dramatized in this play belongs to interpretative motifs and themes that focus on a specific biblical text. The play's obvious point of departure is Genesis 9, a complex biblical passage that makes, despite the play's assumption, no mention of skin color, but stipulates slavery as a punishment for Ham's transgression. In the Pentateuch, Noah curses Canaan to become a "slave of slaves to his brothers." Theologians have puzzled over this passage for centuries.[38]

The artistic license taken by the author of the 1927 play Werner Sollors summarizes may well have been taken by the author(s) of Genesis 9:24. Noah may not have existed as a concrete singular individual. Like "Adam," "Noah" too may be entirely mythic, "a figure we can just discern to be essentially male and patriarchal, but which, if it were not for those human attributes, would rise above our earthly existence and join the ranks of the demi-gods." While for many Adam was the father of the first race of man, Noah was the father of the second. So understood, Noah can be considered a second Adam; in him God presumably reflected upon the future of man.[39]

Ham is the son of Noah whose name is generally set down first and who may have been, though not the eldest, in status the senior of the sons. It was Ham who went to the tent for some reason we are not told. It is not even clear, R. H. Mottram observes, that if we are to assume that the family was still living together, with Noah as its patriarch and daily authority. It was inside Noah's tent that Ham looked at his "revered, heroic" father lying there naked and "dead drunk." Next (we are told, in the Bible not the play) that Ham left the tent and told his brothers (Shem and Japheth), who "took a garment, and laid it upon their shoulders and went backward and covered the nakedness of their father; and their faces were backward and they saw not their father's nakedness." Was their action stimulated by their reverence for the heroic figure? Were they only doing for their father what he had neglected to do for himself? There is no hint of sexual scandal in Mottram's account: "They covered him decently. They did not wake him."[40]

Noah slept it off. When he "awoke from his wine," as the Authorized Version has it, someone (who?) told him what had happened, or so Mottram suggests. Or did he know himself? The narrative only reports: "He knew what his younger son had done unto him." Mottram tells us that Noah knew "that he had been made ridiculous." Or perhaps, Mottram speculates, in the sober mood of one who wakes from a deep and sodden sleep, "what really happened was that he became self-conscious." In any case, Noah concluded, "with a shock, that he had a dignity to maintain, and that it had been treated lightly."[41] "Cursed be Canaan," he cried; "a servant of servants shall he be to his brethren." And he went on: "Blessed be the Lord God of Shem and Canaan shall be his servant." He added: "God shall enlarge Japheth and he shall dwell in the tents of Shem, and Canaan shall be his servant."

Mottram notes that these lines—in which the "curse of Ham" is pronounced—may well have been written long after the event, if there had in fact been any "event" at all. They may have been written once the disparity between the fortunes of the sons of Noah, or those tribes who had become represented by those historic names, had to be explained. In this scenario, the writer created the curse to rationalize the more successful and prosperous as the more devout descendants; *they* had acted in some more properly filial manner toward that legendary figure from whom they all had descended. The name of Japheth suggests that very "enlargement" that was promised him, that of Ham means "dark" and Shem "renown."[42]

Mottram's account is meant to introduce Noah to a general public. It raises more questions than it answers, questions numerous biblical scholars have worked to answer. H. Hirsch Cohen (1974)[43] suggests that the interpretations of many biblical scholars are inadequate because, for starters, they have never explained satisfactorily why the one man thought worthy enough by God to be saved from the waters of the Flood should be portrayed later as a drunk lying naked passed out. While Cohen's account also fails to explain satisfactorily for the curse, it does provide detail an introductory account by definition does not. For instance, Cohen tells us that Noah's nakedness was directly related to his drunkenness; and he argues that both Noah's drunkenness and his nakedness comprise an integral sequel to the Flood story.

The *Zohar,* a medieval book of Jewish mysticism, depicted Noah as having been driven into a drunken stupor by his idealism. The grape vine he had planted, from which the wine he drank would be made, had come, he believed, from the Garden of Eden. He wanted to drink of the vine in order to better understand the sin of Adam, in hopes he might then warn the world. Early Church Fathers Origen and Chrysostam excused Noah for a different reason. They suspected the old patriarch had not known what wine could do. Drinking without knowing its effect, Noah quickly became overwhelmed in the inebriating power of the fermented grape.[44]

Cohen characterizes Michelangelo's famous fresco of the drunken Noah in the Sistine Chapel "as the tragic confrontation between youth and old age." He points to the "listless and aging body" of the reclining Noah as symbolizing the "infirmity and weakness of age." The "athletic bodies" of his sons represent the incarnation of youth in its prime.[45] To the homosexual Michelangelo, these were, perhaps, more than merely symbols of youth in its prime. Moreover, the (homo)erotics of the relationship between Ham and Noah may have occurred to Michelangelo.

Cohen recounts ancient Egyptian and Greek associations between alcohol and virility. It is this special power ascribed to wine that suggests to Cohen a justification for Noah's intoxication. Cohen's is no "deficiency of character" thesis in explanation of Noah's state (a curiously Protestant view of the matter in any case). Rather, Cohen speculates that Noah believed that the wine would replenish his supply of semen and would thereby allow him to obey the command he had received from God upon disembarking from the Ark. Recall that when Noah left the ark with his family and all living creatures, he built an altar and there burned an offering. God then promised never again to destroy all life on earth. He blessed Noah and his sons with what, as Cohen points out, must be regarded as more of a command than a blessing:

Be fertile and increase, and fill the earth. (Gen. 9:1)

God was, Cohen notes, explicit: He wanted Noah and his sons to begin the job of replenishing the earth with the human species. (There seems to be no mention that heterosexual incest is involved here, given that Noah's sons had to sleep with their mother, unless they themselves were hermaphroditic or intersexual.) After observing God destroy the world, except for them and the occupants of the ark, these men must have taken their responsibility of repopulating a decimated earth seriously indeed. Curiously, as Cohen notes, God's order was carried out only partially:

> These three were the sons of Noah, and from these the whole world branched out. (Gen. 9:19)

This sentence, Cohen reminds, directly precedes the section describing the drunkenness of Noah. It should, he thinks, anticipate what would transpire in the verses to follow. Instead, the sentences introduce the subject of procreation. Significantly, Noah's name is missing. We are told that the whole world would branch out from the three sons of Noah, not from Noah *and* his three sons. Cohen concludes that Noah failed to carry out God's wish, even though the command to repopulate was issued to all four men. In that sense, then, did Noah fail as a man?

That Noah may have failed does not mean, Cohen points out, that he did not *try* to comply with God's command. Cohen thinks he made a "stupendous effort." Despite that effort, Noah failed, perhaps due to his age; Cohen reminds us that he was then six hundred years old. Whether or not Noah's advanced age was an issue, Cohen speculates that he must have approached his task with resolve—even if his procreative capacity was past its peak. To shore up his supply of semen, Cohen suggests, Noah decided he would consume wine, and in considerable quantity. To follow the command of God the Father, then, Noah (Cohen speculates) "planted a vineyard to produce the fiery substance so necessary to increase his supply of seminal fire and thereby enhance his generative capacity."[46] But it would appear the old man overcompensated:

> . . . and he drank of the wine, and became drunk, and lay uncovered in his tent. (Gen. 9:21, RSV)

There are many interpretative possibilities here, several of which we will examine later, but, for the moment, let us stay with Cohen.

A rabbinic homily, Cohen reports, divined Noah's intent as conjugal—to have sexual intercourse with his wife "in his tent." Because "tent" has a consonant ending generally denoting the feminine gender, the rabbinic interpreter understood the word as meaning "her tent," namely the tent of Noah's wife, presumably in order to "cohabit with her."[47] But "tent" could connote Noah's own split-off self, in other words, his "feminine self" or even his feminized sex organ, his anus. Cohen is not about to go there.

Cohen's interpretative strategy involves linking the drunkenness of Noah with the drunkenness of Lot and the destruction of Sodom and Gomorrah, another biblical tale in which, lay readers concluded, homosexual desire provoked the father's (in this case God the Father's) curse. (Scholarly interpretations of the episode tend to stress slander and inhospitableness as the "sins" of Sodom.) Recall that only four people escaped the destruction of those cities: Lot, his wife, and his two daughters. Fleeing Sodom just before its destruction, Lot and his family reached the town of Zoar, where Lot's wife was turned into a pillar of salt when she ignored the prohibition against gazing upon the scene of destruction. Fearing that Zoar was not safe either, Lot and his daughters fled to the hill country and finally found refuge in a cave (Gen. 19).

Lot's older daughter felt certain, evidently, that the whole world had gone up in flames. The thought that she, her father, and her sister were the sole survivors prompted her to suggest to her younger sister an incestuous plan to save the human species from extinction, obviously a recurring theme in Genesis:

> Our father is old, and there is not a man on earth to consort with us in the way of all the world. Come, let us make our father drink wine, and let us lie with him, that we may maintain life through our father. (Gen. 19:31–32)

The daughters plied their father with wine until he drank himself into such a semi-conscious state that he was, apparently, unaware that he had had sex with his older daughter. The following night the scene was repeated, this time with the younger daughter.

Lot's experience replicates Noah's in a number of significant details, Cohen suggests, evidently missing a rather obvious difference between the two episodes, namely that it was Lot's daughters who "raped" the patriarch and in Noah's case, if there was penetration, it was by his son. But Cohen is focusing on the fact that Lot, like Noah, survived a disaster of cataclysmic proportions, with the result that he believed that he and his children were the sole survivors on earth. Second, Cohen offers, Lot too was considered to be an old man at the time of his escape from catastrophe. His age differs from Noah's in years only. Third, Lot too became intoxicated to the point of being (sexually) vulnerable. "Such close similarity of detail," Cohen concludes, "suggests that the factors resulting in Noah's drunkenness were the same that caused Lot's intoxication."[48] One must surmise that heterosexism is at work in Cohen's eagerness to make parallel the two very different stories.

Finished with situating the event, Cohen is ready to move "inside the tent." He begins by acknowledging that considerable interpretative energy has been expended by biblical exegetes in a centuries-long effort to decide what happened to the drunken, naked Noah inside the tent, "whetted by the enigmatic statement" that Noah, upon recovering consciousness, "knew what his youngest son had done unto him" (Gen. 9:24). "Apparently," Cohen writes, "more than Ham's voyeurism is involved, but precisely what is is not amplified by the narrator." (The love that dare not speak its name will never occur to Cohen, at least not in print.) Due to the absence of details, Cohen reports, ancient Jewish commentators were compelled to embellish the story with "the lurid details" obviously left out by the narrator.[49]

The rabbinic sages of the Midrash and Talmud came to a different conclusion about what happened: Noah must have been castrated in the tent. Symbolically, then, the great patriarch had been "unmanned," not unlike Daniel Paul Schreber, about whose case we will read in my completed book (but not in this chapter). In reconstructing the incident, Cohen tells us, several rabbis imagined Canaan, Ham's son, entering the tent, looping a cord around his grandfather's exposed testicles, drawing it tight until the deed was done. Informing Shem and Japheth of this "gruesome deed," Cohen continues, these rabbinic sages then imagined Ham responding to his father's castration as if it were humorous. Other rabbis maintained that Ham, not Canaan, castrated his father, causing Noah to cry out: "Now I cannot beget the fourth son whose children I would have ordered to serve you and your brothers! Therefore it must be Canaan, your first-born, whom they enslave."[50]

Other sages denied that Ham was guilty of such foul play, suggesting that in all likelihood a lion castrated Noah, a fantasy not limited to students of sacred texts, evidently, as a poster displayed in many gay bars a decade or so ago portrayed a lion "castrating" (via anal penetration) a (white) man. But evidently these sages' imagination was not so bestial. Instead of consensual intercourse, they imagined an accident. As Noah disembarked from the ark, a lion—ill perhaps from the voyage, they suggested—struck Noah's genitals with an inadvertent swipe of his paw, so that he never again could perform "the marital act."[51] In this version, the tent and the wine are irrelevant.

Many modern scholars agree, Cohen reports, that the story of Noah and Ham bears the signs of biblical editors, and, consequently, tend to regard the episode of Noah's drunkenness and the curse of Canaan as a transitional passage, connecting the Yahwist (J) account of the Flood with the Table of Nations in Genesis 10. The episode then becomes a splinter of a more lengthy narrative, in which the roles of Ham and Canaan had to be "telescoped."[52] Perhaps due this abbreviation of events, the passage remains cryptic. Questions remain: If Ham committed a crime against his father, why did Noah direct his curse against Canaan? Why does the narrator characterize Ham as the youngest son, when the word order of the sons, which to most scholars seems to indicate their order of birth, implies that Ham is the second-born? Cohen agrees that satisfactory answers to these questions have not yet been provided.

Despite the apparent failure of ancient and modern exegetes to make sense of the passage, Cohen believes he can solve the mystery. To solve it, he will assume that no information has been suppressed or lost by abbreviating a much longer and complex story. Rather, he works from the assumption that the narrator presented all the details necessary for an adequate understanding of the episode. In doing so, Cohen locates the "crime" in "the taboo of looking."[53]

Cohen finds evidence for this interpretation in Genesis 9:23. Recall that after hearing Ham report that he had seen his father naked, Shem and Japheth took a garment, walked backward into the tent—in order to avoid seeing their father naked—and covered him. The narrator tells us:

Their faces were turned away, and they did not see their father's nakedness. (Gen. 9:23)

Working from only what the text states, Cohen concludes that Ham's sin consisted solely of gazing upon the naked body of his father.

Shem and Japheth's behavior points to such a conclusion, Cohen argues. Had Ham castrated his father, as suggested by the rabbinic sages, the brothers would have attended to the wound, not simply draped a garment over him. By telling us that the sons did nothing more than cover their father, the narrator seems to be saying that this measure was an appropriate and sufficient response to what had happened. That Shem and Japheth approached their father with their faces averted, Cohen emphasizes, suggests that they were determined to avoid their brother's sin. Focusing on the facts of the text, then, Cohen feels confident that "Ham's offense lay in gazing upon his father's nakedness."[54]

"Looking was not," Cohen writes, "the simple act for biblical man that it is today." It's no simple act today, either.[55] In ancient Israelite culture, the "look" contained the potential of danger. Cohen cites the following examples: God refuses Moses's request to allow him to behold His Presence with the warning that "man may not see me and live" (Exod. 33:20); Manoah, father of Samson, after viewing the angel of the Lord, cries to his wife: "We shall surely die, because we have seen God" (Judg. 13:22): Elijah avoids the sight of God by covering his face with his mantle; and, perhaps most well known, Lot's wife turns into a pillar of salt upon viewing the destruction of Sodom and Gomorrah.

To explain why the act of looking was regarded as perilous, Cohen turns to psychoanalysis, if only for a moment, to suggest that looking implies identification. He quotes Fenichel: "If a man looks upon God face to face, something of the glory of God passes into him. It is this impious act, the likening of oneself to God, which is forbidden when man is forbidden to look at God."[56] Cohen argues that Lot and his family were forbidden to look upon the destruction of Sodom and Gomorrah for a similar reason, a reason related to the dynamics of identification: "Though the ancients never heard of 'identification,' they intuited, judging from even these few examples, that there was something in the act of looking that closely resembled the psychoanalytic concept of identification; that is, by looking at someone, one could acquire his characteristics. In short, looking became an act of acquisition."[57] Acquisition can, of course, imply erotic possession. Moreover, the dynamics of acquisition or identification are hardly free of libidinal politics; Judith Butler argues persuasively that the relationship between the two—identification and desire—is inevitably an unstable one, as identification forever threatens to dissolve into desire.[58]

The Hebrew language reflects the notion that looking can be a means of acquisition. Cohen points to the number of Hebrew words for "see" and "look" that are identical with or closely related to the words for "fence" or "wall." Fence, Cohen asserts, symbolizes ownership: "everyone recognizes that the enclosed object has been acquired at some time in the past and is owned by the person who has erected the fence." Biblical man, he continues, related the word for "looking" to the word for "fence," thereby indicating that something could be encompassed even without the visible signs of enclosure. In other words, the one who is looking—the eye of the beholder—could encompass everything within his range of vision. In this sense, Cohen is arguing, the Hebrew language conveys the idea that looking can mean acquiring that which is viewed. The idea occurs in English in the words "hold" and "behold."[59]

But fence or wall (in poet Robert Frost's sense) can also imply separation and distance, allowing for privacy and space to breathe. Frost suggests, of course, that fences are necessary for good neighbors, not good patriarchs. In ancient Israelite culture, however, to enter someone's property, say a tent or a body, is to transgress the erections that typify patriarchal possession and enclosure. If patriarchy is, in part, about the substitution of property for symbiosis (or relationality), or "having" for "being," then Ham has struck a blow (as it were) for the matriarchal state. Is that why his progeny must be enslaved?

Now that Cohen has defined the act of looking as a means of acquiring, he thinks he can now explain why Ham left the tent to tell his brothers what he had seen. Ham was not trying to undermine his father's honor "by making him the butt of his dirty mouthings," as some commentators contend. Rather Ham was merely trying to make a claim, namely "that by looking upon his nude father, he thereby had acquired his father's potency!"[60] This is similar to the analytic tactic historian Joel Williamson (1984) employs in his brilliant (if heterosexist) effort to explain lynching.[61] It is a tactic that assumes that identification always succeeds in its sublimation of desire.[62]

Perhaps Cohen senses the instability of "identification," senses that in "acquiring" his father's "potency" (a six hundred-year-old man lying passed out, in a drunken stupor, seems vulnerable not potent, does he not?) the son remains in a desiring position, because he moves quickly from the scene of the son gazing upon the naked father. He imagines Noah not as "passive" but as "active," as in, presumably, heterosexual intercourse. "To claim his father's potency would have to mean that Ham caught Noah in the act of procreation," Cohen writes. The text, Cohen acknowledges, says nothing about Noah engaging in (hetereo)sexual intercourse, only that Noah was drunk and naked inside his tent. Yet, Cohen insists, somewhat stubbornly it would seem to me, "from the information given, Noah evidently did have intercourse or intended having it."[63]

Cohen continues his effort to exonerate the patriarch, telling us that Noah's nudity "most likely" was not related to his being drunk. He was naked, Cohen argues, neither because he was incapable of controlling his actions nor because he was overheated from drinking so much wine. Rather, Cohen suggests, Noah's nakedness was preliminary to sexual intercourse. Recall the relation between wine and potency: Noah drank the wine "to obtain the seminal potency necessary for the prodigious task of repopulating the earth." Once sufficiently "fortified," Noah stripped for sex. The narrator, Cohen is forced to acknowledge, "seems to be averse to furnishing further details, since he does not proceed further along this subject."[64] So while the text says nothing to even hint that Ham caught his father having (hetero)sex, Cohen speculates:

> [H]e must have been present throughout the act—until Noah fell asleep—
> peering from his hiding place to assimilate thereby his father's strength in his

gloating stare. Possessing part or all of his father's strength, he would become thereby the most powerful of the sons and consequently would stand to inherit the mantle of leadership on Noah's death.[65]

Curious, given this scenario, why the other sons were not the ones to become angry. After all, would not *they* have felt competitive, wished *they* had been the ones to "acquire" Noah's potency? Why, in this scenario, would Noah become enraged? Should he not have been proud that his son wanted to be potent like his Dad? In the 1927 play, *The First One*, it is the scheming of a woman that sets off the oedipal sequence, resulting in the curse. In Genesis it's all about men: about a father and his sons.

Still immersed in his heterosexual fantasy, Cohen tells us that, after all, "it seems reasonable to infer that Ham had to do something more than tell his brothers what he saw."[66] He had to prove it. How? There is only one piece of evidence, Cohen decides, that no one could deny: the clothing that Noah had shed preliminary to intercourse. Cohen notes that Ham indeed produced Noah's garment, narrated in Genesis 9:23:

> Then Shem and Japeth took a garment, laid it upon their shoulders, and walked backward and covered their father's nakedness. . . .

Cohen notes that the key word in the passage seems mistaken, but that is only apparently so. Instead of "a garment" as in "any old garment," we must read the word as denoting "*the* garment." Though on occasion in the Bible the definite article expresses a general definition, Cohen explains, the definite article in this instance designates something specific, in this case a particular item of clothing. "That specific garment could have belonged to no other than Noah," Cohen concludes. Reconstructing the scene, Cohen is sure that "Ham must have skirted the sleeping, naked Noah, picked up his father's garment that had been cast aside, and stepped outside to show '*the* garment' to his brothers."[67] Perhaps the garment Noah shed was his "gender" as a "man"?

Shem and Japheth appear to be acting more out of fear than respect, Cohen notes. He speculates that they probably feared being "infected" by their father's debility. Or, in a queer reading, perhaps they feared being infected by (incestuous) homosexual desire. Despite Cohen's heterosexist interpretation, a queer undertow is unmistakable. Cohen notes that instead of showing respect for Noah, the brothers appear to regard their father "as irreparably weakened." Is that because he is "spent" after phallic heterosexual intercourse? Or is it because, due to rape or castration or being "acquired" by his son in the gaze, he is now "unmanned," now a "woman"? None of this seems to occur to Cohen, who continues his narration that

Shem and Japheth walked backwards, avoided looking at their naked father, "to protect themselves against possible 'infection.' "[68] Cohen suggests that the biblical narrator evidently regarded the threat of possible infection as key to the event, for s/he stressed the fact that Shem and Japheth could not possibly have seen their father's "weakness":

> [T]heir faces were turned the other way, so that they did not see their father's nakedness. (Gen. 9:23)

Perhaps, Cohen speculates, Noah's "weakness" was the reason he failed to beget any more children, despite the "seminal fire" derived from the wine.[69] What weakness? Cohen suggests that his generative power, once appropriated by Ham's voyeuristic gaze, was, then, too diminished for procreation.

And now, as countless Christians imagined it, the genesis of racialized slavery:

> And Noah awoke from his wine, and knew what his youngest son had done unto him. (Gen. 9:24)

There is no indication in the text that Shem and Japheth felt they must inform their father what happened to him, Cohen notes. There was no need to tell him. He already knew.

Cohen feels he has solved the mystery of Noah's nakedness, except for one item. It is one very significant item. "There remains," Cohen acknowledges, "to be explained the reason why Noah vented his wrath upon the innocent Canaan when Ham was the affronting party."[70] He quotes the relevant lines:

> And Noah awoke from his wine, and knew what his youngest son had done unto him. (Gen. 9:24, JPS)

> And he said:

> "Cursed be Canaan: The lowest of slaves shall he be to his brothers." (Gen. 9:25)

Assuming the text is not "disturbed," that is, does not reflect two different interpretative traditions melded into one narrative, Cohen is ready to resolve this mystery too. He offers that, in his view, Noah's curse—relegating Canaan to the lowest of slaves—was not as "unjust" as it might seem, especially when we consider what Noah could not do. Cohen assumes that Ham presumably knew that once he possessed his father's generative power that Noah would not avenge himself against the now potent son, now able (presumably) to pass along this potency to his son Canaan and his progeny. "To thwart Ham's scheme," Cohen speculates, "Noah—if this hypothesis is correct—would have had to curse Ham's son, Canaan, who was not shielded by any such generative power."[71] Even without being "disturbed" by heterosexism, this interpretation seems a stretch.

Cohen is undeterred. "Far from acting out of vengeance," he writes, "Noah seemingly degraded the future generations of Canaan to frustrate Ham's design of transferring his newly acquired special strength and power to Canaan and his progeny." Why wouldn't a grandfather want that? That question is never raised, as Cohen continues intently within the logic of his speculation, noting that Noah's decree had to be pronounced before Ham could transfer the force of Noah's potency to his son, thereby making him invulnerable. With Ham's scheme blocked, he was, in this scenario, no longer able to threaten the position of Shem and Japheth and their progeny (a problem not raised previously). Cohen concludes, simply: "Noah assured the safe succession of leadership."[72]

Cohen's careful if heterosexist interpretation of Genesis 9:24 reproduces tendencies in the Christian imagination toward the patriarchal valorization of genealogy, acquisition, and possession. Sublimation means identification with an aging and drunken patriarch's vicious defense of "manhood"—cover his naked vulnerable body—while desire, even if expressed only by looking, means paternal dispossession of the not-fully sublimated son. Cohen substitutes virility and generativity for Noah's vulnerability and degeneration, declining to discern even the (homo)erotics of "looking," a violation of ancient Israelite fantasies of an invisible God the Father. Here the body in question is not God's but Noah's, the second Adam. It is his paternal body that must not be noticed, looked at (let alone entered). In the cover-up of oedipal indignation, the sensual son is now banished, cursed, his son enslaved and, later, racialized as "black." Cohen is surely right to assert that Noah assured the "succession of leadership," but it is the "leadership" of a gendered and racialized regime we antiracist educators can expose. The white patriarch has no clothes.

WHAT DID HAM DO?

By staring at a complicated passage in Genesis while experiencing human difference in racial terms, readers may have projected some of their most feared transgressions onto Noah's sons, both as a cause or an explanation and as the result of difference.

—Werner Sollors[73]

We shall see how the emergence of an idea of race is inextricably linked to an increasing preference for these profane stories—the legend of Noah, the curse of Ham—as literal explanations for the origins and divisions of man. Above all, it is a system rooted in a theory of emanation complemented by physiognomical thinking.

—Ivan Hannaford[74]

The literalistic conclusion that Africans' skin color was a result of Noah's curse on Canaan appears to have been developed most fully in the modern world, Werner Sollors reports. Originating sometime near the end of the Middle Ages, the belief has been widely held in Europe and North America for the past four hundred years. There have been Jewish, early Christian, as well as Muslim readings of the text. But the modern notion that the curse of Ham pinpoints the origin of peoples of "color" seems to have become popular not because it had occasionally been in evidence since ancient exegetical literature. The curse of Ham became widely known because it became interwoven with debates about the African slave trade, and that new scientific concept—race—that was to become at times a subcategory of, and at other times a synonym for, species (in its new abstract sense). The *Oxford English Dictionary* gives the first English equivalent for Italian *razza,* Spanish and Castilian *raza,* and Portuguese *raça* in the sixteenth century; for example, Foxe 1570: "Thus was the outward race & stocke of Abraham after flesh refused." This definition, Sollors observes, supports the theory that the obscure roots of race may lie in the word "generation." For some time race and generation remained synonyms in English and French.[75]

Unsurprisingly, proslavery advocates ignored the ambiguity of the biblical passage. In 1818, for example, Senator William Smith (South Carolina) invoked the curse of Ham as divine support for a fugitive slave bill. The idea of a divine and hereditary curse was equivalent to "proof" to proslavery advocates that while blacks may be a part of one human race descended from Adam and Noah, they were a cursed part. And that curse meant that they were forever below the realm of the chosen people, a metaphor that was slowly transferred from religious believers such as Jews, Christians, or Muslims to the religiously neutral and racialized term *whites.* Slavery, southern whites argued, was biblically sanctioned. Furthermore, unlike religious beliefs but like the fantasy of aristocratic blue blood, "whiteness" could not be spread by missionary efforts.[76]

Whiteness was an idea that had first evolved, some suggest, in fifteenth- and sixteenth-century Spain. At this time Christianity was, Verena Stolcke argues, "converted into a natural—and hence, hereditary—

attribute," as the Inquisition scrutinized genealogies for possible "stains." Four centuries later James Weldon Johnson's narrator in *The Autobiography of an Ex-Colored Man* comments bitterly: "Have a white skin, and all things else may be added unto you."[77] This line paraphrases Luke 12:31, "But rather seek ye the kingdom of God; and all these things shall be added unto you."

In Dion Boucicault's play *The Octoroon* (1859), Zoe describes herself as marked by "the ineffaceable curse of Cain," repeating the common Christian confusion between Canaan and Cain. Here the curse is evident in Zoe's ineligibility to marry her white suitor and first cousin George Peyton. In her novel *The Octoroon* (serialized in the 1860s), M. E. Braddon writes about the character named Cora: "One drop of the blood of a slave rain in her veins, poisoned her inmost life, and stamped her with the curse of Cain."[78] Slavery was justified as the punishment for Ham's act, as the fulfillment of Noah's curse. Slowly the curse became a genealogical origin that made whites shudder, a curse they must avoid invoking through marriage. The curse of Ham functioned as both a myth of origins and as a racist depiction of difference. Africans had become black due to some transgression in the biblical past; their blackness was consequence and proof of guilt as well as, in itself, permanent punishment.[79]

Such tautologies circulated outside reason or the facts. Sollors quotes James Baldwin's description of feeling enslaved by the story of Ham's curse in "The Fire Next Time."

> I realized that the Bible had been written by white men. I knew that, according to many Christians, I was a descendant of Ham, who had been cursed, and that I was therefore predestined to be a slave. This had nothing to do with anything I was, or contained, or could become; my fate had been sealed forever, from the beginning of time.

Amending Baldwin, Sollors notes, it was not so much the original biblical passage that had "sealed" his fate as it was a certain tradition of misreading it. "[B]ut for what," Sollors asks, "according to the logic of these stories, was it imagined to be a punishment?"[80] What indeed?

This question—what did Ham do?—has stimulated, as we have glimpsed, much exegetical labor over the centuries. The punishment appears, structurally at least, symmetrical: the son looks at his patriarchal origin and the son's descendants are doomed. Structural symmetry, Sollors notes, does not constitute explanation. A son's gaze at his father's nakedness seems a minor transgression to most contemporary readers. However, as Cohen pointed out, it may have constituted a particularly offensive violation of a special taboo.[81] The Ugaritic epic of Daniel and

Aqhat has been cited in this regard because it suggests that the "disgrace of a drunken father was considered by the Canaanites to be a crime of the utmost gravity."[82]

Yet knowledge of this taboo has not resolved the interpretative controversies regarding the specific behavioral content of Ham's "sin." The feeling has remained among general readers and exegetes that there had to be more to Ham's transgression than the biblical passage revealed. During debates on slavery, abolitionists sometimes felt that they had to deemphasize Ham's transgression, whereas proponents tended to elaborate and magnify it. In opposing the curse of Ham, the American anti-slavery writer Stephen Vail argued that Ham had "just opened his eyes and then turned away as any pure-minded man would." Despite their claims to biblical literalism, proslavery advocates took extraordinary interpretative license in their reinterpretations of the biblical text, as we will see.[83]

In these extrapolations upon the biblical text, there are links between filial disobedience and enslavement, between race and homosexual desire. Sexual desire is suggested by Noah's nakedness. This point was important enough to Roland Barthes, Sollors notes, that he regarded this scene as the mythological origin of the striptease. In classical striptease narrative, Barthes wrote in *The Pleasure of the Text*:

> all the excitement is concentrated in the hope of seeing the genitals (the schoolboy's dream) or of knowing the end of the story (the novelistic satisfaction). . . . [I]t is an Oedipal pleasure to denude, to know, to learn the beginning and the end, if it is true that all narrative (all unveiling of the truth) is a staging of the Father (absent, hidden, or suspended)—which would explain the consubstantiality of narrative forms, family structures, and interdictions on nudity, all brought together in our culture in the myth of Noah's nakedness covered by his sons.[84]

Barthes was not the first to try to make sense of the event by going well beyond a literal reading of the text. For instance, in Josephus's *Antiquities of the Jews* (as well as in *Thousand and One Nights* or, even, in *The First One*), is added Ham's laughing at his father's nakedness. The proslavery writer Josiah Priest, however, managed to see Ham "yelling and exploding with laughter at his sleeping father."[85] According to the *Azhar* of Jalalu 'l-Din al-Suyuti (1445–1505), Ham had looked *shamelessly* at his father while the man was bathing. Other interpretations are even less restrained; indeed, Ham has been found guilty of a variety of remarkable crimes that, presumably, account for Noah's curse upon Canaan.[86]

There is one interpretation that is of special interest to me, an interpretation that points—as do lynching and prison rape[87]—to a homoerotic element at the core of racial fantasy. In the *Soncino Chumash,* the following interpretation of Genesis 9:22 is offered: "Some say that [Ham] castrated [Noah]; others say that he indulged a perverted lust upon him."[88] It is this sexual reading to which James Baldwin alluded in his first novel, *Go Tell It on the Mountain.* Baldwin writes: "Yes, he had sinned: one morning, alone, in the dirty bathroom, in the square, dirty-gray cupboard room that was filled with the stink of his father. Sometimes, leaning over the cracked 'tattle-tale gray' bathtub, he scrubbed his father's back; and looked, as the accursed son of Noah had looked, on his father's hideous nakedness."[89]

Rabbinic opinion has also suggested that it was Canaan who committed the act (castration? fellatio? anal penetration?), suggesting even that Canaan may actually have been Noah's fourth and youngest son. Robert Graves and Raphael Patai merge differing versions into their castration tale, according to which Canaan "mischievously looped a stout cord about his grandfather's genitals, drew it tight, and unmanned him," or Ham himself unmanned Noah, or a sick lion dealt Noah's "genitals a blow." Graves and Patai relate the story to the five Greek sons—among them Cronus, who was later unmanned by his son Zeus, and Hyperion, the father of Helios (sun), Selene (moon), and Eos (dawn)—who conspired against their father Uranus. Arthur Frederick Ide elaborates the sodomitical theme suggested in the *Soncino Chumash:* "Noah did nothing to stop sex from taking place inside his tent, with him as the recipient of at least one phallic advance, as he made no protestation about such activity until his other sons became privy to what happened, and attempted to cover up the buggery." Perhaps the son is not to blame at all; perhaps it was the drunken father who encouraged his son's advances. This would appear to be the view of Charles Carroll, who spoke of Noah's "drunken desire."[90]

Concerning the issue of incest, Frederick W. Basset points out that in Genesis 25 Noah refers to Ham's offense as a deed. He invokes Leviticus 18:8: "The nakedness of thy father's wife thou not uncover: it is thy *father's* nakedness." He suggests that for the ancient Israelites "to see the nakedness of someone" means "to have sexual intercourse with someone." Basset suggests that the redactor or a later editor may have missed the idiomatic meaning and "added the reference to the brothers' covering their father's nakedness with a garment."[91] The passage would also seem to acknowledge that under compulsory heterosexuality the wife is the father's property; to see her naked is to see him naked; to engage her sexually is to sexually assault her husband. The black man's desire for the white woman has embedded within it, Michele Wallace has suggested, an obsession with the white man.[92]

The three—homosexual desire, incest, and race—conflate. Consider the following reconstruction of the original scene, in which what happened inside Noah's tent results in black skin, kinky hair, and a large penis:

> The more important version of the myth, however, ingeniously ties in the origins of blackness—and of other, real or imagined Negroid traits—with Noah's curse itself. According to it, Ham is told by his outraged father that, because you have abused me in the darkness of the night, your children shall be born black and ugly; because you have twisted your head to cause me embarrassment, they shall have kinky hair and red eyes; because your lips jested at my exposure, theirs shall swell; and because you have neglected my nakedness, they shall go naked with their shamefully elongated male members exposed for all to see.[93]

Whether the emasculation occurred sexually (via anal intercourse) or symbolically (via looking), the father was evidently "unmanned" by his son. Regardless which sin Ham committed, Noah rose to the oedipal challenge and, in Genesis 9:24, avenged his unmanning, his feminization. The father's "stud" son—the sexualized son who declined identification and sublimation—is disowned, enslaved, and, later, racialized as black. Those sons who accepted identification and sublimation remained, in the Christian imagination, white. This fundamental fantasy will take many forms, but the racialized and religious binary around which it is structured is: sex or sublimation. Sex is racialized, projected onto the disavowed now black son, cursed to perpetual enslavement, a hostage to his body: in the present, an overdetermined embodiment.

Sex and race were, certainly, conflated in the minds of slavery's supporters. In 1860, for instance, the President of Dartmouth and slavery supporter Nathan Lord expressed his belief in Ham's "forbidden intermarriage with the previously wicked and accursed race of Cain." In April 1860, not long before he would become President of the Confederacy, Jefferson Davis argued in a speech to the United States Senate: "[W]hen the low and vulgar son of Noah, who laughed at his father's exposure, sunk by debasing himself and his lineage by a connection with an inferior race of men, he doomed his descendants to perpetual slavery. Noah spoke the decree, or prophecy, as gentlemen may choose to consider it, one or the other." Davis substituted an inferior race for the generation of Canaan, conflating racial and sexual fantasy.[94]

Anchoring the defense of slavery in scripture, Thornton Stringfellow mixed race, sex, and sin. He argued that a "beastly wickedness" made

Ham's character "a true type of the character of his descendants." This notion—type and character of descendants—may still have been somewhat metaphoric in the antebellum period. By the late nineteenth century, however, the concept of race had moved from biblical generation toward biological species, in the modern sense, and other races could therefore be viewed in extra-species terms. Charles Carroll's *The Negro a Beast* (1900) for example, intended its title literally. Applying this idea to a racially paranoid reading of the Bible, Carroll maintained that at the time of the Flood, Noah and his wife were the only pure whites left on the earth; but there was a pair of Negroes among the beasts on the Ark, and amalgamation resumed after the Flood. Christ was then sent to "redeem man from atheism, amalgamation, and idolatry" and to "rebuild the barrier which God erected in the Creation between man and the ape." Miscegenation here becomes identified with extra-species relationship. Canaan was not only compared with the raven on the ark; in the *Sachsenspiegel* (ca. 1200) he was also presumed to have been the offspring of Ham's copulation with the raven—making his blackness both a proof of and punishment for his father's bestiality.[95]

Bestiality is thus added to incest and miscegenation on Ham's lengthening criminal record, although in some readings he resorted to bestiality after being cursed. Are these rigorous readings or revealing expressions of fantasy? Sollors suggests, carefully: "By staring at a complicated passage in Genesis while experiencing human difference in racial terms, readers may have projected some of their most feared transgressions onto Noah's sons, both as a cause or an explanation and as the result of difference."[96] What is clear from these projections is that sexual—specifically homosexual and incestuous—transgression is embedded in Christian conceptions of racial difference in the West.

Genesis 9:24 provides the founding moment, the imprinting episode, and the basic conceptual structure of this study of race in the Christian mind. What can it mean to us that the founding moment of race may have been one of an incestuous assault upon the father by the son? Or were Ham's advances seductive or even loving? Or did the father invite the son into the tent? Why did Noah respond so viciously? Even if Ham's crime is only looking, the dynamics remain libidinally similar: the father's nakedness, his vulnerability, including his gendered vulnerability (or lack, or castration), become visible to the son. Whether the father is raped or made love to, castrated or simply looked at, the effects conflate: the unmanning of the father is denied by a curse upon the son whose son is enslaved and, later, racialized.

The wound of the forsaken son becomes ritualistically inscribed on the penis in religious ceremony and, later, in medical practice—circumcision.

The sensual naked drunken father is converted into an abstract, other-worldly God-the-Father, whose disembodied presence we presumably experience in prayer and in the afterlife, a Father who is angry or forgiving, but who claims the capacity to curse. For many Christians, the partitions between the abstract and the concrete, the word and the flesh, the holy father and the abject son sometimes leak, as evidenced in those Renaissance religious paintings of the son (Jesus) with an erect penis. Ah, the return of the repressed, wherein the son shall rise again, most especially—and here, I think, is my symmetrical moment (as I imagined prison rape to be the symmetrical opposite of lynching in *The Gender of Racial Politics and Violence in America*)—at the end of the nineteenth century in the West. It is not the historical crisis of masculinity in the United States I will narrate here,[97] but the one in Europe, personified most spectacularly, perhaps, in the case of Daniel Paul Schreber, unmanned lover of God.[98]

Schreber was the (infamous) German judge whose breakdown provided Freud with his original theorization of paranoia as an effect of repressed homosexual desire, a theorization no longer taken seriously by most practicing psychoanalysts, but one I could not resist employing in volume one to suggest a sexual undertow to the hysteria of many white men over the (imagined) threat of (black male) rape in the nineteenth-century American South. Like Noah, Schreber has direct contact with God-the-Father, contact which he finds, against his will, stimulating, sexually stimulating, and which turns him, for brief periods, into a woman. Like Ham, like Jesus, this son too was cursed by a wanton God-the-Father, who took what he wanted and left his sons wounded, enraged, enslaved: "My God, My God, why have you forsaken Me?" (Matt. 27:46).

Forgiveness is, as we say, a necessary but not sufficient condition. A gendered anti-racist education must attack hegemonic white masculinity, as it is the horrific legacy of that mythic drunken night inside Noah's tent. After Kaja Silverman[99] I specify three elements of that masculinity: alterity, specularity, and the denial of lack expressed in a curse. Whether Ham's transgression was sexually penetrating his father or merely looking at the naked body of the father, in both instances he saw his lack, an embodied state of castration, then denied in the curse. Lack denied displaces alterity from within, from the self-same body, projects it onto an Other imagined as different due to anatomical difference, sexual and racial. Our work as antiracist educators is nothing less than to dispel the curse. We cannot perform this pedagogical labor in rational terms only. As Deborah Britzman[100] has made compellingly clear, we must work with the psyche. We—the wounded, circumcised ones—must return to Noah's tent and meet our maker. If we are once again our father's lover, might we sons then become our brother's keeper and our sister's friend?

Unlike Robert Musil, I am not recommending incest as utopian. Musil's fantasy, in *The Man Without Qualities,* was heterosexual incest between brother and sister.[101] For me, Noah's tent is a metaphoric formulation of the hegemonic white male self. To reenter it is to work autobiographically, to regress toward a reexperiencing of the negative oedipal complex, and a subsequent restructuring of internal object relations in which binaries are mixed and merged in the self-same (now also the opposite sexed) body. The inner topography of a Ham not forsaken by his father will have to wait for volume III of my work. For this chapter, one point is clear: To become "race traitors," we white men must become gender traitors. We must reexperience our relation to the internalized father not as disavowed, competitive, and contentious (i.e., as cursed, but as symbiotic and incestuous, that is, homosexual not homosocial). In such a restructuring of the inner topography of hegemonic white masculinity, perhaps the curse of race can be lifted. That would amount to an Emancipation Proclamation for us all.

Acknowledgment: I wish to thank Alan Block for his critical reading and suggestions.

NOTES

1. Vron Ware, 1992, *Beyond the Pale: White Women, Racism and History* (London: Verso), 253.
2. Jonathan Katz, "The Age of Sodomitical Sin, 1607–1740," in *Reclaiming Sodom,* ed. Jonathan Goldberg (New York: Routledge), 43–58, here 49.
3. William F. Pinar, 1991, "Curriculum as Social Psychoanalysis: On the Significance of Place," in *Curriculum as Social Psychoanalysis: Essays on the Significance of Place,* ed. Joe L. Kincheloe and William F. Pinar (Albany: State University of New York Press), 167–186.
4. For an introduction to curriculum as racial text, see William F. Pinar, William M. Reynolds, Patrick Slattery, and Peter Taubman, 1995, *Understanding Curriculum* (New York: Peter Lang), chapter 6; Louis A. Castenell Jr. and William F. Pinar, eds., 1993, *Understanding Curriculum as Racial Text: Representations of Identity and Difference in Education* (Albany: State University of New York Press), and Cameron McCarthy and Warren Crichlow, eds., 1993, *Race, Identity, and Representation in Education* (New York: Routledge). For the notion of "autobiographics," see Leigh Gilmore, 1994, *Autobiographics: A Feminist Theory of Women's Self-Representation* (Ithaca, N.Y.: Cornell University Press). To appreciate the inevitability of practice, see Alan Block, 1997, *I'm Only Bleeding: Education as the Practice of Violence against Children* (New York: Peter Lang).
5. Madeleine R. Grumet, 1990, *Bitter Milk: Women and Teaching* (Amherst: University of Massachusetts Press), and Jo Anne Pagano, 1990, *Exiles and Communities: Teaching in the Patriarchal Wilderness* (Albany: State University of New York Press).
6. Gaile Sloan Cannella, 1997, *Deconstructing Early Childhood Education: Social Justice & Revolution* (New York: Peter Lang); Bernadette M. Baker, 2000, In *Perpetual Motion: Theories of Power, Educational History, and the Child* (New York: Peter Lang); Susan Grieshaber and Gaile Cannella, eds., 2001, *Embracing Identities in Early Childhood Education: Diversity and Possibilities* (New York: Teachers College Press).
7. James Sears, ed., 1995, *Sexuality and the Curriculum* (New York: Teachers College Press); Jonathan G. Silin, 1995, *Sex, Death and the Education of Children: Our Passion for Ignorance in the Age of AIDS* (New York: Teachers College Press); Deborah P. Britzman, 1998, *Lost Subjects, Contested Objects: Toward a Psychoanalytic Inquiry of Learning* (Albany: State University of New York Press).

8. Kaja Silverman, 1992, *Male Subjectivity at the Margins* (New York: Routledge).

9. William F. Pinar, 2001, *The Gender of Racial Politics and Violence in America: Lynching, Prison Rape, and the Crisis of Masculinity* (New York: Peter Lang).

10. Pinar 2001, 21–22.

11. Phil Cohen, 1997, "Laboring under Whiteness," in *Displacing Whiteness: Essays in Social and Cultural Criticism,* ed. Ruth Frankenberg (Durham, N.C.: Duke University Press), 242–282, here 245.

12. Philip Wexler, 1996, *Holy Sparks: Social Theory, Education and Religion* (New York: St. Martin's Press). In addition to Wexler's provocative employment of Jewish mysticism in his recent work, other scholars have also emphasized the significance of Jewish subjects for contemporary curriculum studies. See, for instance, Alan Block, 1998, "And He Pretended to be a Stranger to Them," in *The Passionate Mind of Maxine Greene,* ed. William F. Pinar (London: Falmer), 14–29, and Marla Morris, 2001, *Holocaust and Curriculum* (Mahwah, N.J.: Lawrence Erlbaum).

13. See Stephen O. Murray, 1996, *American Gay* (Chicago: University of Chicago Press).

14. Saidiya V. Hartman, 1997, *Scenes of Subjection: Terror, Slavery, and Self-Making in Nineteenth Century America* (New York: Oxford University Press).

15. John C. Hawley, ed., 1996, *Cross-Addressing: Resistance Literature and Cultural Borders* (Albany: State University of New York Press).

16. Ann duCille, 1996, "The Occult of True Black Womanhood: Critical Demeanor and Black Feminist Studies," in *The Second Signs Reader,* ed. Ruth-Ellen B. Joeres and Barbara Laslett (Chicago: University of Chicago Press), 70–108, here 103.

17. Gayatri Chakravorty Spivak, 1989, "in Praise of *Sammy and Rosie Get Laid." Critical Quarterly* 31(2): 80–88, here quoted in duCille 1996, 76.

18. Melville Herkskovits, 1985 [1928], *The American Negro: A Study in Racial Crossing* (Westport, Ct: Greenwood); 1938, *Dahomey* (New York: Augustin); *The Myth of the Negro Past* (Boston: Beacon); Melville Herkskovits and Frances Herskovits. 1936 *Suriname Folklore.* New York: Columbia University Press.

19. Darlene Clark Hine, 1980, "The Four Black History Movements: A Case for the Teaching of Black History." *Teaching History: A Journal of Methods* 5 (Fall): 115, quoted in duCille 1996, 77.

20. Harriet Jacobs, 1987 [1861], *Incidents in the Life of a Slave Girl, Written by Herself,* ed. Jean Fagan Yellin (Cambridge: Harvard University Press), quoted in duCille 1996, 77.

21. Toni Cade Bambara, 1970, *The Black Woman* (New York: New American Library); Gloria Wade-Gayles, *No Crystal Stair: Visions of Race and Sex in Black Women's Fiction* (New York: Pilgrim Press), 41–42, here quoted in duCille 1996, 77; Jeanne Noble, 1978, *Beautiful, Also, Are the Souls of My Black Sisters* (Englewood Cliffs, N.J.: Prentice-Hall), cited in duCille 1996, 77.

22. For studies of Horace Mann Bond see Wayne J. Urban, 1989, "The Graduate Education of a Black Scholar: Horace Mann Bond and the University of Chicago," in *Curriculum History,* ed. Craig Kridel (Lanham, Md: University Press of America), 72–88; and Wayne J. Urban, 1992, *Black Scholar: Horace Mann Bond, 1904–1972* (Athens: University of Georgia Press); James A. Banks, 1969, A "Content Analysis of American Blacks in Textbooks," *Social Education* 33: 954–57, 963; James A. Banks, 1981, *Multiethnic Education: Theory and Practice* (Boston: Allyn & Bacon); Louis A. Castenell Jr., 1991, "The New South as Curriculum," in *Understanding Curriculum as Social Psychoanalysis,* ed. Joe Kincheloe and William Pinar (Albany: State University of New York Press), 155–66; Patricia Hill Collins. 1993, "It's In Our Hands: Breaking the Silence on Gender in African American Studies," in *Understanding Curriculum as Racial Text,* ed. Louis A. Castenell Jr. and William F. Pinar (Albany: State University of New York Press), 237–241; Beverly Gordon, 1985, "Toward Emancipation in Citizenship Education," *Theory and Research in Social Education* 12(4): 1–23 [reprinted in 1993], *Understanding Curriculum as Racial Text,* ed. Louis A. Castenell Jr. and William F. Pinar (Albany: State University of New York Press) 263–84; Cameron McCarthy, 1990, *Race and Curriculum* (London: Falmer); Cameron McCarthy, and Warren Crichlow, eds., 1993, *Race and Identity in Education* (New York: 1993); William Watkins, 1993, "Black Curriculum Orientations." *Harvard Educational Review,* 63(3): 321–38.

23. Gerda Lerner, 1972, *Black Women in White America: A Documentary History* (New York: Random House), xx, quoted in duCille 1996, 78.
24. duCille 1996, 78.
25. William Wells Brown, 1989 [1853], *Clotel; or, The President's Daughter: A Narrative of Slave Life in the United States* (New York: Carol Publishing); N. F. Mossell, 1988 [1894], *The Work of the Afro-American Woman* (New York: Oxford University Press); both cited in duCille 1996, 78.
26. Anna Julia Cooper, 1988 [1892], *A Voice from the South* (Xenia, Ohio: Aldine); quoted in duCille 1996, 78.
27. Charles Nichols, 1963, *Many Thousand Gone: The Ex-Slaves' Account of Their Bondage and Freedom* (Bloomington: Indiana University Press), quoted in duCille 1996, 78.
28. James Weldon Johnson, 1960 [1912], *The Autobiography of an Ex-Coloured Man* (New York: Hill and Wang); James Weldon Johnson, 1933, *Along This Way* (New York: Viking); David Levering Lewis, 1984, "Parallels and Divergences: Assimilationist Strategies of Afro-American and Jewish Elites from 1910 to the Early 1930s." *Journal of American History* 71 (December), 543–64; quoted in duCille 1996, 79.
29. duCille 1996, 79.
30. duCille 1996, 80.
31. I refer here not only to the nonunitary and inherently unstable status of the "subject" as indicated, for instance, in the well-known post-structuralist notion of "death of the author," but to the speaking ego's necessarily self-contradictory structure indicated by various traditions of psychoanalytic theory.
32. Walter White, 1929, *Rope and Faggot: A Biography of Judge Lynch* (New York: Alfred A. Knopf), 33, quoted in Pinar 2001, 156.
33. From Silverman 1992, 33.
34. Werner Sollors, 1997, *Neither Black nor White yet Both: Thematic Explorations of Interracial Literature* (New York: Oxford University Press), 79.
35. Quoted passages in Sollors 1997, 79.
36. Quoted passages in Sollors 1997, 79.
37. Quoted passages in Sollors 1997, 80.
38. Paraphrased from Sollors 1997, who translates the phrase "slaves of slaves." Alan Block (personal communication) writes that "In my translation, the phrase is "slave of slaves to his brothers. That links him genetically (and therefore racially) to Shem and Japeth."
39. R. H. Mottram, 1937, *Noah* (London: Rich & Cowan, Ltd., 1937), 2–3, paraphrased from H. Hirsch Cohen, 1974, *The Drunkenness of Noah* (University, Ala.: University of Alabama Press).
40. Mottram 1937, 188.
41. Mottram 1937, 191.
42. Mottram 1937, 192.
43. Paraphrased from Cohen 1974.
44. Paraphrased from Cohen 1974.
45. Cohen 1974, 1.
46. Cohen 1974, 8.
47. Cohen 1974, 8.
48. Cohen 1974, 9. In linking homosexual desire with the curse of God in the Sodom and Gomorrah tale, I underline that it is "lay readers" who have made this link. As Alan Block points out, there is a considerable body of commentary that suggests that the sins of Sodom and Gomorrah had more to do with slander than with sexual promiscuity, let alone homosexual desire.
49. Cohen 1974, 13.
50. Cohen 1974, 13; Robert Graves, and Raphael Patai, 1964, *Hebrew Myths: The Book of Genesis* (Garden City, N.Y.: Doubleday), 121, quoted in Cohen 1974, 13.
51. L. Ginzberg, 1909, *The Legends of the Jews* (Philadelphia: The Jewish Publication Society of America), 1:165, quoted in Cohen 1974, 13.
52. Cohen 1974, 14.
53. Cohen 1974, 14.
54. Cohen 1974, 15.

55. Cohen 1974, 15. See Lisa Disch, and Mary Jo Kane, 1996, "When a Looker Is Really a Bitch?: Lisa Olson, Sport, and the Heterosexual Matrix," in *The Second Signs Reader,* ed. Ruth-Ellen B. Joeres and Barbara Laslett. Chicago: University of Chicago Press, 326–356.

56. O. Fenichel, 1953, "The Scoptophilic Instinct and Identification," in *The Collected Papers of Otto Fenichel* (New York: Norton), 391, quoted in Cohen 1974, 15.

57. Cohen 1974, 15.

58. Judith Butler, 1997, *The Psychic Life of Power: Theories in Subjection* (Stanford, Calif.: Stanford University Press).

59. Cohen 1974, 15.

60. Cohen 1974, 16.

61. Joel Williamson, 1984, *The Crucible of Race: Black-White Relations in the American South since Emancipation* (New York: Oxford University Press).

62. Butler 1997.

63. Cohen 1974, 16.

64. Cohen 1974, 17.

65. Cohen 1974, 18.

66. Cohen 1974, 18.

67. Cohen 1974, 19.

68. Cohen 1974, 21.

69. Cohen 1974, 21.

70. Cohen 1974, 29.

71. Cohen 1974, 29.

72. Cohen 1974, 30.

73. Sollors 1997, 102.

74. Ivan Hannaford, 1996, *Race: The History of an Idea in the West* (Baltimore, Md.: Johns Hopkins University Press), 133–34.

75. Quoted in Sollors 1997, 92, paragraph paraphrased from Sollors 1997.

76. Quoted in Sollors 1997, 92, paragraph paraphrased from Sollors 1997.

77. Verona Stolcke, 1994, "Invaded Women: Gender, Race, and Class in the Formation of Colonial Society," in *Women, "Race," and Writing in the Early Modern Period,* ed. Margo Hendricks and Patricia Parker (New York: Routledge), 272–86; here 277–78, quoted in Sollors 1997, 95; Johnson 1960 [1912], 155, quoted in Sollors 1997, 95.

78. Dion Boucicault, 1970 [1859], *The Octoroon* (Upper Saddle River, N.J.: Literature House); M. E. Braddon, N.d. *The Octoroon* (New York: Optima Printing).

79. Paraphrased from Sollors 1997.

80. James Baldwin, 1985 [1963]. "The Fire Next Time," in *The Price of the Ticket* (New York: St. Martin's Press), 333–79, here 347, quoted in Sollors 1997, 96; Sollors 1997, 96, 80.

81. Howard Eilberg-Schwartz, 1994, *God's Phallus. And Other Problems for Men and Monotheism* (Boston: Beacon Press).

82. Quoted in Sollors 1997, 96.

83. Paraphrased from Sollors 1997.

84. Roland Barthes, 1973, *Le Plaisir du Texte* (Paris: Editions du Seuil), published in 1975 as *The Pleasure of the Text,* trans. Richard Miller (New York: Hill and Wang), 20, quoted in Sollors 1997, 78.

85. Quoted in Sollors 1997, 96.

86. Paraphrased from Sollors 1997.

87. See Pinar 2001, especially chapters 1–3, and 16–17.

88. Cohen 1974, 47; see also Graves and Patai 1964, 120–124.

89. James Baldwin, 1985 [1953], *Go Tell It on the Mountain* (New York: Dell-Laurel), 197.

90. Graves and Patai 1964, 121; Arthur Frederick Ide, 1992, *Noah and the Ark* (Las Colinas, Tex.: Monument Press), 49; quoted in Sollors 1997, 98; in Sollors 1997, 110.

91. Quoted passages in Sollors 1997, 100.

92. Michele Wallace, 1978, *Black Macho and the Myth of the Superwoman* (New York: The Dial Press).

93. Harold D. Brackman, 1977, *The Ebb and Flow of Conflict: A History of Black-Jewish Relations through 1900,* Unpub. Ph.D. dissertation (Los Angeles: UCLA), 80–81, quoted in Tony

Martin, 1993, *The Jewish Onslaught* (Dover, Mass.: Majority Press), 34–35; in Sollors 1997, 445 n47.

94. Quoted passages in Sollors 1997, 101.
95. Charles Carroll, 1900, *The Negro a Beast* (St. Louis: American Book and Bible House); quoted passages in Sollors 1997, 101–102; paragraph paraphrased from Sollors 1997.
96. Sollors 1997, 102.
97. See Pinar 2001, especially chapter 6.
98. For documentation of sexuality in Renaissance paintings of Jesus, see Lee Steinberg, 1996 [1983], *The Sexuality of Christ in Renaissance Art and in Modern Oblivion.* 2nd ed. (Chicago: University of Chicago Press 1996 [1983]).; for portraits of the European crisis of masculinity see Gerald N. Izenberg, 2000, *Modernism and Masculinity: Mann, Wedekind, Kandinsky through World War I* (Chicago: University of Chicago Press); Daniel Paul Schreber, 2000 [1903], *Memoirs of My Nervous Illness,* (New York: New York Review of Books).
99. Silverman 1992.
100. Britzman 1998.
101. Robert Musil, 1995, *The Man without Qualities.* Trans. by Sophie Perkins and Burton Pike (New York: Knopf). For an insightful discussion of the utopian function of the incestuous relationship between Ulrich and Agathe, see Stefan, Jonsson, 2000, *Subject without Nation: Robert Musil and the History of Modern Identity* (Durham: Duke University Press).

8

Queer Pedagogies:
Camping Up the Difference

MARLA MORRIS

> *Curriculum as symbolic representation refers to those institutional and discursive practices, structures, images, and experiences that can be identified and analysed in various ways, i.e. politically, racially, autobiographically, phenomenologically, theologically. . . . We can say that the effort to understand curriculum as symbolic representation defines . . . the contemporary field.*
>
> —Pinar (1995, 16)

Drawing on Pinar (1995), I suggest that thinking differently about our pedagogies begins by thinking more symbolically and metaphorically about what it means to be pedagogically Other. Autobiographical text, which is a form of symbolic representation, allows me to rethink who I am against the backdrop of my (em)placement in the South as a queer teacher. Thus, this is a story about my struggle to understand who "I" am and how I might rethink what it means to talk about pedagogical practices as the site of difference.

The (un)self, in these poststructural, (post)-whatever times, webs within and between the complexities of story retelling, wandering, wondering. Teaching in the rural South, my sense of (un)self only grows more uncertain. As a queer Jewish Carpetbagger, I feel more and more schizophrenic and monstrous. I am Jewish, queer, and a Northerner through and through. To my students, I must seem alien. The notion of my (un)self has become monstrous. My (un)self is situated against the backdrop of my student (body), my classroom filled with bodies. Who are my students? Rural Southerners. Many of them have confided in me that they are conservative, and many admit that they dream of erasing the pedagogical experience of the face-to-face, they dream of online courses, wishing our presences absent. They wish that they did not have to face me, perhaps they do not want to look at me, or face what they see, or face what they see within themselves. Ah, the d-generation: Digital.com.

These presences, my students, embodied and troubled, haunted by a Southern past, wish that I (queer-Jewish-carpetbagger) would teach methods, recipies, and offer online, digital assignments. Their phantasies of erasing differences, erasing difficulties of the face-to-face, erasing bodies dis(turbs) my pedagogical sensibilities. Bodies matter. Their wish to disappear into cyberspace con-fuses. The Luddite within says, no. The face-to-face of embodiment becomes key to queering up and camping up our pedagogies. Do our pedagogies address body-to-body engendered, fleshy sexual sites of difference within the classroom, or ignore, tune out, channel surf, and avoid what is right there in front of the drama of education lived out in real time, with real life stories begging to differ, in-difference within-the-difference making-a-difference. Or do we turn back, turn our backs, turn toward becoming, as David Smith (2000) says, a "Neo-Gnostic culture" of no-body? Is our (post)un(destiny) to become once again (dis)embodied through virtual this and virtual that, or to become more enfleshed, fleshy. Whoever the (un)self is, she is somebody or wants to become somebody, some-body, who is not only engendered but sexual.

Can our pedagogies handle this fleshy creature, the monstrousness of embodiment? Queer pedagogies camp up the difference. Queer pedagogies perform the difference. Queer pedagogies trope up the difference through different forms of symbolic representation. In this chapter I camp up pedagogical difference by troping up queer-camp-neo-gothic-vampires.

BECOMING QUEER IN A (POST) HISTORICAL HER-STORY

Gayatri Chakravorty Spivak remarks that "The story of one's life, is to 'recognize' oneself as also an instantiation of historical and psychosexual narratives that one piece together, however fragmentary" (1993, 6). History is written by men—for men. The narratives of history, the stories of homosexual, homophile, gay, and queer men are more visible, more well respected and told more often than the her-stories of lesbian/queer women. From Foucault (1990) to John Boswell (1980, 1994) queer male histories are more well known, well respected, cited more often. Gay men are more well known, period. Gay writers, musicians, artists, and politicians come to mind immediately: Oscar Wilde, Truman Capote, Aaron Copland, Lytton Strachey, Harvey Milk.

From Christine Downing (1989) to Lillian Faderman (1999), lesbian/queer her-stories get erased and become subjugated knowledges. Queer women writers and artists are less well known. Lillian Hellman, Gertrude

Stein and who else comes to mind? Even when women seem queer or appear to be queer, even if they are not, their legitimacy is questioned. Randall (in Piggford 1999) points out that when Annie Lennox's gender/sexuality was questioned by MTV officials in the 1980s, she had to "prove" that she was a "woman" and not a transvestite in order to allow her to perform on TV. But David Bowie, whose appearance is just as slippery as Lennox's, never had to prove that he was actually a "man" to be able to perform on MTV. Women have always been second class citizens, but queer women and women of color have been (in)visibilized.

When we trace briefly the history of homosexuality, John Boswell (1980) suggests that the term itself was virtually unknown in the pre-modern world. Boswell tells us that in the pre-modern world the word "homosexual" did not exist. Historians agree that this term arrived on the scene in the nineteenth century. Naming queers homosexual had of course negative consequences, as is well known, since the pathologizing, criminalizing, confessionalizing led queers to insane asylums and prisons (Foucault 1990). Even before the shock "therapies" of the twentieth century, more shocking are ancient punishments. Boswell reports that,

> In France [around 1252–1284], the legal school of Orleans issued a code containing a synthesis of both Spanish laws, requiring first offense [of sodomy] by a male castration, for the second, dismemberment; for the third, burning. This provision, unlike almost all other legal approaches of the 13th century, specifically mentions female homosexuality as well, stipulating dismemberment for the first two offenses and burning for the third. (1980: 289–90)

Witchcraft hunters haunt lesbian/queer his/herstories. One of the complaints of the clergy and other so-called educated persons was that homosexuals (or whatever term was used to signify difference) simply were not "natural." Boswell points out the slipperiness of this signifier "natural": "Historical ethical systems based on 'nature' opposed shaving, growing flowers indoors, dyeing garments, regular bathing" (1980: 15). What is considered "natural" changes over time. This term is highly changeable and contingent.

Boswell (1994) admits that when writing history it becomes difficult to include women because during "antiquity or during the Middle Ages," lesbian/queer women are virtually absent from the annals of historiography. Boswell has been criticized for not digging deeply enough (Downing 1989). Women have always already been absented from historiography. But there is another place to turn.

Mary Aswell Doll (2000), in a groundbreaking study on the mythopo-etics of curriculum, argues that it is to the myths we must turn to under-stand the complexities of women's inter-relations and her-stories. Sappho remains our goddess. Demeter and Persephone our teachers. Lilith? Do we turn to Myth to tell and retell our stories? Some might say yes. Do we mythologize herstory? Or is history and herstory always already mythologized?

Part of the mythologizing begins with living underground, living in an underworld, a netherworld of secrets, lies. Being hated, targeted, scape-goated, othered requires that one live an underground life. The bars are the underground world for queers. The bar culture represents the meeting place, the place where one can feel a bit of relief from heteronormativity. Secret lives played out in bars have protected many from persecution, criminalization, and even murder. But it is well known that bars are also the site of raids and police brutality. Thus, many remain totally invisible, remaining completely underground, remaining hidden. Thus, doing his-torical work around queer life becomes difficult because so many people are scared to come out. Queer historiography is largely a question, then, of allowing for lacks and empty spaces in the historical record. Karen Quimbly and Walter Williams (2000) point out that,

> The very act of historicizing or claiming gay existence presents the unique problem of a subject always already obscured through the demands of the closet. In gay historical inquiry, therefore, there can be no myth of an authen-tic or completely knowable subject that has, in the past, informed much mainstream historical investigation. (181)

Queering up sites of historiography require mythologizing tendencies, though. Imagining(s) of lack and (in)visibility become key. Tropes of dif-ference can be found through our myths, folklore, and storytelling. The trajectory from Lilith and Sappho to the trope of the vampire are part of this mythological herstory, as we will see later on in this chapter.

My own recalling and rememory, my own historical memory of grow-ing up queer is a bit fuzzy. I remember (in-vagueness), the Harvey Milk murder. But Milk's murder was overshadowed by the People's Temple and Jim Jones. Because I came out in the 1980s I missed the entire Gay Liber-ation Movement of the 1970s. I was still watching *Rocky and Bullwinkle* and *The Brady Bunch* in the 1970s. I read about (what seems to be ancient history) the Stonewall riots and have heard the older ones in the lesbian community shout (at the younger generation) that we don't know how good we have it because the elders fought on the front lines. I know all about the butch-femme rule of the 1950s crowd. I know the younger ones call themselves lipstick lesbians, much to the horror of the stone butches. I know the politics of the bar scene. I have lived through the arguments over separatism, inclusion, and mixed bar life. I know how tough it is to be a queer youth in an urban public high school. As Jim Sears (1991) points out,

> Stymied by fear and shame, these teens' psychological growth and development languishes. In lunchrooms, adolescent gossip and crude comic stereotypes violate their human dignity. In classrooms, the exceptional teacher expresses concern about their hurt and hardship. With not-so-hidden expectations, the school institutionalizes heterosexism while homophobia exerts a heavy psychological price. (16)

So repressed was I, that I didn't dare come out. I didn't dare breathe a word of anything to anybody. I couldn't even articulate what was "wrong" with me, or what I thought was wrong with me. Images of black and white films kept popping up in my mind's eye about the wicked witch of the west. That's who I was!! At least that is who I identified with at the time. I pushed down my feelings so much that when I did finally come out, I became emotionally paralyzed for two days. I sat and stared against a wall, motionless. I never did acknowledge my sexuality in high school, it was just too dangerous. But I remember the day I came out; it was my first year of college. I sat on the floor in a dorm at Carnegie-Mellon for two days, paranoid, emotionally paralyzed, scared, confused. Like Ezekiel I remained speechless. Twenty-some years ago, I decided that I could live a lie no longer.

The queer youth of my generation, though, is radically different from the queers of the 1950s. I experienced much of this tension especially when I moved to New Orleans. I had trouble finding kindred spirits because there seemed to be such divisiveness between the young and old. Elisabeth Young-Bruehl points out that "Historians and anthropologists have also begun recently to notice that lesbianism . . . varies enormously within cultural contexts. This notice has been slow in coming because in many cultures . . . lesbianism is much less apparent, more hidden, silent, than male homosexuality" (1996, 146). Even within the bar scene in New Orleans, I noted the generational divide. I never felt welcomed. I never did break into that lesbian world in New Orleans. The gay community in New Orleans is extremely separatist. There are not many bars that are mixed. I remained isolated for many years in my French Quarter apartment reading vampire novels and studying esoteric texts.

Much to my surprise, queer life in Savannah is mixed: young and old, African American and white, Hispanic, Latino, Latina, queer, gay, lesbian, transgendered, transsexual—all hang out together. Club One is the only game in town and so it perhaps forces this intermixing and more inclusive atmosphere, which I would prefer over the separatist culture of New Orleans. But there is more to queer life than the club scene. There is also academic work to be done.

As a relative newcomer to academe, I have joined the ranks of queer theorists in the academy and have joined my local chapter of GLSEN. I have experienced the demise of identity-politics. I have heard many say that the Gay Liberation movement was a failure; assimilationism is disastrous. AIDS turned the tide away from assimilationism to an angry down right campy in-your-face, we aren't taking it any longer mentality. As Sue-Ellen Case (2000) tells us we can no longer afford to be "good girls" fighting for civil rights. Instead, the queer movement demands "taking back the insult—inhabiting the 'bad girl'—playing the monster" (25).

This queer monster has visited the Stonewall Bar in New York City. I have walked the streets of Chelsea. I have walked the Castro. And as the bad girl, I must confess that I have witnessed gay male misogyny both on the streets and in the halls of academe. I have witnessed gay males in the academy act hatefully and stupidly toward women. I have witnessed terrible acts of sexism by queer men. But gay/queer male mysogyny is nothing new. Yolanda Retter (2000) declares that,

> Within weeks of the Stonewall Riots, the New York City Gay Liberation Front (GLF) had organized, and within six months the Southern California GLF was founded at the first "in your face" gay/lesbian political action group in Los Angeles. However, by the summer of 1970, co-gender groups had divided over the issue of sexism. Daughters of Bilitis (DOB) leader and homophile veteran Del Martin wrote a scathing letter to gay men arguing that their culture was as oppressive to lesbians as heterosexual culture was to homosexuals . . . (2000: 198–99)

There are divisions among men and women within queer culture, and now there are more distinctions and divisions articulated among the various sexualities. Those who call themselves Gay, lesbian, transgendered, transsexual, intersexual, queer, agree on little.

NON (IDENTITY): QUEERING UP THE (UN)SELF

Queer theory arrived on the scene during the early 1990s, a movement frustrated with the do-nothing attitudes of politicians while the AIDS crisis raged and still rages. Tired of peaceful demonstrations during the 1970s, activists tried new tactics in the 1990s. Angry, in-your-face queers act up and act out. Blurring the line between activism and scholarship, queer theory seeks to do its work to undo oppressive, heteronormative surveillance. The older generation of gay men and lesbian women, however, may not be happy with the next generation taking back the term queer. John Rechy (2000) says,

> Many of you have chosen to call yourselves "queers." I believe that this trend, entrenched, will divide our own ranks disastrously. I and others of my generation and later will never use the word queer to identify ourselves or each other, because we will never be able to erase its association with the twisted faces of gay bashers, including cops; that word, for us, will always belong to the violent enemy. (130)

But "our ranks" have always already been divided. There are basic divisions within the queer community that have been well established partly because of mens' pervasive sexism. The queer community is not a monolithic entity. There has always been tension between men and women, people of color and those of European descent, between Christians and Jewish queers, between working class and upper class, between the older and younger generations.

Some argue that the term queer actually works to undercut the notion of difference. Trevor Holmes (1997) argues that

> Queer at once radical, productive, and multiple . . . many now see it as a liberal whitewashing term that erases differences even as it attempts to form alliances . . . queer means nothing if queer can include happy heterosexual couples with children in tow who retreat to their nice middle-class homes in suburbia. (182)

Queer, the slippery umbrella term for gay/lesbian, bisexual, transgendered, transsexual, intersexed people, is at once too inclusive and yet not inclusive enough.

Some argue that the term queer has cast the shadow of the object of (in)visibility over women once again. Joseph Boone (2000) sounds a worry that is echoed by many in the queer community. He says,

> [O]ne of the pitfalls often attributed to the concept of queer . . . of much queer theory and praxis, from which many women, including lesbians, feminist activists, and gay sympathetic women, have at times felt excluded or, in spite of their participation, rendered more or less invisible by a movement that is most often associated, especially in the media, with white, urban gay men. (2000: 8)

The notion of queer is supposed to signify slippery sexualities and the social construction of sexuality and gender. Unlike the feminist movement, which has largely utilized the category, gender, to talk about social injustice, queer theory/activism turns on issues of the body and sexuality. Sexuality is slippery and sexed bodies refuse categorization.

Essentialist concepts of identity (lesbian/gay) become problematic in this post(modern) post(everything) landscape. I don't like the word lesbian—I never did. When people call me lesbian it infuriates me. I don't like others naming me. I choose to self-identify as queer. Queer signals something more (post), more complicated, more in your face, more slippery, more performative. Queer is more virtual, less essentialized.

Sue-Ellen Case remarks that it is no accident that identity is slip slidin' away at this historical cyberjuncture. Case (1996) says that, "The virtualizing of identity has occurred in many critical, practical, and technological discourses, but this work focuses on the evacuation of identity in both electronic and poststructuralist discourses" (6).

But the "evacuation of identity," seems undercut by much psychoanalytic discourse which has not moved beyond foundationalism and structuralism. It is thought by many in the psychoanalytic community that women who are queer are somehow pre-oedipal. This position smacks of pre (post) structuralism. It is interesting to note that much of the talk around pre-oedipality can be attributed to Freud, although Freud did not think homosexuals pathological (Young-Bruehl 1996). Diana Fuss suggests that we need to be careful about taking for granted the discourse around pre-oedipal. Fuss (1995) argues that "In the history of psychoanalysis female homosexuality is theorized almost exclusively in terms of the "pre": the pre-oedipal, presymbolic, the prelaw, the premature, even the presexual" (58). Many versions of psychoanalysis from "Sigmund Freud to Julia Kristeva" mark queers as nonpersons, or persons who are not quite persons—prepersons (Fuss 1995: 59). How can queers be (pre) anything in a (post) era? Aren't we beyond meta-narratives? Aren't we beyond stories of the whole self? Wholeness of selves? Heteronormative selves? Girls identify with mothers and desire fathers? Boys identify with fathers and desire mothers? Girls identify with fathers and desire mothers? Boys identify with mothers and desire fathers? Identification and desire, the psychoanalytic mantra may be too simplistic for this post-whatever era, especially as we learn more about intersexual-hermaphroditic, queer performativity.

The discourse of pre-oedipality is really a concern around the question of "what causes one to be queer." I always wondered why we don't ask heterosexuals the same question. What causes heterosexuals to be straight? It amazes me—and actually horrifies me—that questions of etiology still rage into the twenty-first century. John Boswell points out that,

> In regard to the question of etiology, it should be noted that what "causes" homosexuality [or other kinds of sexualities] is an issue of importance only to societies which regard gay people as bizarre or anamalous. . . . Since very few people in the ancient world considered homosexual behavior odd or abnormal comments about its etiology were quite rare. (1980: 48–49)

Queerly, the question of cause is still here and still the subject of heated debate. This question is troubling. It is irrelevant. It is not the question we should be asking.

A more interesting question is, What do we do with intersexed bodies? Morgan Holmes tells us that,

> Intersexual bodes [or hermaphroditism]—when understood as those that do not fit into the symbolic realm of Western culture—have been physically and literally cut, bound, and sutured in order to appear, in a most violent paradox, "normal" even if not "natural." (2000: 84–85)

The violence of literality! There is no "both" "and" thinking in Western culture. One must be either this or that, girl or boy. Medical doctors cut the difference with a knife. Intersexuality signals the unthinkable and because it is unthinkable it must be altered to become more thinkable. Altering alterity literally with a knife.

Like hermaphrodites, transsexual persons, as Jill St. Jacques (2000) suggests, confuse. St. Jacques says that transsexuals are like rhizomes: "The "trans" elements of the linguistic rhizome are "shifters"; they allow the rhizome of identity to slide between male-to-female, female-to-male" (114). I wonder why it is that when we walk down the street we simply must know what or who is coming toward us, is that a boy or girl? If we cannot determine, frustration sets in. But in these post-whatever times, why can't we just let it be, let the person walking toward us be a whatever, boy-girl, girl-boy, androgyne.

Along with transsexuals, queer women work to confuse as well, especially when they are excessively masculine. Elisabeth Young-Bruehl (1996) claims that

> [W]omen who act male—that is, "active" female homosexuals as homophobic people understand them—are more intrinsically, less directly threatening . . . they demonstrate that the phallus is not necessary for doing what men

do. They confuse the fact of anatomical difference, they upset the world of sexual identity concepts. (36)

Some argue that masculine queer women are not queer at all because they act just like men. Others suggest that femme women who are queer are not queer at all because they act just like women. Some others argue that lesbians are not women at all. Whoever we are, we are a symptom of excess.

The discourse of desire signifies excess. Queer signifies this excess. Queer signifies the inability to name otherness. Some older gay and lesbian activists are uncomfortable with this because it undermines stability. Yet there is no stability of self, no reference for identity, no grounding for consensus, no foundation.

QUEER PERFORMANCE: CAMPING UP THE VAMPIRE

Sue-Ellen Case (2000) says, "i-dentity once gone, as visibility, promotes the new sense of performativity in which the body is a trope" (33). Performance is local, it is agency, an agency that is outrageous. Queer performance is angry, funny, sad, and down right campy. Queers are no longer marching politely along city streets and chanting liberation mantras of the 1970s. Queers have noticed that civil rights are not fully extended to our queer nation, at least here in this queer United States. Queers are still rounded up in parks, gay bashing is still popular. The GLF has failed. Queers are acting out a counternarrative, engaging in a counteragency.

Queer theorists/activists have largely abandoned the notion of identity politics, since it is difficult to say what identity is. Identity is the code word for stability. Identity is not a stable foundation, it is rather a performance, a shifting signifier. Performativity signals slippery movement. But what are queers performing? What is the drama? Can the drama be the drag show? Of course. Queering by acting out. Performing the queer. Literal performances yes.

I would like to turn, though, to the metaphorical and the mythological, the metatextual performances of queer readings, metatexts on queer texts, queer mythologies, fictions, and folklores around the trope of the other, the trope that is queer, the trope of the queer-campy-neo-gothic-vampire. Thinking through difference at this highly symbolic and performative level, pedagogues might be able to turn their thinking upside down and inside out, camping up pedgagogies of difference.

CAMPING: A QUEERY

Performing camp is an aspect of queer life. Not all queers perform camp, but some do, some express a sensibility that performs this drama. Camp is difficult to define. It is theatre, it is excess. It is delightful, it is hilarious.

Camp is parody and exaggeration, it is not straight. There is something about camp that is queer. What that something is, again, is hard to describe. A campy sensibility is one that is completely wordy, embellished, funny. Flabio Cleto (1999) remarks that camp is "a queer, twisted discourse building, the site of an improvised and stylised performance, a proper-groundless, mobile building without deep and anchoring foundations" (9). Camp performance is (post)modern in that it dares to be superficial. David Miller (2000) calls for the (post)modern pedagogue to dare to act out the superficial performance in the spirit of the bricoleur. Dabbling in this and that without reference to deep abiding structures might give our pedagogical practice(s) a space in which to create worlds with our students. But dabbling does not mean working without rigor either. Dabbling is the site of rigorous interdisciplinarity, an interdisciplinarity that calls for breaking through and breaking down taken-for-granted modes of thought.

Camp performance queers up our pedagogies because it calls for breaking down the boundaries between high and low culture. Mark Booth (1999) points out that camp discourse entertains "the trivial, the trashy, the kitsch, the not-terribly-good. Thus in the cultural sphere, to be camp is to be perversly committed to the trash aesthetic" (70). Some of my esteemed colleagues in academe might question the validity of the queer camp performance because it debunks the call to study the so-called great books. Studies in popular culture, however, suggest that academics can learn much from the popular, even if it is considered trashy (Daspit and Weaver 2000). Moreover, academicians can learn much about youth culture(s) from studying their world(s), especially when those worlds include campy vampire novels, for example, or fictions that are not included in the canon(s) of so-called high culture.

Camp parodies not only trash but sexuality. Philip Core (1999) says "CAMP is cross-dressing in a Freudian slip" (81). Queer camp sensibility is one that is able to poke fun. Mark Booth (1999) says, "parody informs the camp persons' whole personality, throwing an ironical light not only on the abstract concept of the sexual stereotype, but also on the parodist him or herself" (69).

Camp has historically been considered a male genre—way of life—aesthetic—performance. But as is noted in the above citation by Booth, women can be just as campy as men. Whatever camp is, it is definitely a part of the urban culture. Jack Babuscio (1999) tells us that "Camp is also urban; it is, in part, a reaction to the anonymity, boredom, and socializing tendencies of technological society" (122). Ironically, there are no rural camp sites. It seems odd that with all the hype around cyberspace and all the stimulation available to young people, youth is indeed bored. My colleagues talk to me about their students sleeping in class. Of course, they might be bored because they cannot channel-surf teachers off of the website of pedagogical space. A campy pedagogy might alter youth boredom.

Camp is anything but boring. It is the collection of trashy art objects, bad kitsch, anything of bad taste. Camp is perfecting exaggerated mannerisms. Camp is dressing ridiculously: Never wearing socks, for instance. Dressing up urban apartments in blood red neogothic furniture and lining the walls with unthinkably bad paintings is the camp symbolic. One true sign of a camp apartment is never having food in the refrigerator but always having "greyhounds" poured in chilled martini glasses ready to go, just in case an interior designer drops over for cocktails. Camp is costume, and costume jewelry is a must. Jack Babuscio (1999) claims that "Four features are basic to camp: irony, aestheticism, theatricality, and humour" (119).

Babuscio (1999) also claims that camp collections might include bad horror flicks. Here I would add that vampire novels and films are part of the campy horror genre and might serve as yet another trope for queering our pedagogies, queering ourselves.

Pedagogical Difference: Queer=Camp=Neo=Gothic=Vampires

Ellis Hanson (1999) suggests that an attempt to study the symbolic significance of vampires might not go over too well with our more conservative academic colleagues. He states that "Needless to say, however, the lesbian [I would say queer] who bites, though commonplace in trashy films and novels, is highly unpopular in critical circles where her kind is likely to be discussed with any degree of scholarly rigor" (1999: 185–86). Many queer women and feminists also take offense to doing work on vampires and queer culture. Hanson (1999) points out that "Marjorie Garber . . . is one of the few feminist critics to acknowledge the radical appeal of vampire films, however tenuously" (185).

I attribute the scholarly skepticism to doing work around vampires to literalism. Some scholars might think that (literally) the vampire is just plain stupid. It is stupid if it is analyzed stupidly. However, if the trope of the vampire can be used to make scholars think differently, especially around notions of difference, then it is useful and can be treated rigorously, just like any other scholarly topic of analysis. I use the metaphor of the queer campy gothic vampire as a trope of difference, a metaphor of living life queerly, a metaphor of the outsider, a metaphor of the symbolic other. But in order to analyze the vampire metaphorically, I think first it is important to turn briefly to the historical record to see how the vampire has been conceptualized and represented.

Pam Keesey (1995) points out that in the Jewish tradition we can trace vampire images back to Jewish folklore. Keesey says,

> Lilith is a recurring figure of Jewish talkes of the supernatural, and her resemblance to the vampire is strong. She is said to dwell in darkness, with dark hair and eyes and luminescent skin. She has the ability to change herself into any form she wishes, human or animal. (13)

Lilith is a countercultural figure in Jewish lore. She is the seductress, the one who can shapeshift, the one who gets marginalized out of Jewish narratives. She represents difference, she is the Other.

European folklore is repleat with vampire tales. Katharina M. Wilson (1998) points out that "There are four clearly discernible schools of thought on the etymology of vampire, advocating Turkish, Greek, Slavic, and Hungarian roots for the term" (3). Vampires are sometimes dubbed the undead, because they return as ghosts from beyond the grave. Some folkorists, as Nina Auerbach (1995) tells us, suggest, in fact, that vampires and ghosts, at one time, were thought to be one and the same thing. Auerbach claims, "Folklorists use vampires interchangeably with revenant or ghost. Only gradually did vampires lose their identification with the human world to acquire the menace of a separate system" (20). John Fine (1998) remarks that the belief in vampires, at least in Serbia, was not "limited to the ignorant peasantry" (65). In fact, Fine points out that the clergy did not even wonder if vampires existed, they were mainly interested in what to do with vampires, how to get rid of them.

Paul Barber (1988) remarks that according to folkore, vampires are born in odd ways. Barber states that,

> In Roumania it is reported that by flying over a corpse a bat can create a vampire. This circumstance deserves remark if only because of its rarity, for as important as bats are in the fiction of vampires, they are generally unimportant in the folklore. (33)

In Roumania there are tales about how to tell whether one will turn into a vampire. Agnes Murgoli (1998) states that,

> It is known that a man is a vampire if he does not eat garlic. . . . When a child dies before it is baptized, it becomes a vampire at seven years of age. . . . Men who swear falsely for money become vampires six months after death. If a vampire casts its eye on a pregnant woman, and she is not disenchanted, her child will be a vampire. When there are seven children of the same sex, the

seventh will have a little tale and be a vampire. A dead man becomes a vampire, if a cat jumps over him. (20)

Philip D. Jaffe and Frank DiCataldo (1998) tell us that in Eastern Europe there are "Telltale signs indicating a possible vampire . . . birthmarks, infants born with teeth, red-haired and sometimes blue-eyed children, tall and gaunt people, and epilepsy" (145). Usually vampire folk tales have emerged from cultures where burial takes place. Paul Barber (1998) has done an interesting study on death and decaying bodies and points out that much of the folklore on vampires may have arisen because improperly buried bodies do strange things and sometimes even pop up out of the ground; they might even make weird noises and give off a weird glowing light. When bodies begin pushing up from underneath the grave (because decaying bodies tend to bloat) horses and other animals sense this and get spooked around graves. One of the popular tales about vampires concerns horses freaking out at grave sites. If a horse starts acting in a bizarre fashion near or around a grave it is a sure sign that a vampire (in)habits the plot.

Who gets to be em(plot)ed as a candidate for vampirism? Paul Barber (1998) says that in Eastern Europe, "people who are different, unpopular, or great sinners are apt to return from the dead. It may be merely a corollary of this role that in Eastern Europe alcoholics are regarded as prime candidates for revenants" (29). Revenants haunt because they represent difference. Difference is considered dangerous. People who are different are not only dangerous in this life, but they are also potentially dangerous in the next. The psychological mechanism that triggers these irrational fears and paranoia about the (un)dead is clearly projection. Paranoia and fear are projected out onto scapegoats because the individual who is fearful and paranoid is really fearful and paranoid about his own heart of darkness, his own tendencies toward difference. When one cannot manage one's own difference from within, one projects it out onto the other and demonizes the other, thus creating the scapegoat. Vampires make convenient scapegoats.

But all vampires are not the same. Representations differ in folklore and in fiction. Scholars suggest that the vampire of folklore differs from the vampire of nineteenth century gothic novels. Barber (1998) tells us that,

It is only in fiction that a vampire is likely to be from the upper classes—Count Dracula, for example. Actually, rich and important people tend to be buried properly, and their families have sufficient influence to prevent them from being dug up again. (132)

Those suspected of being vampires, on occasion (especially in Eastern Europe) have been dug up after burial to ensure that they are not roaming around. Surveillance of the (un)dead was a popular site of cultural archaeology in Europe of old. Foucault's work on surveillance perhaps doesn't dig deeply enough. Bentham's panoptican extends beyond the grave.

When doing vampire watching, one may notice that some vampires are loners, while others are out and about. Some vampires are glamour queens. Here I am thinking of the film *The Hunger*. Catherine Deneuve is not your everyday regular gritty alcoholic folklorish, ruddy-faced dumpy vampire. Hollywood vampires are very different from vampires of folklore. Vampires tell us much about our culture and times. As Nina Auerbach (1995) says, vampires reflect who we are and how we manage difference. The title of her book is provocative: *Our Vampires, Ourselves*. Thus it makes sense that the vampires of folklore are nothing like the vampires of Hollywood. An American vampire will reflect American culture, an Eastern European vampire will reflect that culture.

Scandalously, the technology of vampire images is not dissimilar from images of Christ. American versions of Christ reflect our culture. Here Christ is typically white and sanitized. The film *The Last Temptation of Christ* is a good example of a typical American, Hollywood Christ image. An Italian Christ will reflect the Italians. Here I am thinking of Pasolini's scandalous film *The Gospel According to St. Matthew*. Christ is an angry revolutionary, not a compassionate, kind Christ. Many Italians, though, were not pleased when the film came out. Still, there is something to be said about the difference between an Italian representation of Christ and an American one. Likewise, a Mexican representation of Christ is usually covered with blood, not sanitized at all. And so too with vampires. Some are pretty, some are ruddy. Some are monstrous, others are beautiful. Some look old, some are eternally young. Vampire representations are not stable, rather they are reflections of culture and are therefore shifty.

Nineteenth century gothic novels and twentieth and twenty-first century neogothic fictions cast vampires in campy dress, campy rebelliousness, campy symbolics. The fictionalized vampire serves as a trope for the other. J. Gordon Melton (1999) declares that,

> For enthusiasts, today's vampire symbolizes important elements of their lives that they feel are being otherwise suppressed or ignored by the culture. The most obvious role thrust upon the contemporary vampire has been that of cultural rebel, a symbolic leader advocating outrageous alternative patterns of living in a culture demanding conformity. (xxiii)

It is not difficult to understand why youth culture(s) today are so fascinated with the vampires of Anne Rice's fictions. Young people can identify with being othered, alienated. This is what I think the turn to the neogothic is about. Neogothic subcultures symbolize a turning away from slick, cheerful imagery of the cyberspace post (identity) culture. Neogothic captures the gritty underground punk who is angry at the cultural imperative toward conformity, toward heteronormativity. Neogothic-campy vampirism is a social commentary on a culture that insists on having no culture, a whitewashed, post-toastie, uniformed, standardized boredom. Trevor Holmes (1997) suggests that

> Vampires function as more than just metaphors or archetypes in contemporary culture; in the case of at least some subjects in the boundary-crossing moment that is both queer and goth, vampires are sources of self-invention and the very much outstaging of the problematics of gender identification and sexuality. (188)

Vampires serve as tropes that criss-cross sexual desire and represent what is unthinkable in heteronormative culture. More than this though, the vampire is the symbolic re-presentation of a counternarrative to racist, nationalistic, and homophobic discourse. Judith Halberstam (1995) teaches that,

> The Gothic novel of the 19th century and the Gothic horror film of the late 20th century are both obsessed with multiple modes of consumption and production, with dangerous consumptions and excessive productivity. . . . The monster itself is an economic form in that it condenses various racial and sexual threats to nation, capitalism, and the bourgeoisie in one body. (3)

The vampire is a threat. She threatens all notions of stability and niceness. She is campy and queer, she is angry and scary. She crosses boundaries between this world and that, between this sexuality and that, between animal and human. A white squirrel may be a vampire. A bat flying over head may turn a dead body into a vampire. A redhead may become a vampire. Vampires are (post) (post)modern. You never know who is vampire. Perhaps you are!!

We are here and we are everywhere a threat. The vampire is a symbolic other, a symbolic other with whom I identify as a queer pedagogue. The trope of the queer campy gothic vampire is a metacommentary on what it feels like to feel different, to be different and to be considered Other. Teachers and students working together to build more inclusive school culture(s) might begin to think otherwise, to think more metaphorically, more symbolically in order to understand what it is like to be a bat. (This is a campy pun on Thomas Nagel's famous article on phenomenological approaches to cognition.) Pedagogies of difference make a difference because they approach the notion of difference via symbolic representation(s). Literal approaches to difference do not get us thinking differently about our pedagogical practices. Literalism is the death of the (un)dead.

This autobiographical story about campy queer gothic vampires is an attempt to think through pedagogies of difference symbolically. My em(plot)ment in the South as a queer pedagogue is haunted by the struggles I have had encountering homophobia and heteronormativity. In rural Georgia, there are no camp sites. But I bring to the classroom my urban queer campy vampirism. My aim as an educator is to camp up the difference.

REFERENCES

Auerbach, N. 1995. *Our Vampires, Ourselves.* Chicago: The University of Chicago Press.

Babuscio, J. 1999. "The Cinema of Camp (aka Camp and the Gay Sensibility)." In *Camp: Queer Aesthetics and the Performing Subject: A Reader,* ed. F. Cleto, 117–35. Ann Arbor: The University of Michigan Press.

Barber, P. 1988. *Vampire, Burial, and Death: Folklore Reality.* New Haven, Ct.: Yale University Press.

Boone, Joseph A. 2000. "Go West: An Introduction." In *Queer Frontiers: Millennial Geographies, Genders, and Generations,* ed. J. A. Boone, 3–23. Madison: The University of Wisconsin Press.

Booth, M. 1999. "Campe-toi!: On the origins and definitions of camp." In *Camp: Queer Aesthetics and the Performing Subject: A Reader,* ed. F. Cleto, 66–79. Ann Arbor: The University of Michigan Press.

Boswell, J. 1980. *Christianity, Social Tolerance, and Homosexuality: Gay People in Western Europe from the Beginning of the Christian Era to the 14th Century.* Chicago: The University of Chicago Press.

———. 1994. *Same-Sex Unions in Premodern Europe.* New York: Vintage.

Case, S. E. 2000. "Toward a Butch-Feminist Retro-Future." In *Queer Frontiers: Millennial Geographies, Genders, and Generations,* ed. J. A. Boone, 23–38. Madison: The University of Wisconsin Press.

Cleto, F. 1999. "Introduction: Queering the Camp." In *Camp: Queer Aesthetics and the Performing Subject: A Reader,* ed. F. Cleto, 1–43. Ann Arbor: The University of Michigan Press.

Core, P. 1999. "From Camp: The Lie that Tells the Truth." In *Camp: Queer Aesthetics and the Performing Subject: A Reader,* ed. F. Cleto, 80–87. Ann Arbor: The University of Michigan Press.

Daspit, T., and J. Weaver. 2000. *Popular Culture and Critical Pedagogy: Reading, Constructing, Connecting.* New York: Garland Press.

Doll, M. A. 2000. *Like Letters in Running Water: A Mythopoetics of Curriculum.* Mahwah, N.J.: Lawrence Erlbaum Associates, Publishers.

Downing, C. 1989. *Myths and Mysteries of Same-Sex Love.* New York: Continuum.

Dundes, A. 1998. "The Vampire as Bloodthirsty Revenant: A Pyschoanalytic Post Mortem." In *The Vampire: A Casebook,* ed. A. Dundes, 159–78. Madison: The University of Wisconsin Press.

Faderman, L. 1999. *To Believe in Women: What Lesbians Have Done for America—A History.* New York: Houghton Mifflin.

Fine, J. V. A. 1990. "In Defense of Vampires." In *The Vampire: A Casebook,* ed. A. Dundes, 57–65. Madison: The University of Wisconsin Press.

Flynn, C. 1999. "The Deaths of Camp." In *Camp: Queer Aesthetics and the Performing Subject: A Reader,* ed. F. Cleto, 433–57. Ann Arbor: The University of Michigan Press.

Foucault, M. [1978]. 1990. *The History of Sexuality. Volume I: An Introduction.* Trans. R. Hurley. New York: Vintage Books.

Fuss, D. 1995. *Identification Papers.* New York: Routledge.

Halberstam, J. 1995. *Skin Shows: Gothic Horror and the Technology of Monsters.* Durham: Duke University Press.

Hanson, E. 1999. "Lesbians Who Bite." In *Outtakes: Essays on Queer Theory and Film,* ed. E. Hanson, 183–222. Durham: Duke University Press.

Holmes, M. 2000. "Queer Cut Bodies." In *Queer Frontiers: Millennial Geographies, Genders, and Generations,* ed. J. A. Boone, 84–110. Madison: The University of Wisconsin Press.

Holmes, T. 1997. "Coming Out of the Coffin: Gay Males and Queer Goths in Contemporary Vampire Fiction." In *Blood Read: The Vampires as Metaphor in Contemporary Culture,* ed. J. Gordon and V. Hollinger, 169–88. Philadelphia: The University of Pennsylvania Press.

Jaffe, P. D., and F. DiCataldo. 1998. "Clinical Vampirism: Blending Myth and Reality." In *The Vampire: A Casebook,* ed. A. Dundes, 143–58. Madison: The University of Wisconsin Press.

Keesey, P. 1995. "Introduction." In *Dark Angels: Lesbian Vampire Stories,* ed. P. Keesey, 9–22. Pittsburgh, PA: Cleis Press.

Melton, J. G. 1999. *The Vampire Book: The Encyclopedia of the Undead.* Detroit, Mich.: Visible Ink Press.

Miller, D. 2000. "The Bricoleur in the Tennis Court: Pedagogy in Postmodern Context." *The Journal of Curriculum Theorizing.* 16 (2): 49–62.

Murgoci, A. 1998. "The Vampire in Roumania." In *The Vampire: A Casebook,* ed. A. Dundes, 12–46. Madison: The University of Wisconsin Press.

Piggford, G. 1999. " 'Who's that girl?' Annie Lennox, Woolf's Orlando, and Female Camp androgyny." In *Camp: Queer Aesthetics and the Performing Subject: A Reader,* ed. F. Cleto, 283. Ann Arbor: The University of Michigan Press.

Pinar, W., W. Reynolds, P. Slattery, and P. Taubman. 1995. *Understanding Curriculum: An Introduction to the Study of Historical and Contemporary Curriculum Discourses.* New York: Peter Lang.

Quimbly, K. and W. Williams. 2000. "Unmasking the Homophile in 1950s Los Angeles: An Archival Record." In *Queer Frontiers: Millenial Geographies, Genders, and Generations,* ed. J. A. Boone, 166–95. Madison: The University of Wisconsin Press.

Rechy, J. 2000. "The Outlaw Sensibility in the Arts: From Drag and Leather to Prose: The Mythology of Stonewall, and a Defense of Stereotypes." In *Queer Frontiers: Millennial Geographies, Genders, and Generations,* ed. J. A. Boone, 124–34. Madison: The University of Wisconsin Press.

Retter, Y. 2000. "Lesbian Activism in Los Angeles, 1970–1979." In *Queer Frontiers: Millenial Geographies, Genders, and Generations,* ed. J. A. Boone, 196–221. Madison: The University of Wisconsin Press.

Sears, J. T. 1991. "Growing Gay in the South: Race, Gender, and Turnings of the Spirit." Binghamton, N.Y.: Harrington Park Press.

Smith, D. 2000. "Introduction to George Buck." *The Journal of Curriculum Theorizing.* Winter 16 (4).

St. Jacques, J. 2000. "Embodying a Transsexual Alphabet." In *Queer Frontiers: Millennial Geographies, Genders, and Generations,* ed. J. A. Boone, 111–23. Madison: The University of Wisconsin Press.

Spivak, G. C. 1993. *Outside in the Teaching Machine.* New York: Routledge.

Young-Bruehl, E. 1996. *The Anatomy of Prejudices.* Cambridge: Harvard University Press.

Wilson, K. M. 1998. "The History of the Word Vampire." In *The Vampire: A Casebook,* ed. A. Dundes, 3–11. Madison: The University of Wisconsin Press.

9

Toward an Integrative Approach to Equity in Education

ROXANA NG

INTRODUCTION

The call for diversity, inclusivity, and equity in education in Canada is the result of two major forces: the legislation of employment equity by the federal government in 1984, on the one hand, and pressure from marginalized groups on the other. For many people, the notion of equity represented a major shift in thinking and acting on the historical inequalities that have formed part of Canada's social fabric. Whereas equality implies that people who receive equal treatment are or should be the same, equity takes differences into account. It shifts the debate from equal treatment to that of access and removal of barriers for historically disadvantaged groups.[1]

Employment equity addresses issues such as the elimination of barriers in employment, and supportive measures in work environments. It is results-oriented, and uses quantitative measures to gage results (West-moreland-Traore 1999). Educational equity, on the other hand, is more nebulous. It encompasses general notions of respect for diversity, inclusive curriculum, and warming up the chilly climate some experience in educational settings (see Haig-Brown 1997; Manner 1998; Young 1999). Translated into practice, educational equity means many things to many people. Gender equity recognizes the historical inequality of men and women in the educational process and encourages the inclusion of gender neutral materials into the curriculum and into school practices. Multicultural education and antiracist education are aimed at issues of cultural diversity and racism in the school system (see Thomas 1987). Inclusive education, according to Manners (1998), has often been viewed as a separate initiative targeted at students with special needs[2] that runs parallel to multicultural education and antiracist education. While valuable in addressing inequalities and problems in their specific areas of concerns, these equity measures do not intersect. Indeed, in confining to their specific areas, they overlook the fact that, in reality, people's experiences are complex and multi-dimensional. In his critique of antiracist education, which is applicable to other forms of equity and inclusive education, Gus John points out that "[a]nti-racist approaches . . . begins from a perspective that sets up a hierarchy of oppression, with 'race' at the pinnacle, and places racial oppression outside the range of other oppressions in society" (John 1990: 4). Thus, taking up only one issue serves to reinforce differences constructed along lines of gender, race, and ability. We need an approach that makes links across these domains of social life—an approach that integrates race, gender, class, and other differences in dealing with equity.

This chapter recommends an approach to educational equity that is capable of addressing multiple axes of inequality and difference. I argue that we need to see differences as power relations that are produced in interactions. Understanding power as a relational property is therefore key to working with inequality and difference in education. I begin this chapter with a discussion of my conceptualization of power. To illustrate this conceptualization, I discuss how power operates in terms of race, gender, and class, and hint at how ability can be similarly conceptualized. To conclude this chapter, I tentatively put forward an approach that I call "against the grain," one that seeks to make power relations explicit in the educational process. By way of a conclusion, the implications of this approach are explored.

POWER AS RELATION

In sociology power is viewed frequently in macro terms, as a property of social structures and institutions. For example, the police have the power and authority to charge and arrest people who are seen to be breaking the law; policemen are empowered by law to keep order and arrest those deemed to be disrupting the social order. Men have power over women by virtue of their historical control over major societal institutions and structures. This is a common way to understand power sociologically.

Here, I put forward the notion of power as a dynamic relation, which is enacted in interactions. My understanding is derived from theorization and empirical investigations in interpretive sociology, beginning with the work of Weber and more recently in ethnomethodology. Max Weber (1969) defines power as the ability and chances of an actor to impose his or her will on another in a social relationship. Berger and Luckman (1967) take this notion further to suggest that particular people have the power to construct and impose their definition of reality on others. More recently, researchers in ethnomethodology and social linguistics have begun to analyze how power in enacted microsociologically. For example, Thorne and Henley (1975) mapped how men dominate women through the use of language. From a different but equally important tradition, Foucault (1979, 1990) draws attention to how power is not only over-and-above but enacted in local sites; this he calls the microphysics of power. These theorizations locate power not only in institutions (where of course it is), but in interactional settings where institutional life is lived and enacted.

To give an illustration, I draw on Pamela Fishman's analysis of conversations between intimate couples, which illustrates succinctly how unequal power between women and men is enacted, established, and maintained in interactional settings. In her study, Fishman (1978) analyzed the conversational patterns and strategies of five heterosexual couples by tape recording their conversations in their homes. The couples had the right to turn off the tape recorder or edit out conversations as they liked. On the whole, Fishman felt that the tape recording represented conversations that occurred in natural settings. In analyzing these mundane conversations, she found marked differences in women's and men's conversational strategies and patterns. Men tended to make more statements and control the topics of conversations. Women tended to support conversations by using minimal responses such as "hmm," whereas men used them to end conversations. In conclusion, Fishman argued that gender relations are not givens; they are negotiated on an ongoing basis. Her analysis and that of other researchers demonstrates that power and hierarchical relations are not abstract forces operating on people. Power instead is a human accomplishment, situated in everyday interaction; thus, both structural forces and interactional activities are vital to the maintenance and construction of social reality.

It is this notion of power as a dynamic relation, which is negotiated continuously in interactional settings, that I want to draw attention to here. I make a distinction between "power" and "authority." *Power* is an individual property that is subjected to negotiation interactionally. *Authority*, on the other hand, is formal power granted to individuals through institutional structures and relations. Thus, the police have legal authority to take certain courses of action. Teachers have authority over students as a consequence of their ascribed role in the educational system. But in an interactional setting, this authority can be challenged by those without formal power.

RACE, GENDER, ABILITY, AND CLASS ARE RELATIONAL

Race, gender, ability, and class are frequently treated as fixed and immutable categories of social differences. Although they are not compatible analytic categories, frequently they are used in tandem and as competing categories for determining social status. The issue for social analyses and their applications is to see which "variable" or "factor" is more important in people's experiences. A common problem I encounter in my teaching is that most students feel they have to decide whether to work on race, gender, class, or ability first and foremost. This decision, I suggest, is highly influenced by the discourses that segment people's experiences into separate domains for social analysis and action, including the way in which various inequalities are taken up in education as mentioned in the introduction. As Goli Rezai-Rashti (1997) observes,

> At the school level, issues of equity in education are usually discussed (if at all) as separate subjects. The work of those who deal with equity issues is often compartmentalized so that systematic analysis of the relational nature of gender, race, and social class is lost to students. While it is commonplace to assume that the understanding of one equity issue can lead to understanding of and empathy for other ones, our experiences shows this might not necessarily be true in the everyday life of school. (24)

Thus, in the 1970s, following the rediscovery of poverty in Western nations after the post-war boom, class inequality was seen to be the primary persistent issue in education. This was the concern of much of the sociology of education literature, such as the cultural reproduction school. In Toronto, for instance, progressive school trustees and teachers worked relentlessly to get rid of destreaming and to develop curriculum that reflected the experiences of working-class children in this period. In the 1980s the struggles waged by feminists finally made inroads into the school system, and gender equity was instituted in the policies of many boards of education in Canada. In the 1990s in Ontario, with the election of the New Democratic Party (NDP) government and until the Progressive Conservative Party defeated the NDP in 1995, issues of racism and racial equity became the primary concern, and antiracism was on the official educational agenda. Sadly, these initiatives were pitted against each other—coming and going with the political climate. There doesn't seem to be a sustained way of working on social differences simultaneously.[3]

This is largerly because people subscribe to a way of knowing that treats these elements as fixed categories. Here I recommend a way of knowing that moves away from treating race, gender, class, and ability as *categories* designating different and separate domains of social life, to discovering how they are features that arise in human interactions. That is, they are *relational properties* located in time and space. We do not have to decide, a priori, which variable is more important. I will show that they are concrete social relations that are interwoven and discoverable in the everyday world of experience.

The term "race" is usually used to point to differences among groups of people on the basis of biology or culture. Following major breakthroughs in theorizations of race (e.g., Li 1990; Miles 1989), I argue that race is a purely imaginary social fabrication whereby people's physical and phenotypical differences are made into absolute differences. Similar to the construction of gender differences, the aim of constructing races is to establish a hierarchy among people. This is very clear in the history of North America. In the process of imperialist expansion and colonization by the Europeans, the myriad tribal groups who inhabited the continent were made into an inferior race—the Indians. Indeed, it is in this period of Canadian history that the Metis, children of European and Indian parents, came into being as a new race. Whereas marrying Indian women and the children of mixed raced marriages were used as a way of gaining access to Indian communities initially for purposes of trade and colonizing the Indians, once these objectives were secured the Metis were cast aside (see Bourgeault 1991). This process of racialization, based on inferiorizing groups of people for purposes of domination and control, is called racism (see Ng 1993).

In terms of the educational system, Nancy Jackson's (1987) study on ethnicity and vocational choice illuminates how racial differences are relations through which the unequal experiences of individuals are organized in the educational process. Her research shows that in Vancouver boys from a Chinese background were advised by guidance counselors to take accounting courses in vocational programs based on the stereotypical notion that they are good at math. Here, the *ability* these boys developed prior to their immigration to Canada was treated as a *cultural trait;* it is thus that ethnic and racial differences, as well as ability, are constructed. Although the counselors acted out of good intention, streaming Chinese boys into vocational programs restricted their future opportunities. It is through this sort of process, a daily occurrence in the everyday world, that a racially differentiated educational system and labor market (that is, class system) is produced and maintained. Thus I argue that racial differences, as well as differences in ability, are accomplished rather than given. They arise in relations of domination and subordination and for the purpose of establishing social and economic hierarchies.

Similarly, gender differences are constructed. Unlike race, gender is a term developed by feminists in the 1970s to distinguish it from biological sex differences. It refers to the process(es) whereby sex differences are made real or objectified as differences between men and women, and where these differences are valorized in differential ways. Thus, encouraging girls to take subjects such as secretarial training and home economics in fact prepares them for a labor market segregated by gender and for a life as wife, mother, and caregiver. Schooling, then, is part of the process whereby a social division of labor according to gender is produced *and* maintained. Furthermore, in the labor force the skills women acquire in domestic and educational settings are seen to be based on their "natural" ability, and less value is assigned to these skills. My own research on sewing machine operators in the garment industry, most of whom are women, is a case in point. Whereas pattern cutters are mainly men, and pattern cutting is seen to be skilled work, sewing is treated as unskilled and is paid less because it is seen as something that women know how to do naturally (Ng 1998). Here we see that the social attributes of men and women are treated *as if* they were natural and biological in the establishment of an occupational and wage hierarchy. This is sexism.

Finally, my understanding of the term class is consistent with the way in which Marx uses the concept in *The German Ideology* (Marx and Engels 1970) and *Das Kapital* (Marx 1954). Class is not used to indicate status in terms of occupation, salary, education, and the like (which is how stratification analysts use the concept). Instead, class is used to refer to a *process* whereby people's lives are organized and transformed in terms of the relation and means of production. Although this transformation hinges on economic relations in a capitalist society, it is not simply an economic relation. Thus, in the examples of the streaming of boys from Chinese background and the treatment of female garment workers above, we see that race and gender are attributes used in creating a gender and racially segregated educational system and labor market. These processes are the organization of class in contemporary society. There is a convergence of gender, race, and class as relations that arise in the schooling process and in the process of slotting people into the labor market. Seen in this way, class pinpoints the process whereby people's livelihood is (re)organized.

It is in the process of developing a labor market for the purpose of commodity production that the issue of ability and disability arises. In the development of a progressively elaborated and differentiated labor market, skills needed in the production process are formalized. Education is a major mechanism through which people acquire skills, which they then sell in exchange for wages in the labor market. In standardizing training for paid employment, those whose learning does not fit into the standardized classroom format are seen as problematic. Again, we see how something that originates in the social process becomes a person's personal attributes (abilities).

In the school system, the term "special needs," or "special education," has been developed to capture the multiple and unique problems of student performance according to a standardized curriculum and classroom practices. Isrealin Shockness, a consultant of special education for Toronto schools and tutor for students with special needs, found that frequently those students classified as special need in fact perform well or adequately in other areas of life, but have problems functioning in a standard classroom environment. Withdrawal to special education classes stigmatizes the students, thereby exacerbating the problem (Shockness 1999). By contrast, but along a similar line of observation, Rita Manners, a teacher in Toronto, criticizes the superficiality of mainstreaming special needs children based on her experience of inclusive education. Teachers are supposed to treat these students as if they were regular students. She writes, "What I see in classrooms is that these students generally tend to hang out or sit with each other due to their familiarity [with] previously separate classes. They participate very little in oral discussions and try very hard to conceal their poor writing skills" (Manners 1998: 70). Equal treatment in this case in fact highlights the "disabilities" of these students, thereby rendering them deviant in an environment that aims at standardization and uniformity.

These examples lend further support to my argument that "ability" is socially constructed. Instead of treating student abilities as given, therefore, we need to interrogate how they arise in the social organization of the school. We need to analyze how labeling students as having special needs based on perceptions about their abilities, seen to be their personal attributes rather than socially produced properties, is consequential, not only for their schooling experience, but for their eventual participation in the labor market. When we see that producing a hierarchical labor market is part of the organization of class in our society, we in turn see how gender, race, ethnicity, and ability are integral to the organization of the labor market and class relations.

In sum, if we see gender, race, class, and ability as relations that come into being in interactions, then we do not need to treat them as variables whose importance needs to be ranked—nor do we have to try to capture them by means of indicators. These relations are concrete, intersecting, and complicated because they converge and diverge in people's everyday lives, but they can be observed and described. Also from the examples given above, we see how education is part of the process through which these relations of differentiation and inequality are enacted and inscribed as properties that reside in individuals; that is, these features of the everyday world are ongoing social accomplishments in which we participate.

Finally, I want to show how these relations of inequality become systematized over time and how we are implicated in their creation and reproduction. I focus on racism, sexism, and classism as systems of domination and subordination.[4] As can be seen, this arises out of the way in which race, gender, and class are implicated in the organization of a capitalist labor market. Racism, sexism, and classism are based on ideas of the superiority of one group (be they Europeans, men, or the bourgeoisie) over others, that developed over time. In North America sexism, racism, and classism were entrenched as systems of domination in the process of colonization and nation building so that certain *practices* become normalized as "this is the way things are done." These "isms," therefore, include *both* the ideology *and* practice of domination and subordination. They become the norm and are taken for granted as ways of doing things.

I use the term "common sense," after Gramsci (1971), to refer to those unintentional and unconscious acts that result in the silencing, exclusion, subordination, and exploitation of groups of people based on normalized courses of action. Gramsci uses this term, contrasting it with "good sense," to refer to the incoherent and at times contradictory assumptions and beliefs held by the mass of population when an ideology becomes hegemonic. Even though dominant ideas may contradict actual experiences, they are taken to be "that's the way things are," and are thus generally not open for questioning. Over time, dominant ideas become common sense; that is, they are naturalized or normalized. Thus it is perfectly "natural" for vocational counselors to encourage boys from Chinese backgrounds to go into accounting courses and girls to take secretarial courses due to their perceived "natural" abilities. In turn, students come to see how certain subjects may facilitate their entry into the job market, thus sustaining a labor market segregated by race and gender. Processes of labeling (for lack of a better shorthand) and identity construction are therefore interactive and dynamic. They are not one-way processes.

If we superimpose my formulation of "power as relation" on the discussion concerning race, gender, class, and ability as relations, we then begin to see how we may work with social differences simultaneously. When I assert that sexism, racism, and classism are relations of domination and subordination, I imply that they are relations of power. In an educational context, the exercise of power is accomplished in interactions (i.e., in a social organization), manifesting itself as acts of exclusion, marginalization, silencing, and so forth. Thus, paying attention to how power operates along axes of gender, race, class, and ability (that is, recognizing that social differences are not given, but are accomplished in and through educational settings) is a step toward educational equity.

AGAINST THE GRAIN: TOWARD AN INTEGRATIVE APPROACH IN EDUCATION

What does the above discussion mean in the educational context? It means that in the interactions of teachers with students in the classroom, or in other contexts, attention needs to be directed toward how dominant and subordinate relations (be they based on race, gender, class, or ability) permeate these contexts and intersect in complicated ways to produce inequality and marginalization. The frequently used and well-meaning phrase, "I treat everyone the same," often used by teachers and administrators to indicate their lack of bias in a diverse educational setting, in fact *masks* unequal power relations. Similarly, educational policies that assume that people are the same or equal may serve to entrench existing inequality precisely because people enter into the educational process with different and unequal experiences. These attempts, well meaning though they may be, tend to render inequality invisible, and thus work against equity in education.

In her exploration of white privilege in higher education in the United States, Frances Rains (1998), an aboriginal-Japanese American woman, states emphatically that these benign acts are disempowering for the minority person because they erase his or her racial identity. The denial of racism in this case is in fact a form of racism.

Thus, in moving toward equity in education that allows us to address multiple and intersecting axes of difference and inequality, I recommend that we try to think and act "against the grain" in developing educational policies and handling various kinds of pedagogical situations.[5] To work against the grain is to recognize that education is not neutral; it is contested. Mohanty puts it as such:

> ... [E]ducation represents both a struggle for meaning and a struggle over power relations. [It is] a central terrain where power and politics operate out of the lived culture of individuals and groups situated in asymmetrical social and political positions. (Mohanty 1990: 184)

We need to develop a critical awareness of the power dynamics operative in institutional relations—and of the fact that people participate in institutions as *unequal* subjects. Working against the grain is to take a proactive approach to understanding and acting upon institutional relations, whether in the classroom, in other interactions with students, or in policy development. Rather than overlooking the embeddedness of gender, race, class, ability, and other forms of inequality that shape our interactions, working against the grain makes explicit the political nature of education and how power operates to privilege, silence, and marginalize individuals who are differently located in the educational process.

In her exploration of feminist pedagogy, Linda Briskin (1990) makes a clear distinction between nonsexist and antisexist education critical to our understanding here. She asserts that nonsexism is an approach that attempts to neutralize sexual inequality by pretending that gender can be made irrelevant in the classroom. Thus, for instance, merely asserting that male and female students should have equal time to speak—and indeed giving them equal time—cannot adequately rectify the endemic problem of sexism in the classroom. One of Briskin's students reported that in her political science tutorials that when the male students spoke, everyone paid attention. When a female student spoke, however, the class acted as if no one was speaking (13). Neutrality is an attempt to conceal the unequal distribution of power.

An against the grain approach would acknowledge explicitly that we are all gendered, racialized, and differently constructed subjects who do not participate in interactional relations as equals. This goes beyond formulating sexism, racism, abilism, and class privilege in individualist terms and treating them as if they were personal attitudes. Terry Wolverton (1983) discovered the difference between nonracism and antiracism in her consciousness-raising attempt:

> I had confused the act of trying to *appear* not to be racist with actively working to eliminate racism. Trying to appear not racist had made me deny my racism, and therefore exclude the possibility of change. (191)

Being against the grain means seeing inequality as systemic and interpersonal (rather than individual), and combatting oppression as a collective responsibility, not just as a personal attribute (so that somehow a person can cleanse herself or himself of sexism, racism, abilism, or class bias). It is to pay attention to oppression as an interactional property that can be altered (see Manners 1998).

Roger Simon (1993) suggests, in his development of a philosophical basis for teaching against the grain, which shares many commonalities in how I think about an integrative approach to equity in education, that teaching against the grain is fundamentally a moral practice. By this he does not mean that teachers simply fulfill the mandate and guidelines of school authorities. He believes that teachers must expose the partial and imperfect nature of existing knowledge, which is constructed on the basis of asymmetrical power relations (for instance, who has the power to speak and whose voices are suppressed?). It is the responsibility of the teacher or educator to show how dominant forms of knowledge and ways of knowing constrict human capacities. In exposing the power relations integral to the knowledge construction process, the educator, by extension, must treat teaching and learning as a mutual and collaborative act between teachers and students.

What may this ideal look like in practice? Marilyn Cochran-Smith (1991) also explores the notion of teaching against the grain in her research on how teachers and students worked together in a preservice program in the Philadelphia area. Borrowing from Gramsci's formulation that action is everyone's responsibility, she asserts that teaching is fundamentally a political activity. In practical terms, she outlines what it may mean to teach against the grain in an actual teaching and learning situation. Her succinct articulation is worth quoting at length:

> To teach against the grain, teachers have to understand and work both *within* and *around* the culture of teaching and the politics of schooling at their particular schools and within their larger school system and communities. They cannot simply announce better ways of doing things, as outsiders are likely to do. They have to teach differently without judging the ways other teach or dismissing the ideas others espouse. . . . [They] are not at liberty to publicly announce brilliant but excoriating critiques of their colleagues and the bureaucracies in which they labor. Their ultimate commitment is to the school lives and futures of the children with whom they live and work. Without condescension or defensiveness, they have to work with parents and other teachers on different ways of seeing and measuring development, connecting and dividing knowledge, and knowing about teaching and schooling. They have to be astute observers of individual learners with the ability to pose and explore questions that transcend cultural attribution, institutional habit, and the alleged certainty of outside experts. They have to see beyond and through the conventional labels and practices that sustain the status quo by raising unanswerable and often uncomfortable questions. Perhaps most importantly, teachers who work against the grain must name and wrestle with their own doubts, must fend off the fatigue of reform and depend on the strength of their individual and collaborative convictions that their work ultimately makes a difference in the fabric of social responsibility. (Cochran-Smith 1991: 284–85)

For me, to be against the grain is therefore to recognize that the routinized courses of action and interactions in all educational contexts are imbued with unequal distribution of power that produce and reinforce various forms of marginalization and exclusion. Thus, a commitment to redress these power relations (i.e., equity in education) involves interventions and actions that may appear "counter-intuitive."[6]

Undoing inequality and achieving equity in education is a risky and uncomfortable act because we need to disrupt the ways things are "normally" done. This involves a serious (and frequently threatening) effort to interrogate our privilege as well as our powerlessness. It obliges us to examine our own privilege relative though it may be, to move out of our internalized positions as victims, to take control over our lives, and to take responsibilities for change. It requires us to question what we take for granted, and a commitment to a vision of society built on reflection, reform, mutuality, and respect in theory and in practice.

Teaching and learning against the grain is not easy, comfortable, or safe. It is protracted, difficult, uncomfortable, painful, and risky. It involves struggles with our colleagues, our students, as well as struggles within ourselves against our internalized beliefs and normalized behaviors. In other words, it is a lifelong challenge. However, as Simon (1993) puts it, teaching against the grain is also a project of hope. We engage in it with the knowledge and conviction that we are in a long-term collaborative project with like-minded people whose goal is to make the world a better place for us and for our children.

NOTES

This chapter is based on a keynote address, bearing the same title, I gave at the Sociology of Education Association annual conference at Pacific Grove, California, February 26–28, 1999. I thank Dr. Gilda Bloom for inviting me to test out my ideas there. An earlier version of this chapter was circulated as a discussion paper at the Seminar on Social Justice organized by the Centre for Policy Studies in Education, University of British Columbia and the Department of Canadian Heritage in Ottawa (June 14–16, 1999). I thank Dr. Reva Joshi for inviting me to submit the paper, and for the participants of the Education Workshop for their invaluable comments.

1. For a detailed explication and historical overview of this debate, see Westmoreland-Traore (1999).
2. The term "special needs" is a rather vague term that includes students labelled disabled as well as students whose mother tongue is not English or French in Canada. In other words, these are students who do not "fit" into a "normal" classroom or who have difficulties with the standard curriculum.
3. For an excellent example of this, see a series of articles published in the *Journal of Moral Education* in 1986 and 1987 (Troyna and Carrington 1987; Walkling and Brannigan 1986) on ethnomethodology. Max Weber (Weber 1969) defines power as the ability and chances of an actor to impose his or her will on another in a social relationship. Berger and Luckmann (Berger and Luckmann 1967) take this notion further to suggest that particular people have the power to construct and impose their definition of reality on others. More recently, researchers in ethnomethodology and social linguistics have begun to analyze how power is enacted microsociologically. For example, Thorne and Henley's work (Thorne and Henley 1975) mapped how men dominate women through the use of language. From a different but equally important tradition, Foucault (Foucault 1979, 1990) draws attention to how power is not only over-and-above, but is enacted in local sites; this he calls the microphysics of power. These theorizations locate power not only in institutions (of course it is), but in interactional settings where institutional life is lived and enacted.
4. I have to confess that I am still struggling with integrating "ability" into the conceptualization I am developing here. Thus I do not address the issue of ability directly in this discussion. However, I maintain that a similar analysis can be done with regard to ability.
5. I hasten to add two things: First, an integrative approach is not without problems. One critique is that working on multiple issues dilutes the significance of any one dimension of power in people's experiences. While this may be so, emphasizing only one dimension, such as gender or race, has as many drawbacks as an integrative approach, as we have seen in the Introduction of this chapter. Secondly, I emphasize that my notion of against the grain is but one of many attempts to address multiple inequalities. One model is social justice, for example. While these two approaches are not contradictory, against the grain focuses on the relational dimension in the production of inequality, thus emphasizing that we are co-participants in the (re)construction of social reality.

6. The term "counter-intuitive" is borrowed from Linda Briskin. She used this term in a workshop on "Negotiating power in the inclusive classroom," which we co-facilitated for the Toronto Board of Education on January 21, 1993. Similar to being against the grain, to be counter-intuitive is to interrogate what we take for granted as the natural ways of doing things.

REFERENCES

Berger, Peter, and Thomas Luckmann. 1967. *The Social Construction of Reality.* New York: Anchor Books.

Bourgeault, Ron. 1991. "Race, Class and Gender: Colonial Domination of Indian Women." In *Race, Class, Gender: Bonds and Barriers,* ed. Jesse Vorst et al. Toronto: Garamond Press & Society for Socialist Studies.

Briskin, Linda. 1990. *Feminist Pedagogy: Teaching and Learning Liberation.* Ottawa: Canadian Research Institute for the Advancement of Women.

Cochran-Smith, Marilyn. 1991. "Learning to Teach against the Grain." *Harvard Educational Review* 61:279–310.

Fishman, Pamela. 1978. "Interaction: The Work Women Do." *Social Problems* 25:397–406.

Foucault, Michel. 1979. *Discipline and Punish.* New York: Vintage Books.

———. 1990. *The History of Sexuality. Volume 1: An Introduction.* New York: Vintage Books.

Gramsci, Antonio. 1971. *Selections from the Prison Notebooks.* New York: International Publishers.

Haig-Brown, Celia. 1997. "Gender Equity, Policy, and Praxis." In *Dangerous Territories: Struggles for Difference and Equity in Education,* ed. Leslie G. Roman and Linda Eyre. New York: Routledge.

Jackson, Nancy. 1987. "Ethnicity and Vocational Choice." In *Breaking the Mosaic: Ethnic Identities in Canadian Schooling,* ed. Jon Young. Toronto: Garamond Press.

John, Gus. 1990. "Anti-Racist Education and Its Limitations." Unpublished manuscript.

Li, Peter. 1990. "Race and Ethnicity." In *Race and Ethnic Relations in Canada,* ed. Peter Li. Toronto: Oxford University Press.

Manners, Rita. 1998. "Inclusive Education vs. Equity in Education." M. Ed. Major Research Paper, Sociology & Equity Studies, OISE/UT.

Marx, Karl. 1954. *Capital.* Moscow: Progress Publishers.

Marx, Karl, and Frederick Engels. 1970. *The German Ideology.* New York: International Publishers.

Miles, Robert. 1989. *Racism.* London: Routledge.

Mohanty, Chandra T. 1990. "On Race and Voice: Challenges for Liberal Education in the 1990s." *Cultural Critique.* 179–208.

Ng, Roxana. 1993. "Racism, Sexism and Nation Building in Canada." In *Race, Identity, and Presentation in Education,* ed. Cameron McCarthy and Warren Chrichlow. New York: Routledge.

———. 1998. "Work Restructuring and Recolonizing Third World Women: An Example from the Garment Industry in Toronto." *Canadian Woman Studies* 18:21–25.

Rains, Frances. 1998. "Is the Benigh Really Harmless? Deconstructing Some 'Benign' Manifestations of Operationalized White Privilege." In *White Reign: Deploying Whiteness in America,* ed. by Joe L. Kincheloe, Shirley R. Steinberg, Nelson M. Rodriguea, and Ronald E. Chennault. New York: St. Martin's Press.

Rezai-Rashti, Goli. 1997. "Gender Equity Issues and Minority Students: Connections of Race, Gender and Social Class." *Orbit* 28:24–25.

Shockness, Isrealin. 1999. "The Social Construction of a Special Education Student in Ontario." Term paper for SES Social Organization of Knowledge, Sociology, and Equity Studies, OISE/UT.

Simon, Roger I. 1993. *Teaching against the Grain: Texts for a Pedagogy of Possibility.* Toronto: OISE Press.

Thomas, Barb. 1987. "Multicultural vs. Anti-Racist Education." In *Breaking the Mosaic,* ed. Jon Young. Toronto: Garamond Press.

Thorne, B., and N. Henley. 1975. *Language and Sex: Difference and Dominance.* Rowley, Mass.: Mewbury House.

Troyna, Barry, and Bruce Carrington. 1987. "Antisexist/Antiracist Education—A False Dilemma: A Reply to Walkling and Brannigan." *Journal of Moral Education* 16:60–65.

Walkling, Philip H., and Chris Brannigan. 1986. "Anti-Sexist/Anti-Racist Education: A Possible Dilemma." *Journal of Moral Education* 14:16–25.

Weber, Max. 1969. *The Theory of Social and Economic Organization.* New York: Free Press.

Westmoreland-Traore, Juanita. 1999. "Educational Equity: No Turning Back." In *Equity and How to Get It: Rescuing Graduate Studies,* ed. Kay Armatage. Toronto: Inanna Publications and Education Inc.

Wolverton, Terry. 1983. "Unlearning Complicity, Remembering Resistance: White Women's Anti-Racism Education." In *Learning Our Way: Essays in Feminist Education,* ed. C. Bunch and S. Pollack. Trumansburg, N.Y.: The Crossing Press.

Young, Allison. 1999. "Linking Employment and Educational Equity." In *Equity and How to Get It: Rescuing Graduate Studies,* ed. Kay Armatage. Toronto: Inanna Publications and Education Inc.

10

Toward a Deconstructive Pedagogy of *Différance*

PETER PERICLES TRIFONAS

> *"Subjectivity—like objectivity—is an effect of différance, an effect inscribed within a system of différance."*
>
> —Jacques Derrida[1]

Différance is perhaps Jacques Derrida's most radical contribution to Western epistemology. Upon it turn the philosophical wheels of deconstruction as a "post-critical pedagogy"—that is, as a way of reconceptualizing what it means "to know" about the self and the other beyond the certainty of empiricism and rationalism and their methods of teaching and learning.

The occidental foundations of pedagogy stand by erecting a monument to the "knowing subject." Education itself is the archive of knowledge to be transmitted from generation to generation as based, on the one hand, upon the logic of measurable sense perceptions in relation to natural phenomena and, on the other, upon the autotelic coherence of reflection in relation to the subjective experiencing of real world structures. A "knowing subject" knows itself in relation to the perceived boundaries of the self and the limits placed upon its actualization of knowledge by an Other. This reciprocity of the phenomenological exchange between the self and other, thus defined, is what makes a moment potentially educational. Because, as the categories of "intellect" and "experience" become changed, linked, or altered by the representation of external signs to the self, learning is said to occur as a growing of understanding or insight into the phenomena of the real word that are experienced in life. The "conditions of possibility" necessary to attain knowledge are articulated through the ability of the subject to synthesize empirical and conceptual differences among its apperception of the signs of the world. In theory and in practice, the performative dimensions of knowing are pedagogically tied to the capability of the subject to produce a clarity of conceptions that unifies and bridges differences of perception. Consequently, illumination and enlightenment are always the product of learning because teaching is linked to a rewriting of the empirical perceptual categories of the "knowing self" in relation to a body of knowledge that is taken for granted and legitimated as common knowledge. What makes pedagogy unjust, in this sense, is that *a rewriting of the self* through the apperception of signs and of natural phenomena is limited to the boundaries placed on knowledge by the epistemico-cultural conventions of philosophy and science. Hence, all knowing whose frame of reference is outside the epistemico-culturally determined "conditions of possibility" for attaining and reproducing knowledge does not formally qualify as education or learning. And its by-products are not legitimated as knowledge or given epistemic status. Where does that leave the education of the subject and the rewriting of the self in relation to a deconstructive pedagogy of *différance?* It becomes necessary to look at the place of writing in deconstruction and how it informs the notion of *différance.* But first we must begin by detailing the dimensions of a "pedagogy of the voice." Or the tradition deconstruction works against and resists.

A PEDAGOGY OF THE VOICE: LOOKING BEYOND CRITICAL THINKING

For Jacques Derrida, Claude Lévi-Strauss—like Ferdinand de Saussure, Plato, Aristotle, and Jean-Jacques Rousseau before him—among others, excluded writing from philosophy and pedagogy "as a phenomenon of exterior representation, both useless and dangerous."[2] This, of course, was a metaphysical judgment safeguarding the reduction of the exteriority of the sign for the sake of the voice. Writing poses a danger to the cultural archive of knowledge that is the domain of the teacher as purveyor of truth. It erases the pedagogical intentions by opening up the semantic and experiential field of interpretation via a text. Writing supplants the teachers, yet also supplements teaching. It does so by giving up control over meaning-making to the subject, who must make sense of signs. But a pedagogy of the voice would bring teacher and student in a face-to-face relation where attempts to control differences of interpretation could be made in order to inculcate desired learning outcomes. The logocentric mode of this dialogical exchange favors the seeming presence of the *phone* over the absence of the *graphe.* The teacher is not made redundant, but is the pastoral guide to knowledge through discourse. Learning happens through the use of pedagogical master narratives, which students must memorize, mimic, and repeat. Speaking is supposed to be more transparent than writing, and therefore morally and ethically superior to writing as an educational tool because it articulates presence and explains itself through the power of the voice. The voice does not deceive, is not empty like a cipher bereft of essence. Speech has a body behind it and therefore its ethical connection to the subject of knowledge is seen to be closer, more direct, and full. As such, the metaphysics of presence driving logocentrism constructs the *cultural politics of the sign* through the power of the voice. Or the ethical imperative of valuing speech over writing in human communications for the purpose of moral and truthful exchanges. Because writing challenges the cultural logic of a pedagogy of the voice, the implication is as follows:

> Writing should erase itself before the plenitude of living speech, perfectly represented in the transparency of its notation, immediately present for the subject who speaks it, and for the subject who receives its meaning, content, value.[3]

Differences of meaning therefore must be negotiated face-to-face in order to make the exchanges of meaning like those characterizing the acts of teaching and learning more efficacious. Saussure supported and justified the pedagogical model of a "phonetic-alphabetic"[4] script as a way to delimit the semantic slippage of language. Such a mode of communication could both sustain the impression of *presenting speech* while simultaneously erasing "itself before speech."[5] Truth thus becomes obvious or self-evident via the socio-political exigencies of the realm of language through the projection of voice.

After Saussure, Derrida has tried to show "there is no purely phonetic writing, and that phonologism is less a consequence of the practice of the alphabet in a given culture than a certain ethical or axiological experience of this practice."[6] In Western culture, for example, the assumption is that the struggle over differences of meaning can be averted by making language transparent. Any axiology must be clear so as to make it possible for consensus to occur in a public sphere. Differences of interpretation have the potential to cause dissensus and breakdown the ethical structure of communities. Ideology is dangerous. A pedagogy of the voice and its critical apparatus focused on language attempts to neutralize differences of meaning by providing a succinct definition of what it means to be an educated being capable of ethical discourse with others. The unique practicability of its teaching of language, language of teaching—and the tranquilizing effects it has on the articulation of interpretative differences—reinforces the cultural politics of the sign. The ethico-theoretical hierarchy of an edifying speech constructs the conditions of possibility for maintaining the binary structure of Western critical thought and sustaining its pedagogy of the voice.

To continue with an example, the tradition of critical thinking revolves around the question of epistemic adequacy. Proof is related to fixed criteria for reckoning truth. Being critical entails finding faults in arguments (e.g., identifying generalizations), watching for fallacies of logic (e.g., tautologies), gauging reliability (e.g., testing assumptions), distinguishing authority (e.g., privileging experience), judging evidence (e.g., weighing perspective), and so on. Under the methodological categories of logic, conceptual analysis, and epistemology, critical thinking aims to nurture the human dispositions for knowledge and self-knowledge. It upholds the epistemological principle of noncontradiction as a moral imperative. Ultimately, critical thinking depends on the transparency of language that a pedagogy of the voice dictates in order to uphold a view of the world that unites representation and truth in the concept of reality. The point is to nullify the distractions of subjectivity that taint the ability of the subject to be able to perceive the lifeworld in its full presence as it is. The logic of critical thinking is based on a method of rules intended to habituate the subject to a ready form of analysis. It is designed around the premise that to elucidate errors of meaning and interpretation has moral implications for living.

Critical thinking is a learned behavior and not innate. The skills of reasoning must therefore be discreet for the purpose of transmitting the tradition in order to facilitate a moral society by enabling the subject to engage in an ongoing examination of the assumptions undergirding everyday life. The repeatability of the process of analysis is crucial to the spread of the tradition of critical thinking via education. The hope is that such education will facilitate the growth of the subject from the simple acquisition of thinking skills to gaining the lifelong habits of the examination of knowledge for moral purposes.

Deconstruction resists a critique of reason or rationality that comes down on one side or the other of right and wrong as a judgment made by appealing only to methods of analysis. The efficacy of critical thinking is not at all useful or moral when it dismisses modes of reckoning that do not adhere to its system of inquiry. In such a case, it becomes a misleading endeavor to seek an ethical refuge in the evaluative power of a binary form of metaphysical reasoning pitting the good against the bad, essentialism against anti-essentialism, Eurocentrism against anti-Eurocentrism, and so on. The sorry endwork of such a critical task of analysis without an openness to thinking, freely places blame or adjudicates value for the sake of a castigation or rejection of worth. The moral judgments of critical thinking are performed too quickly and easily from a deconstructive per-spective. Decisions are rendered by and appeal to the dictates of a univer-salist conception of reason and its demotic (and not at all democratic) corollary of common sense to thereby construct the ideologico-conceptual grounds of what is good and what is bad. The judgmental edifice of criti-cal thinking is an *either/or* rationale that presumes a lack of interpretative complexity in developing an understanding of the lifeworld. Truth is sup-posed to be plain, totally transparent, common, and obvious to every-one—a clear-cut and unarguable claim to knowledge made with no possibility of opposition or exemption to the moral rule of law. One life-world, one reality, one truth are the philosophical hallmarks informing the tradition of critical thinking and the ethical hierarchy of its deontology.

The metaphysical value of this ethic of perception and its monologi-cal model of representation determines the nonoppositional grounds of truth. Anything outside of this frame of reference is irrational and dan-gerous to the moral fabric of society. Conditional and definitive limits thereby demarcate the freedom of what it is possible to know and to think and what it is possible to say without offending the much guarded sensi-bilities of reason and good taste. However these values might be con-structed and articulated, the ideals of commonly held responses to cultural institutions and practices remain static and timeless as eternal truths. Dif-ference is abdicated in favor of a community of shared interpretative responsibility and the unethical hegemony of its "majority rules" attitude that bids one to erect barriers against diversity while seeming, at the same time, to tolerate it as a foil to the cultural hegemony of knowledge—that is, to see and talk about things only as they *are* or *could be*. The priority of clarity as an ethical prerequisite of a "responsible response" is, without a doubt, everything when the analytical imperative is nothing but an exer-cise of choosing sides. Deconstruction offers a more productive approach to the rewriting of the subject by opening up thinking to the post-critical possibilities of reaffirming the utility and necessity of recognizing the pres-ence of an other beyond a pedagogy of the selfsame based on the immedi-acy of the voice.

REWRITING THE SELF: TOWARD A DECONSTRUCTIVE PEDAGOGY OF *DIFFÉRANCE*

Reacting to the ethical implications of sustaining a pedagogy of the voice, the most significant point for Derrida is "not to privilege one substance—here the phonic, so called temporal, substance—while excluding another—for example, the graphic, so called spatial, substance."[7] This radical modification of Saussure's theory is enigmatic to the focus Western edu-cational philosophy puts on the power of the voice to quell differences of interpretation in the public sphere. Deconstruction, as a *pedagogy of différance,* deconstitutes and dislocates the linear expressivity of the sign of speech upon which a dialectic of instruction relies when learning is the product of an enlightened discourse. Rethinking the primacy of voice in teaching reinforces the need to ask a question: How can deconstruction be introduced into pedagogy when *différance* seems to neutralize "every substance, be it phonic, graphic, or otherwise?"[8] We may possibly receive the following answer from Derrida: "Of course it is not a question of resorting to the same concept of writing and of simply inverting the disymmetry that now has become problematical."[9]

To be more specific, the broader and more radical redefinition of writing—that is proposed by deconstruction encompasses every kind of expression, communication, and coding (phonic, graphic, artistic)—"can be called *gram* or *différance.*"[10] In relation to pedagogy, the distinguishing characteristic of the scene of teaching would be an exchange of signs, a *semio-scriptology* involving a "play of differences" and meaning deferrals, the interweaving of syntheses and postponed references, that occur in the process of teaching and learning. A simple or uncomplicated notion of signification "present in and of itself, referring only to itself"[11] as the auto-affective arbiter of complete, unmitigating, and unrelenting, sense without *différance* would be undone.

As such, the text and textuality of this deconstructive writing of the scene of teaching is a *chaining of signs.* But not simply a layering of *sign-functions* standing in for a (cultural) center of mediated meaning, as "everywhere, differences and traces of traces,"[12] within pedagogical acts of communication would come to undo the secure reference points of even the most general signs circulating in that milieu. The semiological constitution of the scene of teaching would therefore be reconstituted through *différance* as the ground of grammatology. A post-critical wherein communication is open to interpretation like a text. This clarifies the outline of what Derrida has presented for the *"science of a new writing"* upon which a post-critical or deconstructive pedagogy of *différance* can be articulated.

Since the gram "is a structure and a movement no longer conceivable on the basis of the opposition presence/absence"[13] and flourishes within the codic play of differences and meaning deferrals, it is as *différance* that the grammatological conversion of a "pedagogy of the voice" takes place via deconstruction to cleave open the realm of self-certainty and epistemic adequacy that has governed the institution of education in the West. We can now begin to evaluate the implications of this claim—the effectivity of why and how it is made—for the phenomenality of the writing of *being,* the being written of the self. That is, for all that relates deconstruction and the institution of pedagogy in the cultural politics of the sign and undoes the ethical emphasis the Western tradition of philosophy and science has placed upon the voice. There are some crucial sticking points, however, that we must address, since, it would seem, that the ethico-axiological agency of the "being-present" of the sign, *its being as presence,* is forever undercut by deconstruction as such. And with it, is summarily extinguished the metaphysical light of both the educational edifice of a valuation of truth and the psychological comfort of a sense of origin.

Différance is incompatible "with the static, synchronic, taxonomic, ahistorical motifs in the concept of structure"[14] and yet, contrastingly, it is *not* astructural. Derrida insists on this. Because the "systematic and regulated transformations"[15] in the specificity of its general workings are able to develop, in certain cases, "the most legitimate principled exigencies of 'structuralism' "[16] upon which a pedagogy of the voice depends. That would be, for example, in the extended concatenation of sytagmatic units of expression whose traces are deferred and multiplied to some degree within the differential or fragmented proportionality of discursive or narrative structures. And here we come to the crux of the matter we must next follow to gauge the ethicity of the sign in this mode of an always already immanently refracted referentiality, as Derrida defines it. It cannot be said, from this vantage, that some "present and in-*different* being"[17] in any shape or form "precedes *différance* or spacing,"[18] for example, a subject "who would be the agent, author, and master of *différance,*"[19] or upon whom *différance* would impose itself. Why? Because, to reiterate the quotation from the beginning of this chapter, "Subjectivity—like objectivity—is an effect of *différance,* an effect inscribed within a system of *différance.*"[20]

The most affable text for engaging the complexity of these ramifications is "Différance," the lecture Derrida addressed to the *Société Française de la Philosophie* on January 27, 1968.[21] As is noted in the preamble to the discourse "proper," the French verb *différer,* like the Latin *differre,* suggests two meanings of association, "to differentiate" and "to delay," thus, relating the idea of difference in two unsimilar ways:

> On the one hand, it indicates difference as distinction, inequality, or discernability; on the other, it expresses the interposition of delay, the interval of a spacing and temporalizing that puts off until later what is presently denied, the possible that is presently impossible. Sometimes the *different* and sometimes the *deferred* correspond [in French] to the verb "to differ." This correlation, however, is not simply one between act and object, cause and effect, or primordial and derived.
>
> In the one case "to differ" signifies non-identity; in the other case it signifies the order of the *same.* Yet there must be a common, although entirely *différante,* root within the sphere that relates the two movements of differing

to one another. We provisionally give the name *différance* to this *sameness* which is not *identical.*[22]

Using the letter "a" from the present participle of the verb *différer,* for example, "*différante,*" Derrida constructs the noun *différance.* A new word, a nonword, that is, in his estimation, a nonconcept—profoundly ametaphysical—precisely because it cannot be either narrowed-down or fixed to a single part of both of its meanings. It is perhaps the penultimate of deconstructive terms, if that were possible in this *post-structural* sense, given that the difference of *différance* is only perceptible *in writing,* since the change of spelling is inaudible—the "e" for which the "a" is substituted being silent to the (French) ear. Thus, the *semanteme* that is "neither a *word* nor a *concept*"[23] expresses both meanings of differentiation as spatio-temporality and as the movement that structures each kind of dissociation in the "middle voice" between passivity and activity like the penumbra of an irreducible origin of production. It is perhaps the offspring of the monstrosity Derrida predicts at the end of his famous lecture at Yale University, "Structure, Sign, and Play in the Discourse of the Human Sciences" (1966). Deconstruction already having given form in itself to a *species of nonspecies marking the unnamable in the alterity of a philosophical subject metaphysics cannot stomach or mouth.* And here it would be tempting—yes it is—to consider *différance* an operating principle. That is, a means to an end rather than to a beginning of meaning-making or interpretation. To criticize it as the ambivalent counterpart to a philosophy of origin upon which the other must rely or fall. But this would also be to misunderstand what Derrida has said is possible at some minimal parameters of signification.[24] Not to do justice to the interpretative possibilities of a "doubling commentary" by representing *différance* as external to the formations of identity instead of it being always already within the nonindicative self-relation of the being written of being, modifying the *here* and *now* "at the zero-point of the subjective origin."[25] What *différance* does to the sign—for our purposes *the trace of the writing of the Self as Other*—is evident in the semiological prospectus of signification: the structural necessity of its repeatability, or reiteration, beyond a single, unitary point of expression. If we acknowledge, as we should, a sign can signify *only through the force of repetition,* the consequences of *différance* render the sign relational rather than identical (e.g., not the selfsame, or iconic, possessing the properties of its referent). Thus, *différance* prevents the possibility of bringing the what a sign indicates (a referent) into line with the terms of expression and undoes the Husserlian idea of a "pre-expressive intentionality" of pure consciousness. It breaks down the notion that a pedagogy of the voice is the privileged source of accurate and therefore truthful representation.

This line of argument decenters the education of the subject as a curriculum of speech with a full presence, brings it out of the shell of the Cartesian *cogito* that shelters its attempt at realizing the security of a self-discourse with itself. *Différance* shows how a pedagogy based on the immediacy of the voice is an instance of non-communication, a case of failed transmission. By equating self-hood with self-presence, the Other is effaced to the point where an inner-monologue with one's self is not really an instance of transmissibility at all, but the self-deceptive verification of the desire for auto-affection—that is, an exercise of the power to hear oneself speaking to oneself at the expense of excluding an Other. An attempt at the reduction of *différance*. In order to ascertain the existence of itself, a subject must refer outside of itself to the world of the signs of the Other using the resources of what does not begin "within" itself. It therefore strives to refrain from obliterating itself just as it seems to have authenticated the uniqueness of its (own) existence. Derrida makes us aware of this relational aspect of subjectivity that a "pedagogy of the voice" enacts and depends upon. The ethical grounding of *différance,* however, refers to the constitutive function of the *sign-trace* of the Other in the formation of the self, the deferring difference between presence and repetition, self and nonself, reveals itself as undecidability at the proliferative core of identity.

Derrida suggests that *différance* is or can stand for "the juncture—rather than the summation—of what has been most decisively inscribed in the thought of what is conveniently called our 'epoch.' "[26] A post-structural pedagogy—of the irreducible play of the sign—marks the delimitation of onto-theology and the decline of the metaphysics of presence (phonologocentrism). That is, the possibility of an ethical opening of the subject toward the difference of the Other. But we must remember however the role of tradition in the formation of new thought. Derrida gives the following examples within the history of metaphysics and the theorizing of difference that led to *différance:*

> . . . the difference of forces in Nietzsche, Saussure's principle of semiological difference, differing as the possibility of [neurone] facilitation, impression and delayed effect in Freud, difference as the irreducibility of the trace of the other in Levinas, and the ontic-ontological difference in Heidegger.[27]

All of these individuals have no doubt figured greatly in the elaboration of the *working of deconstruction.* But more importantly the list displays the discoveries or inventions from the fields of philosophy and theology, linguistics and psychoanalysis, that have changed or altered perceptions of the Western metaphysics and its pedagogy. The exposition of the breadth of the contributions to the theory of *différance* makes a previous point quite clear: *différance* is not only "irreducible to every ontological or theological—onto-theological—reappropriation, but it opens up the very space in which onto-theology—philosophy—produces its system and its history. It thus encompasses and irrevocably surpasses onto-theology and philosophy."[28] The alogicality of its structure also prevents an afore-planned linearity within the reading of the writing of signs, and their teaching. For example, the ordering of a reason of strategy or of finality of purpose, a tacticality toward teleology, philosophical-logical discourse[29] and its symmetrical opposite logico-empirical speech.[30] Master signs, we must remember, are always protected within a self-enclosed system of truth and meaning. The alternative to these more or less traditional discourses of epistemological fortitude and pedagogico-cultural forebearance is a way of knowing that involves acknowledging the play of difference as *différance.* It is a subject Derrida favors and has little difficulty in handling regarding elements of the teachings of Freidrich Nietzsche, Sigmund Freud, Saussure, Martin Heidegger, and Emmanuel Levinas.

With respect to Nietzsche and Freud, both "often in a very similar way, questioned the self-certitude of consciousness"[31] and showed-up the traumatizing elisions of the substantive self that was the product of the teachings of metaphysics, the metaphysics of teaching, designed to center the pedagogical enframing *(Ge-Stell)* of being around the presence of the voice. The main point for Derrida is that this was done "by starting out with the theme of *différance,*"[32] if not the formal notion. An accurate, but nevertheless, audacious claim.

Concerning Nietzsche, the understanding of *différance* is evident to Derrida in his argument that " 'the important main activity is unconscious' "[33] and that "consciousness is the effect of forces whose essence, ways, and modalities are not particular to it."[34] The force determining consciousness, for Nietzsche, is *never present as presence to itself,* but rather, "only [as] a play of differences and quantities."[35] The "postulating" of *différance* in Nietzsche correlates to a "symptomatology" diagnostic of the "adiaphoristic repression"[36] and indifference of a philosophy dedicated to the Same at the expense of the Other, *a pedagogy of the one and only reason, and of the voice.* The post-metaphysical interpretation, however, does qualify *différance,* not as "the disclosure of truth as a presentation of the thing itself in its presence,"[37] but as "an incessant deciphering,"[38] an on-running hermeneutics of *ressentiment* based on a "cipher without truth, or at least a system of ciphers that is not dominated by truth value."[39] The struggle of such a post-critical teaching is to demythologize the objectification of the meaning and the will to the power as it forms and is formed by an *economy of interests weighed against interests* according to the profit of function is consequently "understood, inscribed, and circumscribed"[40] within the history of episteme and philosophy. Nietzsche, Derrida will say, thought "this active (in movement) discord of the different forces and of the differences between forces"[41] is in direct opposition "to a system of metaphysical grammar, wherever that system controls culture, philosophy, and science."[42]

With Freud, another diaphoristics of difference takes places to subdue the power of a pedagogy of the voice. This time it is the primacy of the metaphysical edict of the *phone* that places "presence *qua* consciousness"[43] in direct correlation to each other is transformed and translated via a psychoanalytic questioning of the authority of consciousness, its trustworthiness. The two meanings of *différance* as differentiation and deferral are inextricably fused in Freud's thought, especially in the concepts of the trace *(spur)*, facilitation *(bahnung)*, memory *(erinnerung)*, inscription *(niederschrift)*, and the repressive reserve *(vorrat)* of delay *(nachträglichkeit)*. Derrida emphasizes the open play of this structure of psychic *retardement* as it is developed in *Beyond the Pleasure Principle*. He cites the radicality of Freud's suggestion that the ego's drive toward self-preservation motivates the temporary displacement of the pleasure principle by the reality principle, but without surrendering the drive to an ultimate increase in pleasure, thereby requiring the temporary suspension of gratification through the willful tolerance of displeasure. The vision and certitude of the prevalent system of metaphysical thinking requires the objectification of the value of its content as form in the act of teaching through the voice. The exteriority of language inscribes the interiority of consciousness from the production of the intersubjective violence of a welcomed *socius*. In the image of the mystic writing pad, Freud noted how subjectivity was the product of the indelible traces left upon the conscious and unconscious structures of the mind in relation to the signs of an other. The voice or experience marks consciousness through memory so that it teaches the subject about its relationship to the lifeworld. As writing, the traces of signs embedded within the structures of mind and the permanent as well as the spontaneous relations between them cannot be controlled. Consciousness and unconsciousness become the domain of *différance*.

Derrida details in this lecture of the same title, to offer Saussre as a primary source for a grammatological reconstitution of semiology and of *différance*. Structuralism resurrects the possibility for a rethinking of writing because it draws attention to the historicity of the deferred traces of the difference of the Other that the voice exposes as a weakness in the teachings of metaphysics. The orthographical enframing of knowledge through structural linguistics requires propriety over the means of interpretation. An idea is not an idea, but the idea of an idea well-represented to an Other. Semiology works like this to structure communication as a means of representation articulating differences between a sign, a concept, and what it refers to in the lifeworld. This perspective opens the possibility for an inquiry into how the poststructural, postphenomenological infrastructurality of *différance* contends for an ethics of alterity in a postcritical pedagogy that is beyond the cognitive limits of the teleological trajectory of the subject of metaphysics.

In this sense, where the transitive apportionment of the self to the *infinity of the secret of the* Other needs to be recognized, the thought of Emmanuel Levinas is anything but psychoanalytic. And so Derrida confirms by maintaining that the Heideggerian "forgetting of Being" acknowledges the radicality assigned to *ethics as first philosophy.* An assertion already expressed in Edmund Husserl's conception of phenomenology. In *Speech and Phenomena,* Derrida will have come to deconstructive terms with such a conclusion. On the one hand, the intuition of essence posited as being analogous to perception adequates the act of cognition with "the thing" of its object. On the other, there is the possibility that the apodicticity of evidence requires no adequation of the phenomenality of its apperception beyond the retensions and protensions of experience, a consciousness of a past and future ego. Or a consciousness of Other selves wherein there is a presupposition of the recognition of materiality—for example the body of the Other, physical presence, and the like—because the exteriority of a thing outside the self is not reducible to the presentation of the language of its representation. Derrida accepts this as a justification for the infinite transcendence of the Other. That is, a positive infinitude of the ego involved in the inability to actualize a totality of experience in relation to the structures of perception, but a paralleling of the difference of experience by "analogical appresentation" of the self's relation to the Other as the other's ego to one's own. *Différance* enables this "peaceful" resolution of the rendering of the "sense" of subjectivity through the recognition of difference and the deferral of judgment upon the difference of the Other. The result is that the approximation of experience that solidifies the alterity of the Other—for example the being of the self depending on the being of another ego—does not do violence to the totality of the Other. Derrida nevertheless has reservations against Levinas with respect to acknowledging the difference of being:

> Levinas *in fact* speaks of the infinitely other, but by refusing to acknowledge an intentional modification of the ego—which would be a violent and totalitarian act for him—he deprives himself of the very foundation and the possibility of his own language.[44]

It is not a question of transcendental phenomenology as "metaphysical idealism" or "metaphysical realism" because in the suspension of empirical and metaphysical "factuality" there is at least some semblance of non-neutrality garnered through the intentional quality of the ego as the basis for language and subjectivity that shows-up in the equating of exteriority as an openness to the Other. Is this a paradox or an incoherence with respect to fundamental ontology and a deconstructive pedagogy of *différance?* Derrida comments,

> It is true that Ethics in Levinas' sense, is an Ethics without law and without concept, which maintains its non-violent purity only before being determined as concepts and laws. This is not an objection; let us not forget that Levinas does not seek to propose laws or moral rules, does not seek to determine *a* morality, but rather the essence of the ethical relation in general. But as this determination does not offer itself as a *theory* of Ethics, in question, then it is an Ethics of Ethics. In this case, it is perhaps serious that this Ethics of Ethics can occasion neither a determined ethics nor determined laws without negating and forgetting itself. Moreover, is this Ethics of Ethics beyond all laws? Is it not the Law of laws? A coherence which breaks down the coherence of the discourse against coherence—the infinite concept, hidden within the protest against the concept.[45]

What sort of teaching can be beyond the scope of the law as external to the phenomenological closure of the frame of the logic of reference? There is difficulty in responding to or philosophizing about what is otherwise than being. Especially, for Levinas whose discourse, Derrida reminds us, seems to be all about the ethics of discourse itself, the engagement and aversion of intersubjective violence in the face-to-face relation with the Other. But the concept of "the trace and the enigma [that is also an opening] of absolute alterity, that is, the Other [*autrui*]"[46] certainly parallels the give-and-take of psychic (dis)indications that led to the inscription of the Freudian rebus of the unconscious, a "mystic writing pad" of the mind, discovered by disarming the pedagogical value of the "teaching-being" and the "being-taught" of a face-to-face exchange of hidden memory with the self. Yet, to go further in another direction, Nietzsche occupies a more prominent position in the lecture itself and is held-up in conjunction with the significance of Heidegger for deconstruction, in all probability the intellectual figure to whom Derrida is most closely tied, yet also the furthest from. On the one hand, it must be said that "in a particular and strange way, *différance* [is] 'older' than the ontological difference or the truth of Being,"[47] because in its horizon is borne and bound the play of the deferral of traces demarcating the living-depth of existence. On the other hand,

Heidegger pioneered the "epochality" of textuality and language, the insight making a rethinking of the being of beings possible, but not "actual." Derrida believes that we "must stay within the difficulty of this passage [of ontological difference, recognizing the necessity for it as a *point of reference among others*]; we must repeat this passage in a rigorous reading of metaphysics, wherever metaphysics serves as the norm of Western speech, and not only in the texts of 'the history of philosophy.' "[48] This two-sided "tack" is in itself the responsibility of a deconstructive pedagogy of *différance,* and its ethic of difference and deferral, the nonend of a keeping within to move beyond the present to the future.

Derrida will have asked, here as elsewhere, a more fundamental question of the subject, intriguingly posed to take in the representation of the effectivity of the life-world, after Heidegger and the unfolding of the language of being speaking, exterior to the "installment" of signification: "How do we conceive of the outside of a text?"[49] We could reply to this essentially unanswerable question with another: How do we conceive of the inside of a text? And to, some extent, the thinking of *différance* broaches an impossible answer to the radical opening of the ethics of both of these *aporias* all along.

FOR LOOSE ENDS: AT THE PROXIMITY OF A TEACHING OF THE OTHER

Deconstruction integrates semiological difference within the radical irreducibility of the infrastructurality of *différance* marking the arche-trace of the Other to expose how the telepathy of the *logos* is deferred by the self-effacement, erosion, *phthora,* of the plenitude of the *eidos* of presence. Derrida—complicating the "archive fever"[50] of Western epistemology at the base of its desire to exclude the improper, that which does not belong to the place of consignment,[51] by reintroducing the idea of an outside to the economy of the *arkheion*—begins to address the relative specificity of the larger question of pedagogy around a rethinking of the classical thematizations of the nature/culture opposition of metaphysics, its main pragmatico-logical focus. The engagement of deconstruction with what it means to think, to learn, to teach, to know takes shape in the early texts comprising the biblio-blitz of the collection of writings appearing alongside *Of Grammatology* as a resituating of the intelligibility of the institutionalization of knowledge at the level of the historicity of the sign. Or, what are the socio-theo-philosophical sources of a *nonnatural ethics before and after the letter of writing.* Deconstruction convenes poststructural interventions into topical variations of the educational problematic (e.g., origins, mimesis, nature, primitivism, childhood, reason, etc.) around the issue of the paradoxical stricture of supplementarity, the middle-ground between the fullness of presence and the lack of absence, to show that there is no neutral or apolitical safe-haven of language or representivity, an unmediated, "unpoliced" point of decidable exteriority, from which to approach the horizon of intersubjective violence, the linearist techniques of the repetition of impressionability. The ethico-theoretical hierarchy of the cultural politics of the sign privileging an edifying speech cannot persevere, as such, after the disposition of an ideal of objectivity as dis-continuous with the reality of an ethnocentric deflation of the grapheme exacted at the expense of the heterogeneity of the writing of the Other—that is, the grafting of subjective originarity from within the play of the interiority of consciousness and the exteriority of the projection of being.

What counter-acts the irresponsibilizing drive of metaphysics to secure a teleological trajectory of the subject for its "just completion" along the lines of a teaching of a normative ethics, a normative ethics of teaching, is the deconstructive obligation to grant a vertiginous plurivocity to the retracing of semiological difference as the deferral of the self-presence of the sign, the law of an open-ended justice always already set beyond the divisibility of nature and culture in the order of *différance* and the impossibility of gaining access to a single and determinate truth.

NOTES

1. Jacques Derrida, 1981. *Positions,* trans. Alan Bass. Chicago: University of Chicago Press, 28.
2. Derrida 1981, 25.
3. Derrida 1981, 25.
4. Derrida 1981, 25.
5. Derrida 1981, 25.
6. Derrida 1981, 25.
7. Derrida 1981, 26.
8. Derrida 1981, 26.
9. Derrida 1981, 26.
10. Derrida 1981, 26.
11. Derrida 1981, 26.
12. Derrida 1981, 26.
13. Derrida 1981, 27.
14. Derrida 1981, 27.
15. Derrida 1981, 28.
16. Derrida 1981, 28.
17. Derrida 1981, 28.
18. Derrida 1981, 28.
19. Derrida 1981, 28.
20. Derrida 1981, 28.
21. Although the text of this discourse has appeared in many different places, the version of "Différance" I will be using is found in Jacques Derrida, 1973, *Speech and Phenomena: And Other Essays on Husserl's Theory of Signs,* trans. David B. Allison (Evanston: Northwestern University Press), 129–160. (Translations have been modified unless otherwise indicated.).
22. Derrida 1973, 129.
23. Derrida 1973, 130.
24. See Jacques Derrida, 1988. *Limited Inc.,* trans. Samuel Weber and Jeffrey Mehlman, ed. Gerald Graff. Evanston: Northwestern University Press. The chapter entitled "Afterword: Toward an Ethic of Discussion" is most clear about the misrepresentation of Derridean undecidability and the play of the sign.

25. Derrida 1973, 94.
26. Derrida 1973, 130.
27. Derrida 1973, 130.
28. Derrida 1973, 135.
29. Derrida 1973, 135.
30. Derrida 1973, 135.
31. Derrida 1973, 148.
32. Derrida 1973, 148.
33. Derrida 1973, 148.
34. Derrida 1973, 148.
35. Derrida 1973, 148.
36. Derrida 1973, 148.
37. Derrida 1973, 149.
38. Derrida 1973, 149.
39. Derrida 1973, 149.
40. Derrida 1973, 149.
41. Derrida 1973, 149.
42. Derrida 1973, 149.
43. Derrida 1973, 149.
44. Jacques Derrida, 1981, "Violence and Metaphysics: An Essay on the Thought of Emmanuel Levinas," in *Writing and Difference* trans. Alan Bass. Chicago: University of Chicago Press, 125.
45. Derrida 1981, 111.
46. Derrida 1973, 152.
47. Derrida 1973, 154.
48. Derrida 1973, 154.
49. Derrida 1973, 158.
50. See Jacques Derrida, 1996, *Archive Fever: A Freudian Impression,* trans. Eric Prenowitz. Chicago: University of Chicago Press.
51. Derrida 1996, 11.

Contributors

Megan Boler is Associate Professor of Teaching and Learning and Adjunct Professor of Women's Studies at Virginia Tech. Her work has focused on the politics of emotion in pedagogy, cultural, and media studies, and philosophy of technology. Her book *Feeling Power: Emotions and Education* was published in 1999 and her essays appear in such journals as *Hypatia: Journal of Women and Philosophy, Cultural Studies,* and *Educational Theory.*

Jim Cummins is Professor in the Modern Languages Center at the Ontario Institute for Studies in Education at the University of Toronto. He has published extensively in the area of language rights and antiracist pedagogy.

Manuel Espinoza is a Ph.D. student in the division of Urban Schooling at the University of California, Los Angeles. His research interests center on classroom discourse and philosophy of decolonization. He is currently a graduate student research and teaching assistant in the Center for the Study of Urban Literacies at the Graduate School of Education and Information Studies.

Henry A. Giroux is Waterbury Chair Professor at Pennsylvania State University. He is the author of numerous articles and books including *Channel Surfing* and *Counternarratives.* Among his most recent books is *The Mouse that Roared: Disney and the End of Innocence.*

Kris Gutierrez is Professor in the Division of Urban Schooling and Director of the Center for the Study of Urban Literacies in the Graduate School of Education and Information Studies at the University of California, Los Angeles. Her research concerns itself with the social and cognitive consequences of literacy practices in formal and nonformal learning contexts and the policy issues and implication of urban schooling practices. Across her work, she examines the relationship between literacy, culture, and human development. Issues of equity and excellence are important and recurrent themes throughout her ethnographic studies of urban schools and communities.

Marla Morris is Assistant Professor of Education at Georgia State University. She has published in the areas of psychoanalysis, curriculum theory, holocaust education, and cultural studies. Among her most recent books is *Curriculum and Holocaust: Competing Sites of Memory and Representation.*

Roxana Ng began her academic life as an activist working with immigrant women whose voices and conditions were ignored by society. In addition to researching the lives of immigrant women, she has applied her conception of the interrelation of gender, race, and class to education and has written on the endemic nature of sexism and racism in higher education. Her writings include an edited collection on *Anti-Racism, Feminism, and Critical Approaches to Education.* She teaches at the Ontario Institute for Studies in Education of the University of Toronto.

Michael Peters is Research Professor of Education at the University of Glasgow and has a personal chair at the University of Auckland. He has research interests in education policy and contemporary philosophy with a special emphasis on educational philosophy. He has published more than one hundred academic articles in these fields and is the author or editor of more than twenty books, including *Poststructuralism, Marxism and Neoliberalism, Poststructuralism and Educational Research, Richard Rorty: Education, Philosophy and Politics,* and *Heidegger, Education and Modernity.*

William F. Pinar is St. Bernard Parish Alumni Endowed Professor at Louisiana State University. Pinar has also served as the Frank Talbott Professor at the University of Virginia and the A. Lindsay O'Connor of American Institutions Professor at Colgate University. He is the author of *Autobiography, Politics and Sexuality,* the editor of *Curriculum: Toward New Idenitities, The Passionate Mind of Maxine Greene, Queer Theory in Education,* and *Contemporary Curriculum Discourses.*

Carlos Tejeda is Assistant Professor for the Division of Educational Foundations and Interdivisional Studies at the Charter College of Education—California, State University, Los Angeles. He teaches courses in the social foundations of education, history of education, educational sociology, and qualitative research in education. He is the editor of *Charting New Terrains of Chicana(o) Latina(o) Education*. He serves on the advisory board of the Center for the Study of Urban Literacies/Decolonizing Pedagogies.

Peter Pericles Trifonas teaches Social and Cultural Studies in Education at the Ontario Institute for Studies in Education at the University of Toronto. He has taught at schools and universities in North America and Europe. He has been published in journals such as *Interchange, International Journal of Applied Semiotics, Social Semiotics, Educational Researcher, Discourse: Studies in the Cultural Politics of Education, Educational Theory,* and *Semiotica*. His recent books are *Institutions, Ethics, and the Right to Philosophy* (with Jacques Derrida) and *Good Taste*.

Rinaldo Walcott is Associate Professor of Humanities at York University. He is the author of *Black Like Who: Writing Black Canada* and editor of *Rude: Contemporary Black Canadian Cultural Criticism*. His next book is *Disturbing the Peace: The Impossible Dream of Black Canadian Studies*. He sits on the editorial board of *Topia: A Journal of Canadian Cultural Studies* and *Fuse Magazine*, among others. His writing has appeared in both popular and scholarly periodicals.

Michalinos Zembylas is Assistant Professor of Teacher Education at Michigan State University. His research interests are in the area of emotions in teaching and learning science and technology, science and technology studies, curriculum theory, international comparative science education, and postmodernism/poststructuralism. Currently he is in Cyprus on a two-year research and teaching assignment.

Index